Images of Modern America

LGBTQ CLEVELAND

Front Cover: Cleveland's Terminal Tower (Stephen De Freese)

Upper Back Cover: Rock n Roll City Sisters (Ian Argo; see page 28)

Lower Back Cover (from left to right): Cleveland Pride in 1990 (Brian DeWitt; see pages 60–61), the 2014 Gay Games (Bob Perkoski; pages 42–43), the NAMES Project (Brian DeWitt; see page 72)

Images of Modern America

LGBTQ CLEVELAND

Ken Schneck

ARCADIA PUBLISHING

ISBN 978-1-4671-2921-3

Published by Arcadia Publishing
Charleston, South Carolina

Printed in the United States of America

Library of Congress Control Number: 2017963330

For all general information, please contact Arcadia Publishing:
Telephone 843-853-2070
Fax 843-853-0044
E-mail sales@arcadiapublishing.com
For customer service and orders:
Toll-Free 1-888-313-2665

Visit us on the Internet at www.arcadiapublishing.com

Dedicated to the LGBTQ Clevelanders who fought, shouted, wrote, marched, and celebrated to create what we have today.

Contents

ACKNOWLEDGMENTS

"It takes a village" is unquestionably the theme of this book, both with regard to the stories contained herein and the method by which I gathered them. When I quickly realized my folly of thinking, "Hey, I'll find all these images in one place," the process of spending time with incredible Clevelanders began.

Brynna Fish stacked her photo albums in front of me, marching me proudly through decades of Cleveland Pride via her stunning images and captivating stories. Brian DeWitt proved to be an invaluable trove of images and articles; without Brian and Doug Braun, this book absolutely would not exist. Sally Tatnall sat me down in her living room and shared jaw-dropping and inspiring tales that this book was sorely missing before meeting her. Buck Harris opened his home and steered me toward what was important. I have never met Robert Downing, but when his photographs arrived in the mail one Friday night, my appreciation jig was truly something to behold. John Nosek and Leon Stephens spent time with me in their dining room and provided a validation that bolstered me when I needed it.

There were easily 50 or 60 other LGBTQ and ally Clevelanders who immediately responded when I cried out "help!" or "is this right?!" They are present in the images and words throughout the book.

To Gordana Savic, my first ever Baldwin Wallace University undergraduate research assistant: thank you.

John Skrtic and the staff of the Cleveland Public Library were there supporting me on day one. They did not laugh at me when I tried to thread the microfilm, and for that I will always be appreciative.

The staff of the LGBT Center of Greater Cleveland repeatedly grounded this work with their connections, and the dedicated individuals at the Western Reserve Historical Society patiently (and repeatedly) held my trembling hand throughout the image collection process. I am indebted to both organizations.

And finally, to this wonderful and weird LGBTQ community: previously I did not think I could love you more. Then I worked on this project, and my appreciation increased a thousand-fold. You are my village, and I am proud to live among you.

Special thanks go to the following photographers:

Ian Argo	www.argonianphotography.com
Molly Castle	mollycastlephoto.tumblr.com
Brynna Fish	brynnafish.com
Stephen De Freese	www.swdfphotography.com
Zoë Renee Lapin	zoelapin.tumblr.com
Janet Macoska	www.janetmacoskaphotography.com
Anastasia Pantsios	www.anastasiapantsios.com
Bob Perkoski	www.perkoski.com
Andrew Warren	www.andrewwarren.net
Jacqueline Zema	www.isophotostudio.com

Introduction

As any LGBTQ Clevelander will tell you, Cleveland, Ohio, is as much any Midwestern city in the United States as it is Cleveland, Ohio.

There are no walls isolating the Forest City from the rest of society, no media blackout preventing Clevelanders from witnessing major world events, and no isolation exempting Northeast Ohio from the laws of the nation. Like their LGBTQ siblings across the country, Clevelanders were shocked when Harvey Milk was assassinated, outraged when Anita Bryant crusaded against gay people, devastated by the rampage of HIV/AIDS, and elated when marriage equality became the law of the land. The world influenced LGBTQ Clevelanders, and they responded to that influence.

But they did so in their own Cleveland way: a manner that has evolved greatly over the years.

In February 1979, a writer from the *Advocate* showed up in Cleveland to profile the city for the LGBTQ readership across the nation. The article was a wonderful opportunity to highlight a community coming into its own identity. The section of the four-page spread with the most praise and positive energy read:

> Much like the city itself, Cleveland's gay community also appears divided geographically, socially, and politically, as well as by gender—separatism remains a strong political ideal, I am informed by several lesbians—by degree of openness and participation within the community and its organizations, and by attitudes toward the city. There are those who love Cleveland and those who would love to leave it. Defenders defend it with the same intensity as detractors damn it.

After reading the piece, I felt immediately insulted. I only moved to Cleveland in 2013, but those words did not ring true to my lived, albeit brief, experience. This was not the LGBTQ Cleveland I had come to know and love. The iconic Terminal Tower lit up in rainbow colors across the skyline? An arena full of thousands of cheering international participants at the Opening Ceremonies of the 2014 Gay Games? The throngs of people marching and dancing together annually at Pride? When those images sprang to mind, I embraced our Cleveland tourism bureau's marketing tactics and immediately thought, "#ThisIsCLE."

Seeking validation, I took that paragraph and began sending it out to various lifelong LGBTQ Clevelanders to solicit their outrage. Their responses, however, were significantly less than affronted. In fact, they sounded more like, "yup," "sounds about right," and, "that's us!" Somehow, these 40-year-old words describing a conflicted city not only resonated, but oddly validated. And that . . . well, that is Cleveland, too.

The Cleveland LGBTQ community does not hold hands and speak with one voice. Over the years, there have been intense conflicts, hostile organization takeovers, sharp divisions, stark separatism, and even the occasional intercommunity lawsuit. The Ls occasionally stopped talking to the Gs. The Gs sometimes excluded the Ls from their planning. The Bs did not always feel represented. The Ts were struggling to get their voices to the table. And who the heck even were those Qs?

But that is only part of Cleveland's LGBTQ story. The images on the pages throughout this book tell the tale of a more united Cleveland, a city that repeatedly came together as individuals, groups, and organizations to respond to conflict, fight for equality, and celebrate their identity.

When the Community Center was driven out by arson, barred from operating due to government regulation, and even weathered the occasional bomb threat, the Cleveland LGBTQ community persevered until they found a place they could call home.

When the owner of a gay bar tried to kick lesbians out under the false pretense of a "dress code" in 1988, the Cleveland LGBTQ community protested to successfully restore social inclusion.

When a drunk driver plowed into the crowd attending Dancing in the Streets in 2013, killing one and injuring five others, the Cleveland LGBTQ community grieved together and resolved to not let the spirit of the legendary event be forgotten.

When Cleveland Pride 2016 was suddenly canceled with nothing but a vague explanation of "changing social climate," the Cleveland LGBTQ community organized a city-wide celebration together.

Through it all, Cleveland served as the backdrop. Cleveland's love for music provided countless opportunities for the community to come together to dance and sing. Cleveland's parks, museums, restaurants, and stadiums offered the myriad LGBTQ organizations a place to express their group's identity and bond more closely together. Cleveland's streets and bridges served as the ground beneath the feet for decades of proud marchers declaring their presence for the entire city to behold. Even Cleveland's ethos of gritty determination and hardscrabble fortitude helped fuel the efforts to build, maintain, and celebrate a sense of pride in the face of whatever struggle was set out before the assembled masses.

Then there are the heroes. Metropolis has Superman. Gotham has Batman. Townsville has the Powerpuff Girls. And Cleveland too has its share of heroes, big and small. Jane Daroff quietly created a refuge for parents and friends, while Buck Harris used his microphone to loudly broadcast equality. John Katsaros swooped in to valiantly save a flagging fundraiser, while Mistinguette Smith and Denise Jackson boldly led Cleveland's first "out" group for lesbians of color. Public officials like Matt Zone, Jay Westbrook, Joe Cimperman, and Nikki Antonio spoke passionately in front of the cameras as they worked to change the laws in the community, while countless Clevelanders spoke privately around dinner tables as they worked to change one mind at a time in their families.

The acts of bravery, daring, and courage exist as both well-documented feats and quiet actions that don't end up in the newspaper. There are no images in this book capturing the gay elder coming out to his grandchild, the lesbian writing to her congressperson, or the transgender employee asking his supervisor to update a gendered policy. But those individual achievements create as much change as anything you will see before you on these pages.

Ultimately, this book is an opportunity to pause and reflect on where the Cleveland LGBTQ community has been and most certainly where it can go. Cleveland is a city of hope, conflict, pride, and individuals who have interlocked arms time and time again to be seen and heard. So much has been accomplished, even as there is so much more to do. The moniker "Believeland" may have been coined for distinctly more sports-based purposes, but that core belief is present in every pixel on every page to come. Together, we battle, we bloom, and we believe: #ThisIsCLE.

One

We Connect

Groups and Activities

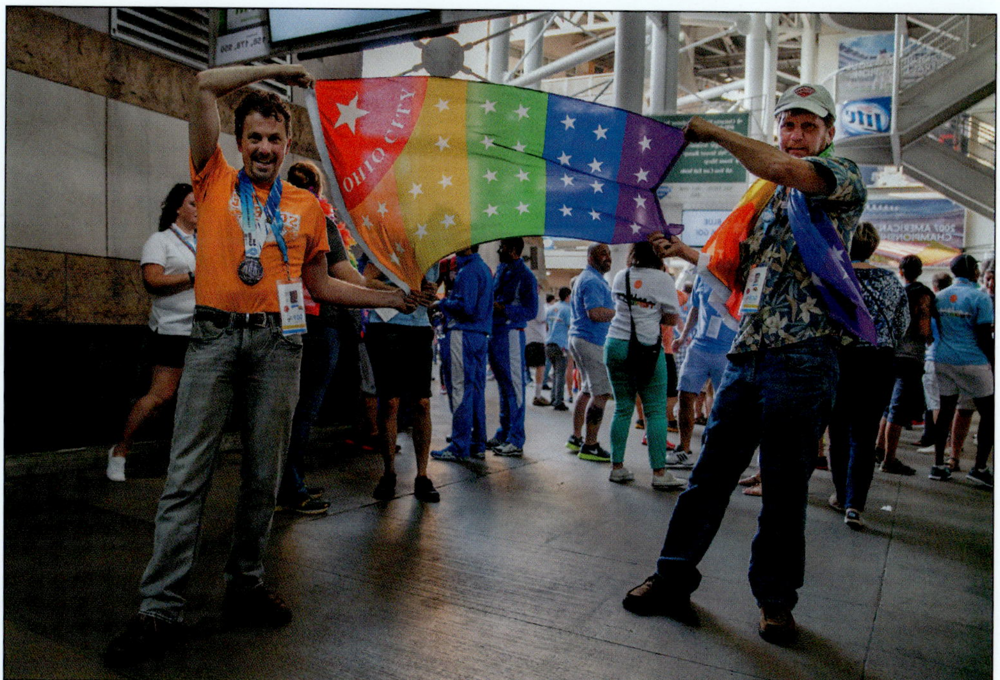

From the Unicorn Motorcycle Club to the Cleveland Irish Les-Bi-Gay Organization, from Insight to GrAY Pride, there has never been a shortage of organizations providing the LBGTQ community an opportunity to come together around common (and sometimes very specific) interests and plan myriad activities to channel their unique and passionate energy. (Bob Perkoski.)

Dayton news

Slightly Older Lesbians organize

By Ruthanne Seaman

From the Dayton Gay Rights Coalition to Dayton Dignity, gay people are finding a place to be themselves. The politically-minded gay person can get involved with the Gay Rights Coalition. The fight for civil rights goes on even though Anita Bryant and others like her are not in the news. The Coalition meets on the first Wednesday of each month. Call Dave at 513-222-8538 for the location and time.

Dayton Gay Center has meetings and potlucks each month. The programs are geared to both gay males and lesbians. For information, call their hotline at 513-228-4875.

Affirmation held their conference here March 30-April 1. Next issue we will have a complete report. Dayton Dignity now has a priest working regularly with them and have scheduled Masses for each month. Call Kay at 513-298-8335 for time and place. Interfaith/Lutherans Concerned has monthly meetings and they can be reached at 513-223-6231.

DAYTON DYKES ON BIKES

Every Sunday morning at 10:00 AM all the lesbian bike enthusiasts are invited to join us at Ann's (for location call her: 513-275-7195). We will start easy and work our way down?! Seriously, all you lesbians, the exercise will only be surpassed by the fun?!

LESBIAN UNITED

Our last coffeehouse of the season will be April 28. All women are invited to participate if you have a special talent or come and enjoy the music and other acts. There will be a surprise talent introduced at that time

We are putting out our newsletter again and need some suggestions for what you want to see. Also some addresses need updating. If you want to receive our newsletter, contact Ruthanne at 513-277-3050 or P.O. Box 303, Dayton, OH 45402.

Come and join us each Sunday evening at 6:00 PM at Dayton Womens Center, 1060 Salem Avenue, St. Andrew Episcopal Church, for our group meetings. The meetings alternate between open rap nights and program nights. We need your input to make these programs successful. For information, call Ruthanne at 513-277-3050.

S.O.L.

Dayton now has a group for Slightly Older Lesbians. You must be 30 or over to join us. If you have younger lover she is welcome to come to the meeting with you. We are just beginning, so until we get organized, we will meet on Sunday evenings, 8:00 PM at Dayton Womens Center. For more information, call Ruthanne at 513-277-3050.

Columbus news

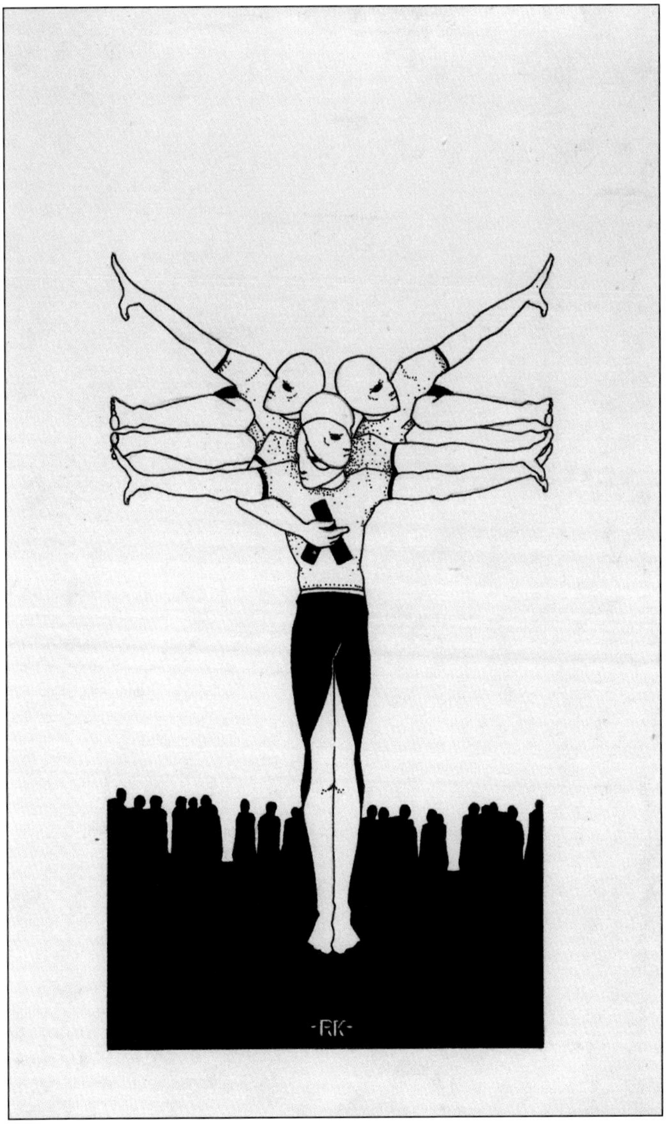

In 1975, the GEAR Foundation launched *High Gear*, an all-volunteer newsletter-turned-newspaper specifically produced for the LGBTQ community. The publication featured a mix of local and national news, coverage of Cleveland and surrounding area events (above), advertising for gay businesses, and quite a few covers featuring original works of art (as seen to the left on the cover in October 1976). The editors sometimes invented pseudonyms to make it appear as if the staff was larger than the small (but mighty) crew that kept things running. The paper was distributed for free to a selection of businesses covering a four-state area and a sizeable subscriber list. The presses stopped on *High Gear* in 1982. (Both, Western Reserve Historical Society.)

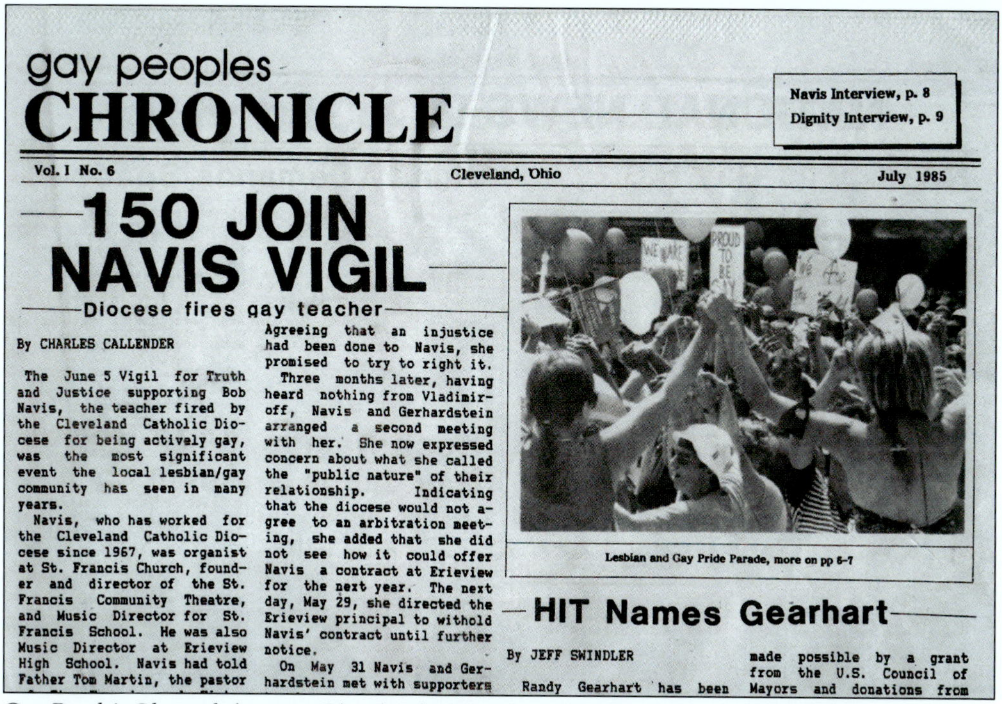
gay peoples
CHRONICLE

Navis Interview, p. 8
Dignity Interview, p. 9

Vol. I No. 6 Cleveland, Ohio July 1985

150 JOIN NAVIS VIGIL

Diocese fires gay teacher

By CHARLES CALLENDER

The June 5 Vigil for Truth and Justice supporting Bob Navis, the teacher fired by the Cleveland Catholic Diocese for being actively gay, was the most significant event the local lesbian/gay community has seen in many years.

Navis, who has worked for the Cleveland Catholic Diocese since 1967, was organist at St. Francis Church, founder and director of the St. Francis Community Theatre, and Music Director for St. Francis School. He was also Music Director at Erieview High School. Navis had told Father Tom Martin, the pastor

Agreeing that an injustice had been done to Navis, she promised to try to right it.

Three months later, having heard nothing from Vladimiroff, Navis and Gerhardstein arranged a second meeting with her. She now expressed concern about what she called the "public nature" of their relationship. Indicating that the diocese would not agree to an arbitration meeting, she added that she did not see how it could offer Navis a contract at Erieview for the next year. The next day, May 29, she directed the Erieview principal to withold Navis' contract until further notice.

On May 31 Navis and Gerhardstein met with supporters

Lesbian and Gay Pride Parade, more on pp 6-7

HIT Names Gearhart

By JEFF SWINDLER

Randy Gearhart has been

made possible by a grant from the U.S. Council of Mayors and donations from

Gay People's Chronicle became Cleveland's second major publication for the LGBTQ community when it was launched in 1985 by Charles Callender, a professor of anthropology at Case Western Reserve University. What began as a free monthly offering soon grew into a distribution of every other Friday. Circulation reached 15,000 copies with availability in more than 300 businesses, every college campus in the state, and every library system in Cuyahoga County. The publication suffered the fate of countless other newspapers across the country whose advertising dollars dried up in the face of internet usage. After a remarkable run of 31 years, printing ceased on December 25, 2015. (Above, Western Reserve Historical Society; below, Brian DeWitt.)

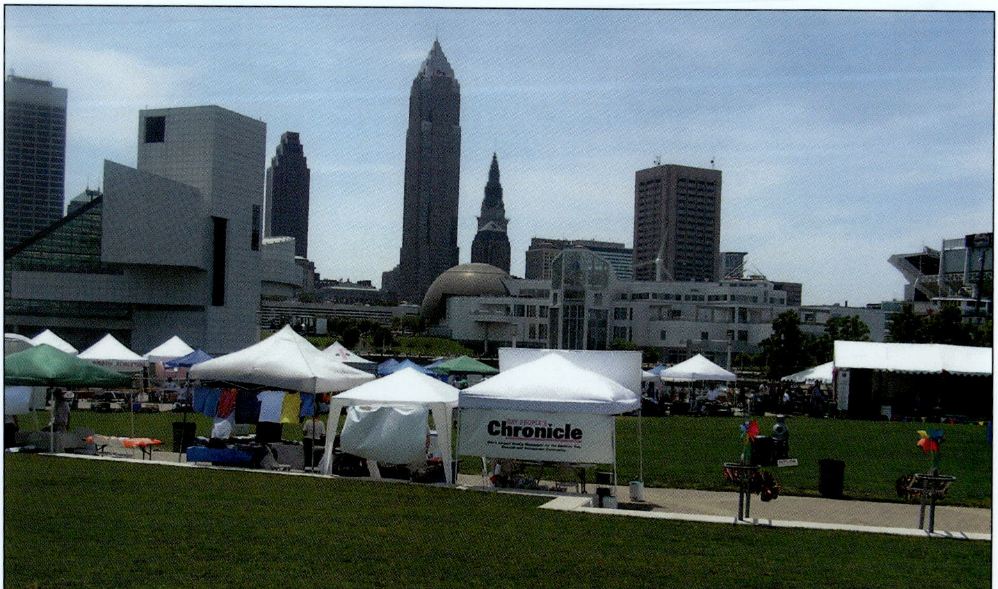

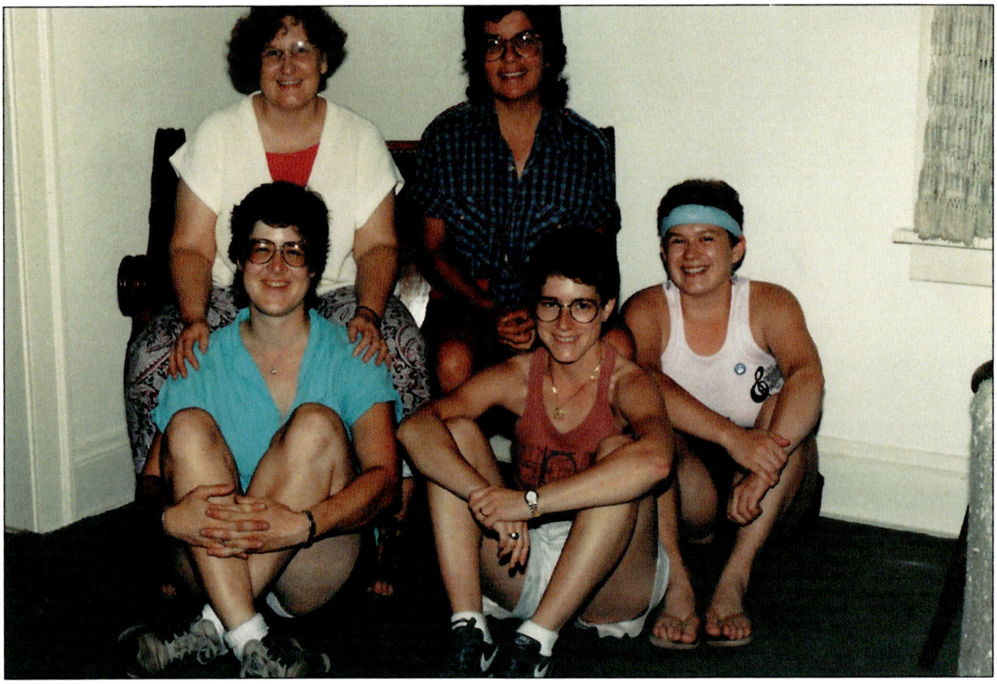

It is simply impossible to overestimate the contributions of Oven Productions to the cultural landscape of both Cleveland and Northeast Ohio. Its humble origins began in October 1975 as a nonprofit collective of six women who wanted to highlight the artistic and musical talents of other women. The organization's efforts quickly coalesced an entire community, and attendance soared over the years at the various events it promotes, which includes art exhibits, films, concerts, dramatic presentations, and of course, the Annual Womyn's Variety Show. Oven Productions' roster of events over 40-plus years is distinguished by both its demonstrated commitment to bringing established voices to Northeast Ohio as well as its unwavering dedication to providing new talent with a microphone for all to hear. (Above, Brynna Fish; below, Sally Tatnall.)

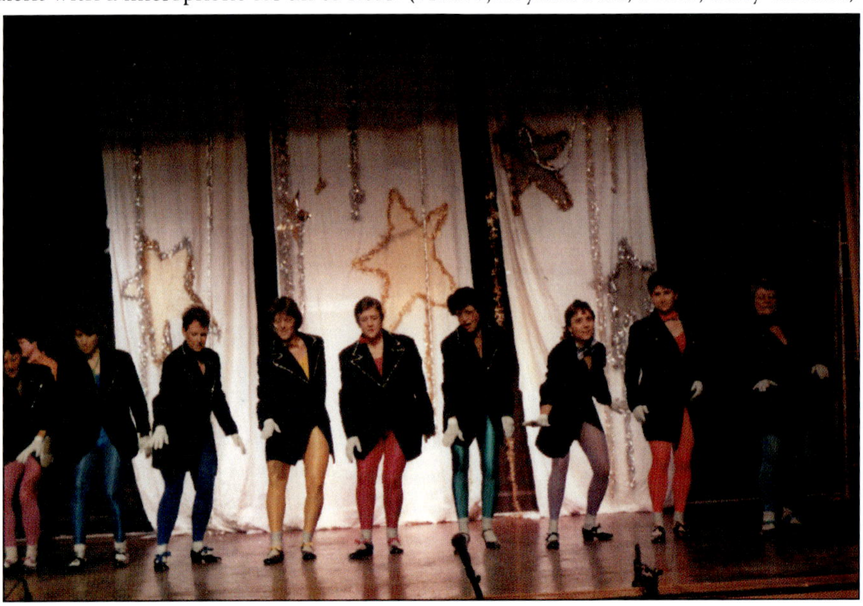

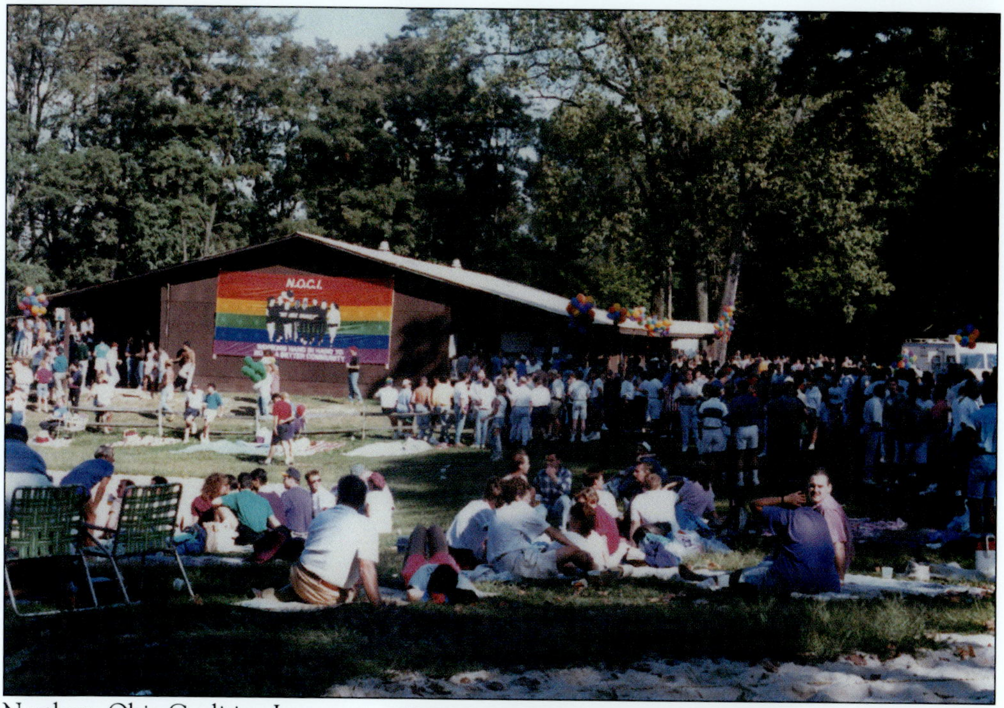

Northern Ohio Coalition Inc. (NOCI) was originally formed in 1978 as an organization of business leaders in the LGBTQ community. An annual highlight in Cleveland was the NOCI Picnic, held for many years at Wildwood Lake Park in Columbia Station. NOCI continues its mission as an all-volunteer, nonprofit organization committed to addressing the financial needs of those living with HIV and AIDS within the LGBT community. (Brian DeWitt.)

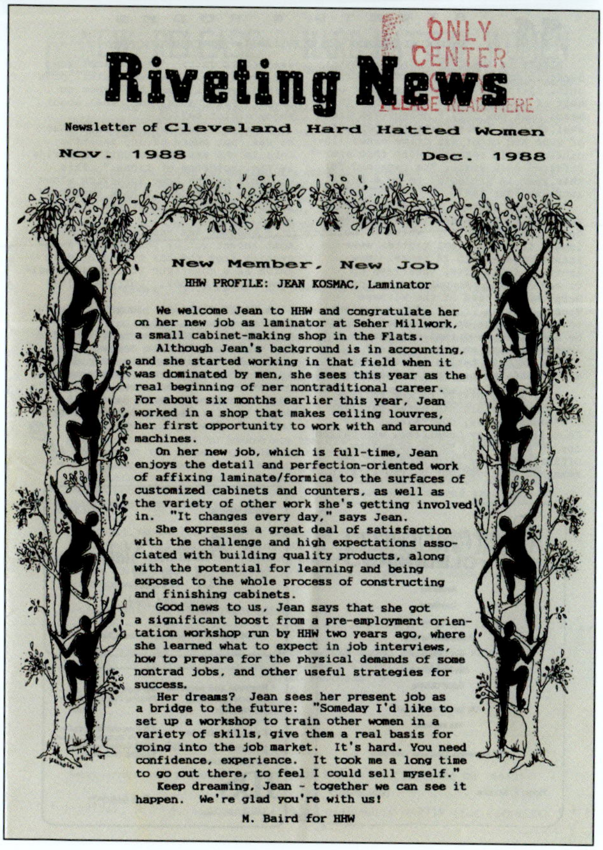

Riveting News

Newsletter of Cleveland Hard Hatted Women

Nov. 1988 Dec. 1988

New Member, New Job

HHW PROFILE: JEAN KOSMAC, Laminator

We welcome Jean to HHW and congratulate her on her new job as laminator at Seher Millwork, a small cabinet-making shop in the Flats.

Although Jean's background is in accounting, and she started working in that field when it was dominated by men, she sees this year as the real beginning of ner nontraditional career. For about six months earlier this year, Jean worked in a shop that makes ceiling louvres, her first opportunity to work with and around machines.

On her new job, which is full-time, Jean enjoys the detail and perfection-oriented work of affixing laminate/formica to the surfaces of customized cabinets and counters, as well as the variety of other work she's getting involved in. "It changes every day," says Jean.

She expresses a great deal of satisfaction with the challenge and high expectations associated with building quality products, along with the potential for learning and being exposed to the whole process of constructing and finishing cabinets.

Good news to us, Jean says that she got a significant boost from a pre-employment orientation workshop run by HHW two years ago, where she learned what to expect in job interviews, how to prepare for the physical demands of some nontrad jobs, and other useful strategies for success.

Her dreams? Jean sees her present job as a bridge to the future: "Someday I'd like to set up a workshop to train other women in a variety of skills, give them a real basis for going into the job market. It's hard. You need confidence, experience. It took me a long time to go out there, to feel I could sell myself."

Keep dreaming, Jean - together we can see it happen. We're glad you're with us!

M. Baird for HHW

Created in 1978, Cleveland Hard Hatted Women (HHW) was formed to provide support and networking to women working in skilled labor positions and industries. Though it was not an organization specifically designed for lesbians, many Cleveland women reported that HHW provided a vital outlet for lesbians to be able to connect with their peers who were having similar experiences in distinctly male-dominated work. (Western Reserve Historical Society.)

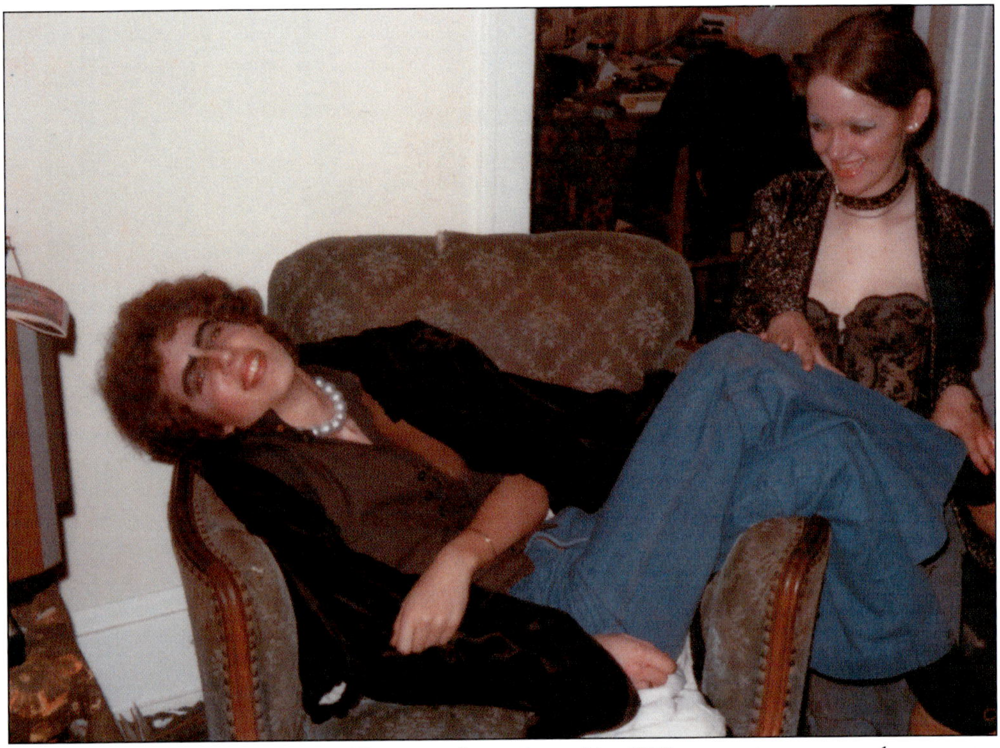

When *The Rocky Horror Picture Show* was first released in 1975, screenings across the country had to be canceled due to low attendance. After midnight screenings were introduced in various cities (coupled with free admission if attendees showed up dressed in costume), the cult following began and continues strongly to this day. With high camp content, cross-dressing antics, and "a sweet transvestite from Transylvania" lead, the film quickly became entrenched within both the LGBTQ community at large and, most definitely, in Cleveland. From Chris and Sadie lounging as Dr. Frank N. Furter and Columbia in 1978 (above) to a group of marchers at Cleveland Pride almost 40 years later (below), it is clear that everyone will continue to do the Time Warp again and again—and again. (Both, Brian DeWitt.)

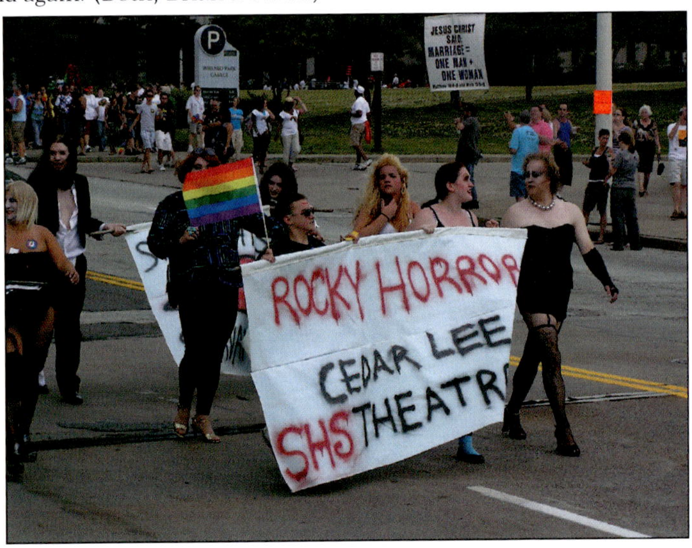

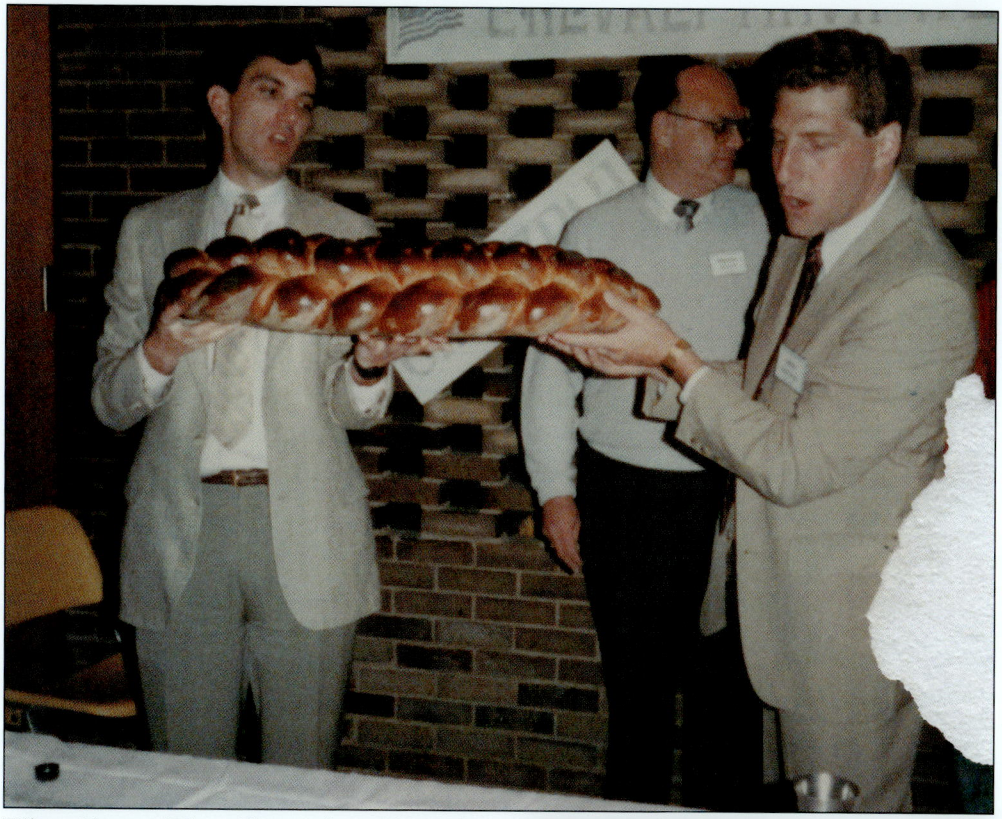

When Chevrei Tikva Chavurah was formed in 1983, it became one of the first congregations in Ohio for LGBTQ Jews. Originally led by student rabbis and lay leaders, they hired their first full-time spiritual leader in 2002 and became part of the Anshe Chesed Fairmount Temple synagogue community in 2005. In July 1988, Cleveland hosted the Midwest Regional Conference of Gay and Lesbian Jews at the Hillel on the campus of Case Western Reserve University (above), attracting Jews from far beyond the borders of Northeast Ohio. Chevrei Tikva hosts an annual Pride Shabbat, and congregants regularly participate in Cleveland Pride festivities. (Above, Victor Karp; right, Santina Cirino.)

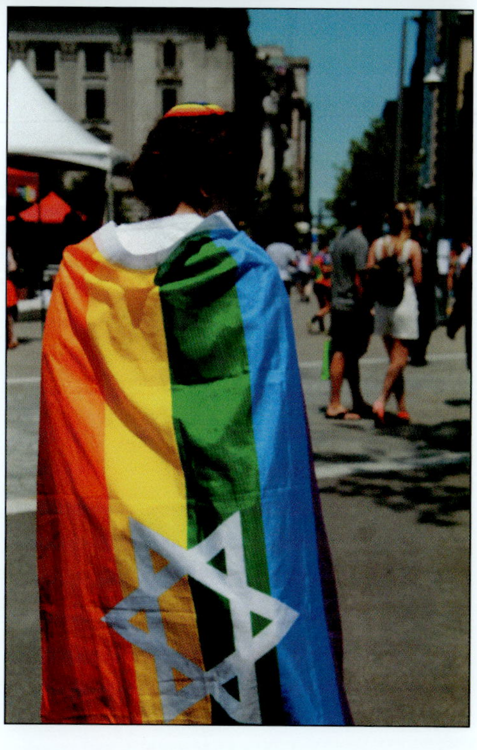

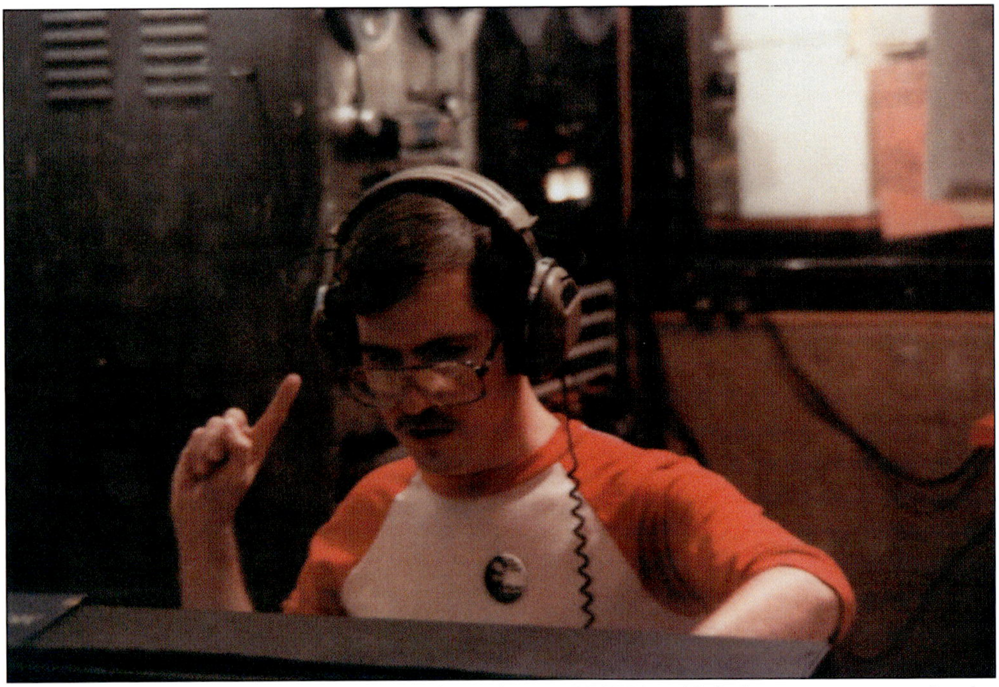

GayWaves is the long-running radio show hosted on WRUW 91.1 FM, the noncommercial radio station hosted by Case Western Reserve University. The show was launched in the 1970s as *Radio Free Lambda* by John Vogel and was rebranded years later as *GayWaves* to carry a more descriptive and obvious name. Billed as "the original gay voice of America's North Coast," *GayWaves* continues to cover the latest news and views, information, and music for the proud and out LGBTQ, intersex, multicultural, and multiracial community of greater Cleveland. The show began broadcasting with 10 watts, a far cry from and a dramatically more limited reach than the 15,000 watts at which the show broadcasts currently. (Both, Brian DeWitt.)

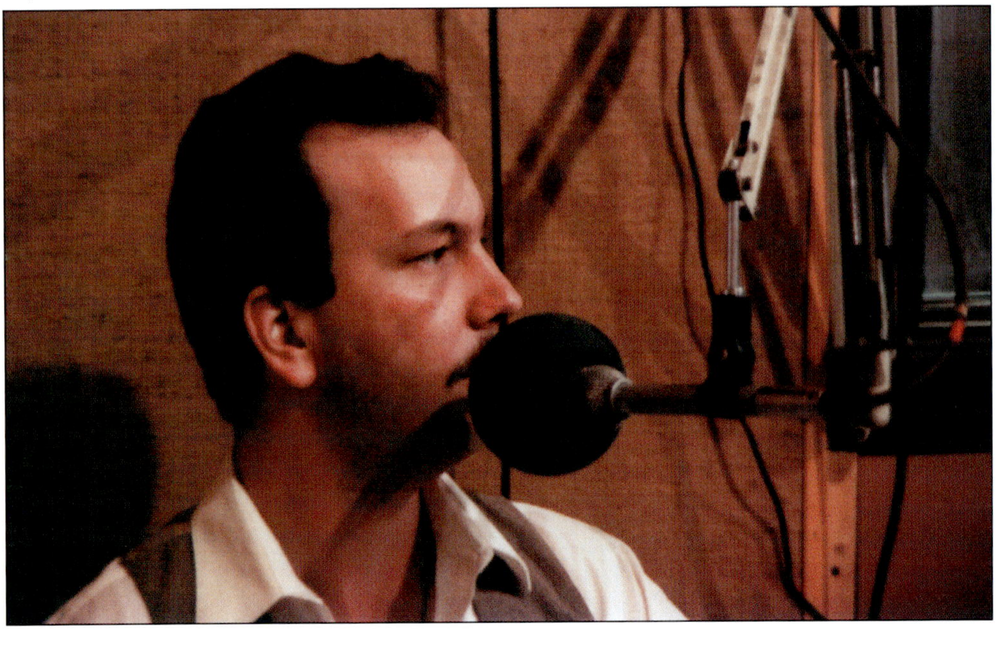

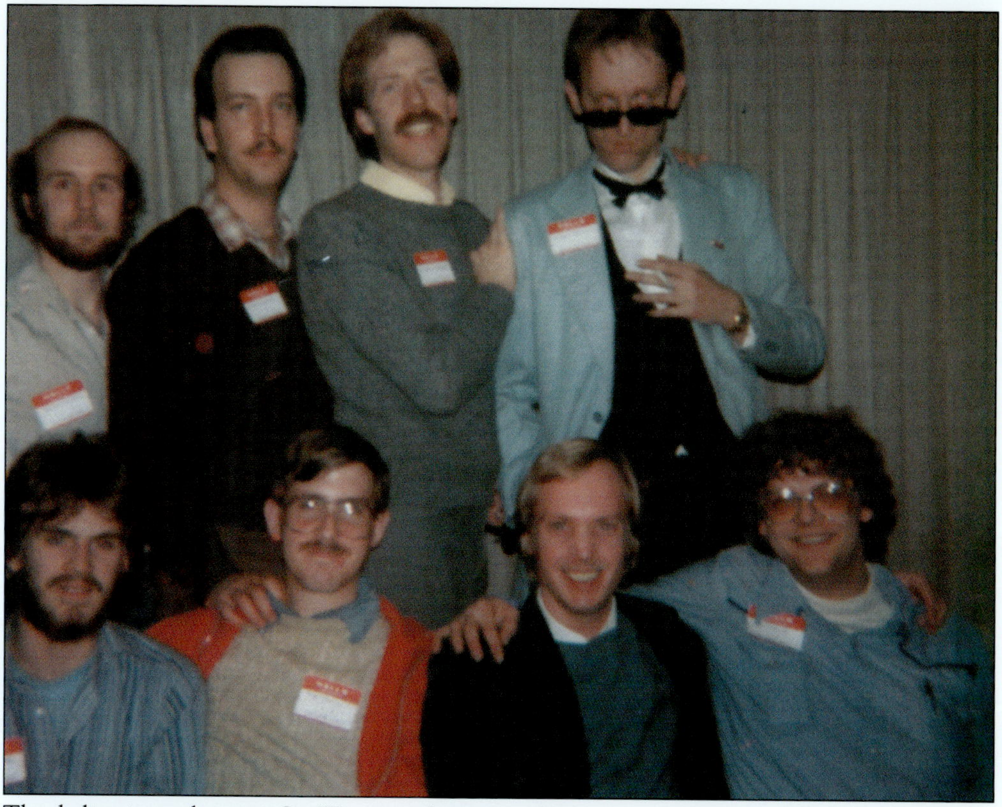

The dedication to keeping *GayWaves* on the air was felt by everyone who stepped foot and worked in the studio. The staff (pictured above in 1984) had different levels of experience with radio from licensed pro to first-time novice, but they shared a passion for broadcasting LGBTQ voices speaking about the issues that mattered most to the community's equality, health, and future. Not even the loss of the studio kept *GayWaves* off the air. When renovations needed to be done at the station, the staff picked up the show and moved it temporarily to the apartment of Brian DeWitt. From a makeshift setup at a dining table (below), the news was covered, the interviews were conducted, and the phone calls came in, as the show must (and did) go on. (Both, Brian DeWitt.)

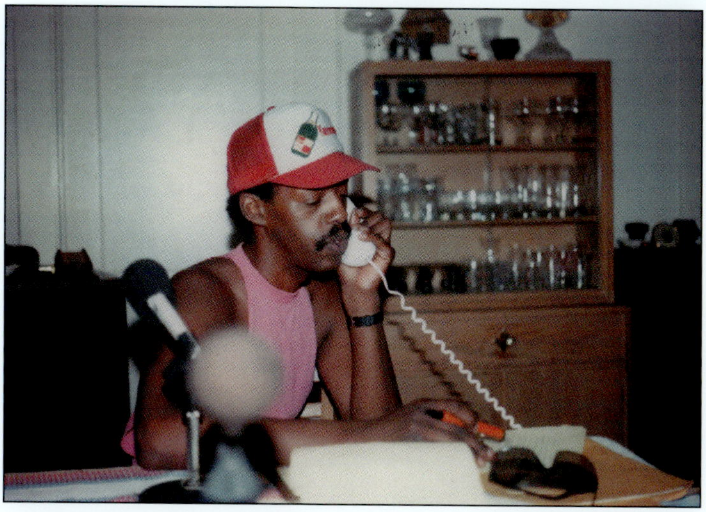

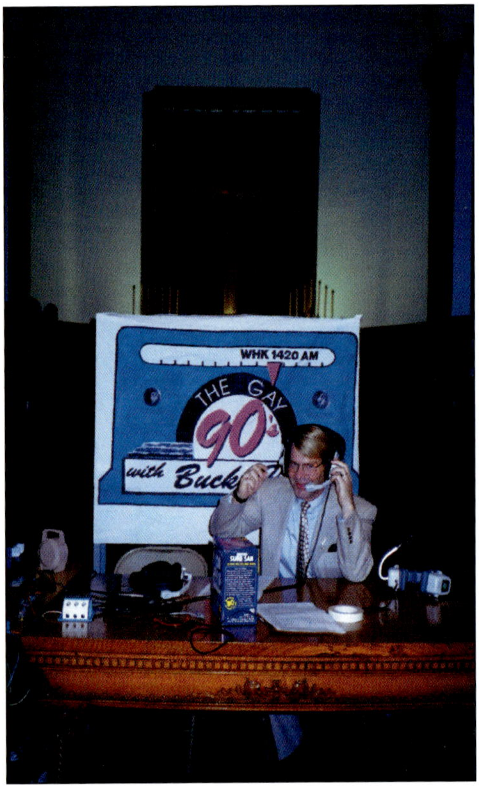

As historian Leda Carol Drake wrote, "The nation's first gay and lesbian talk radio show, *The Gay 90s*, aired from downtown Cleveland, Ohio and started off with a bang. Not literally, but given the bomb threat called in before the show's premier broadcast on WHK 1420 AM, it was a possibility." Hosted by Cleveland native Buck Harris, *The Gay 90s* ran from 1993 to 1999, was heard by roughly 20,000 a week, and featured interviews with everyone from Congressman Barney Frank, to famed activist Quentin Crisp, to singer/songwriter Janis Ian. Buck Harris worked tirelessly, both on and off the air, to advance the equality of LGBTQ Clevelanders, including serving as the Ohio Department of Health's first gay health consultant and demanding that the *Cleveland Plain Dealer* use the word "gay" for the first time (as opposed to pejorative "homosexual," as was their policy at the time). (Both, Special Collections, Michael Schwartz Library at Cleveland State University.)

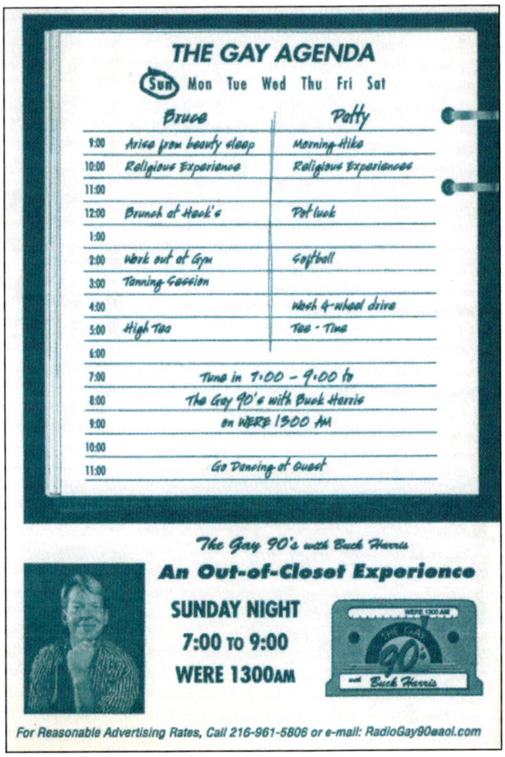

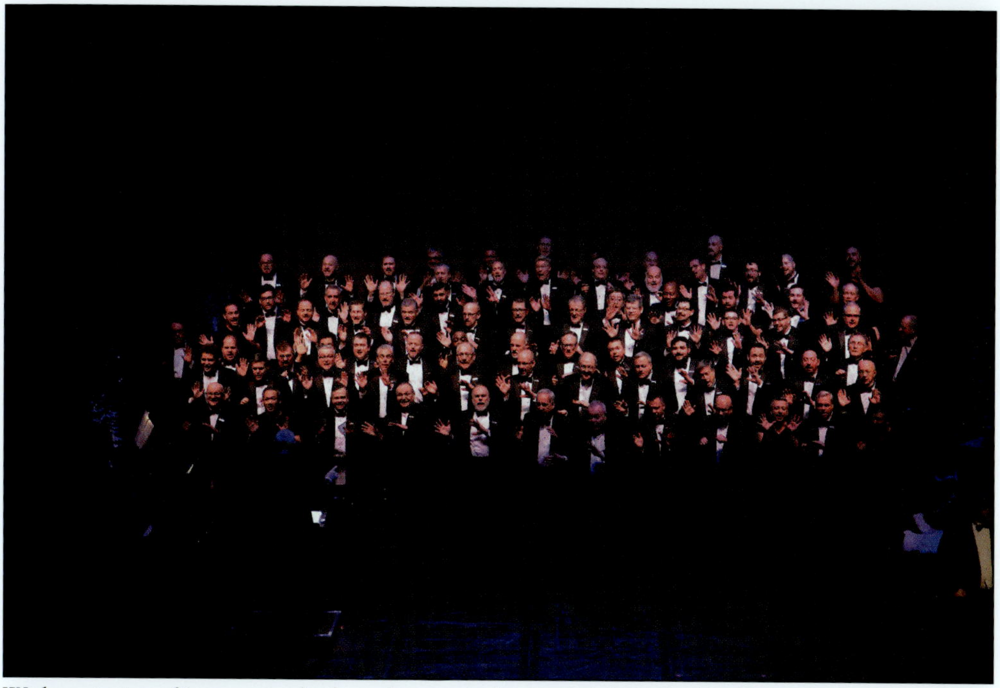

With a mission of "presenting high quality musical entertainment for diverse audiences, promoting a positive influence within and beyond the gay community, and providing a supportive environment for its members and participants," the North Coast Men's Chorus (NCMC) has been delighting Cleveland audiences since 1988. From their humble beginnings as a local group performing in area churches, NCMC has grown into one of the largest gay arts organizations in Northeast Ohio. (Jim Greenfield.)

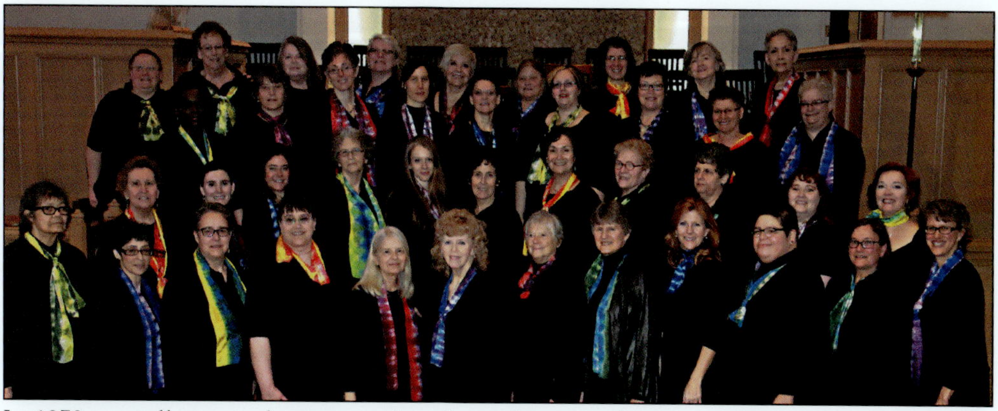

In 1979, a small group of women gathered together as a chorus to perform as a single act for a community event, and Windsong was born. Billing itself as "Cleveland's Feminist Chorus," Windsong seeks to "empower women through their participation in the performance of music" as they "effect social change that is diverse, women-supportive and environmentally responsible." (Amanda Strand.)

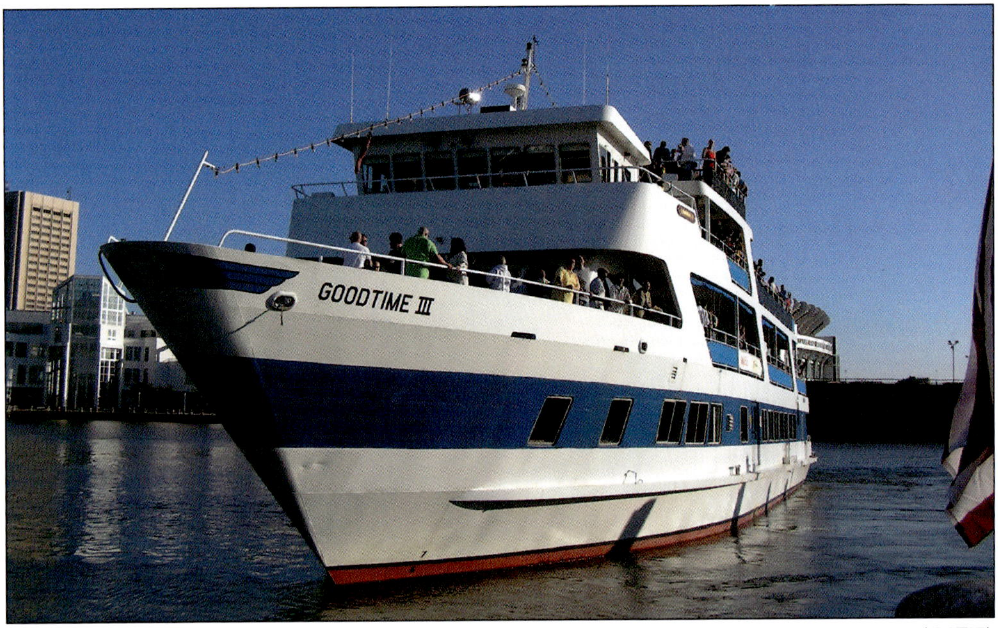

First setting sail in 1989, the Cleveland Gay/Lesbian Invitational Fellowship Tournament (GIFT) Cruise originated as "something unique" for bowlers and guests to do on a Saturday night. Chartered on the *Goodtime III* sailing along the Cuyahoga River and Lake Erie, the event has become one the most well-attended LGBTQ events in Cleveland, with cruises featuring over 700 participants and tens of thousands of dollars raised for local nonprofit organizations. (Brian DeWitt.)

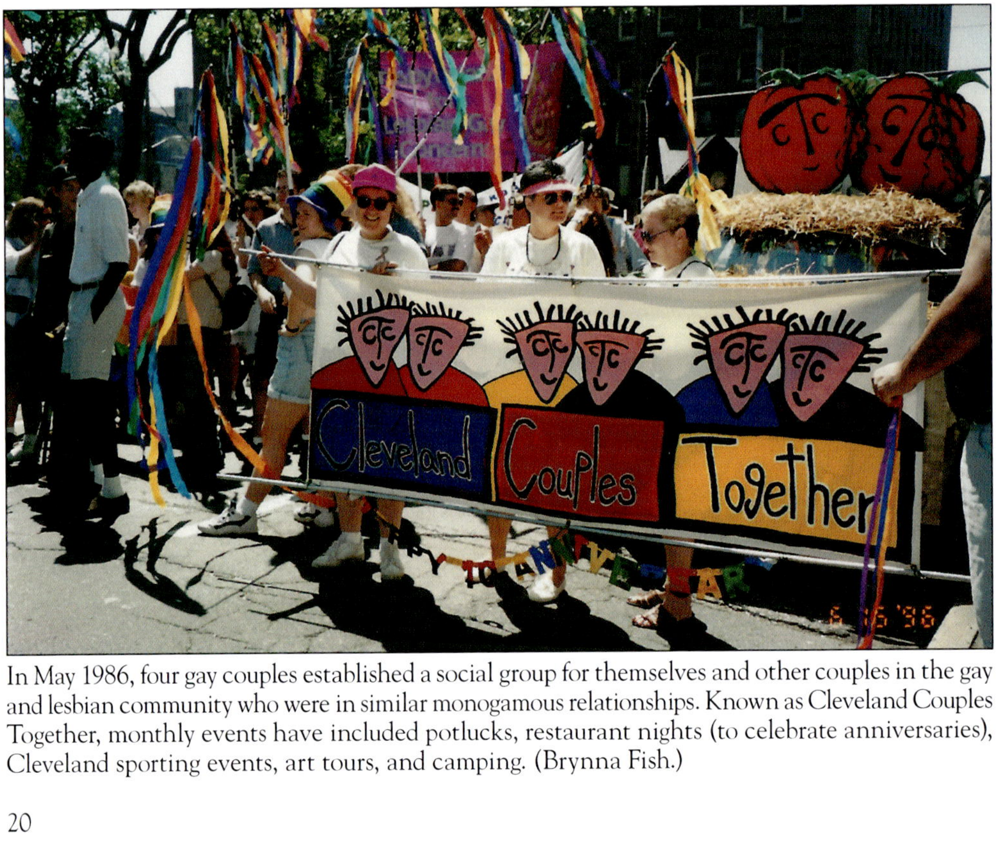

In May 1986, four gay couples established a social group for themselves and other couples in the gay and lesbian community who were in similar monogamous relationships. Known as Cleveland Couples Together, monthly events have included potlucks, restaurant nights (to celebrate anniversaries), Cleveland sporting events, art tours, and camping. (Brynna Fish.)

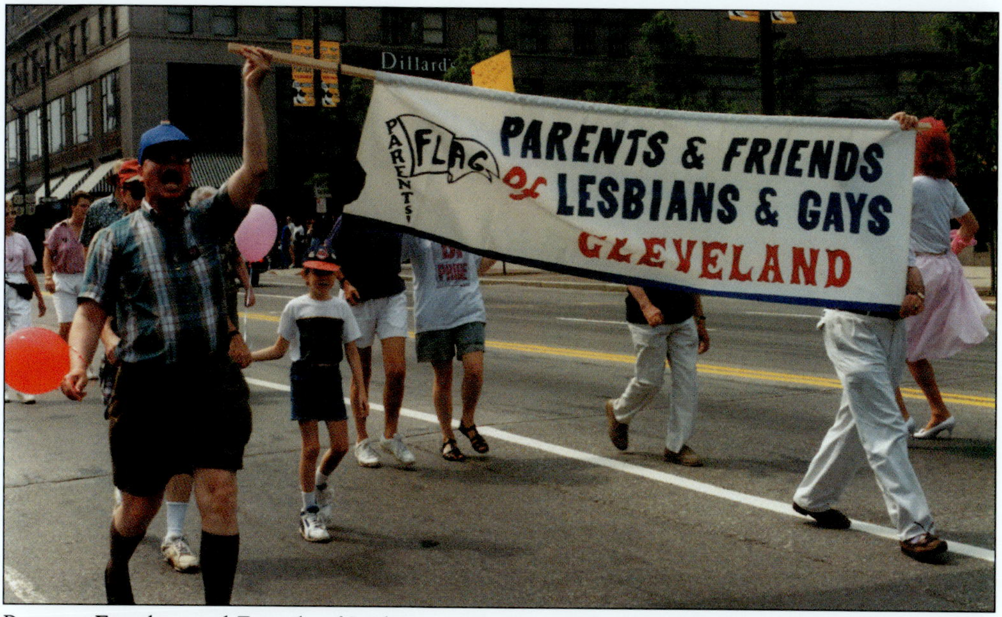

Parents, Families and Friends of Lesbians and Gays (PFLAG) Cleveland held its first meeting in July 1985 at Trinity Cathedral, which agreed to host the group monthly at no charge. Jane Daroff and Jes Sellers founded the chapter to be an educational and emotional support group and fulfill PFLAG's national mission of celebrating diversity and envisioning a society that embraces everyone, including those of diverse sexual orientations and gender identities. (Brian DeWitt.)

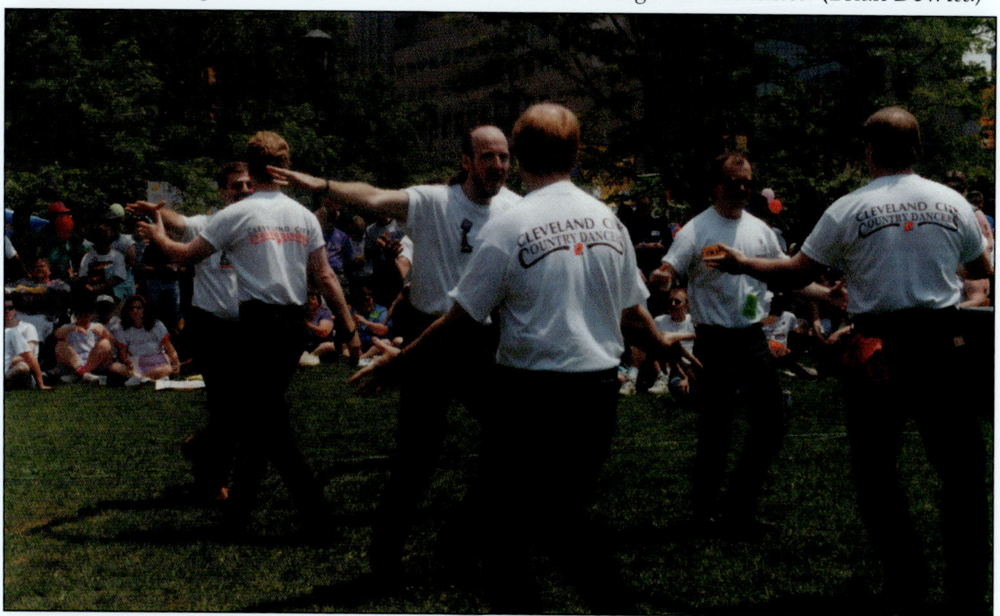

The Cleveland City Country Dancers (CCCD) were formed when Ed Schellhous tried to get a group together to teach them square dancing. The original hoofers struggled to gain participants in the early years, some nights pulling patrons of questionable sobriety into the square. But with a large influx of dancers in 1992, CCCD became the first Ohio member of the International Association of Gay Square Dance Clubs. Weekly lessons, successful fundraising, and a heck of a lot of dancing followed for decades thereafter. (Brian DeWitt.)

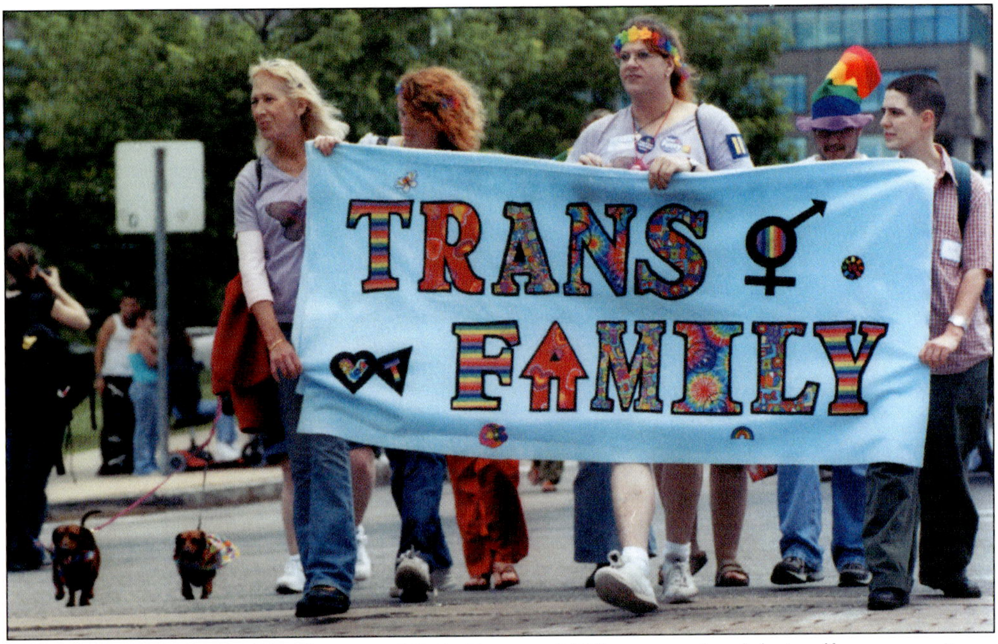

TransFamily was created by Karen and Bob Gross in 1995 as a result of their efforts to navigate their own child's transition. The group provides support, education, advocacy, and outreach for the transgender community, families, friends, partners, and allies of all ages. Their regular group meetings are known throughout Cleveland as a place where everyone is welcome, cared for, and affirmed. (Brynna Fish.)

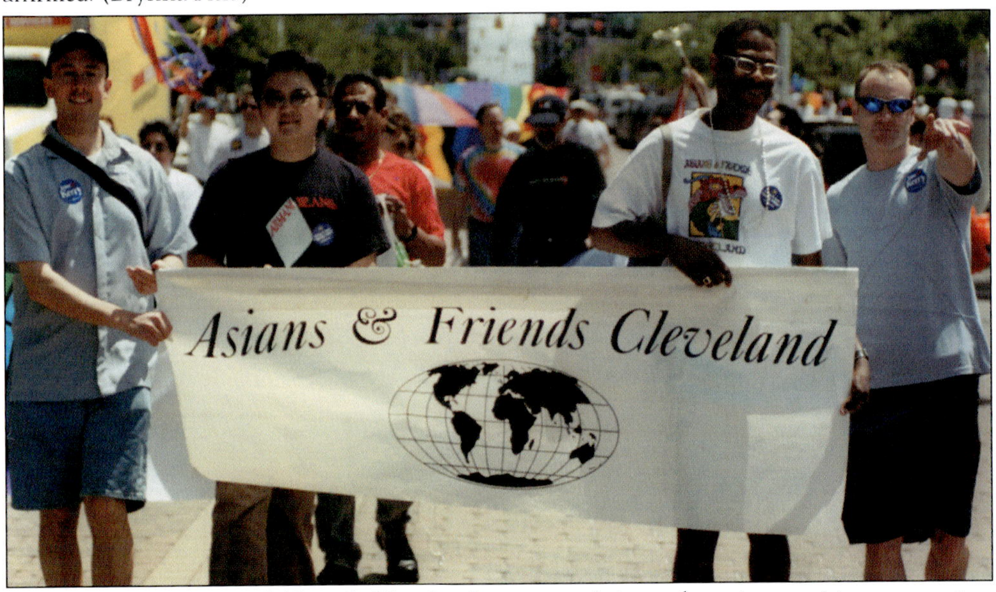

Formed in 1995, Asians & Friends Cleveland promotes Asian culture in a positive, supportive, informative, and fun setting while bridging the gap between various cultures, including contributing to the educational and cultural life of the LGBTQ communities of the Northeast Ohio region. Asians & Friends Cleveland hosted the 1998 International Friendship Weekend, showcasing the whole city of Cleveland for the many attendees of this international social and educational gathering. (Brynna Fish.)

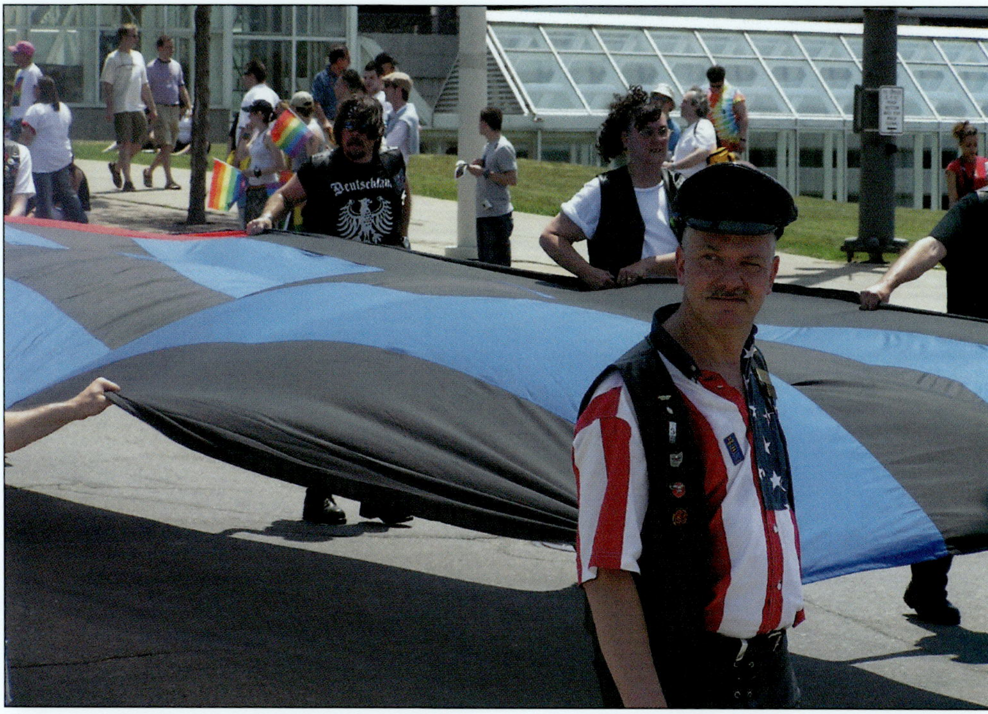

The first Cleveland Leather Awareness Weekend (CLAW) was held in 2002 at the Tool Shed on Detroit Avenue and Twenty-Ninth Street. The event was an enormous success and led to even larger conventions every subsequent year featuring educational workshops, contests, vendors, and fundraising. The weekend is sponsored by CLAW Corp, a nonprofit "dedicated to fundraising, education, volunteerism and all other charitable needs of the adult leather community." Through the convention and smaller events around the country throughout the year, CLAW has raised hundreds of thousands of dollars for charitable organizations, gaining national recognition for both their overall philanthropy as well as their unwavering dedication to the principle that people into leather are normal, happy, and healthy. (Both, Brian DeWitt.)

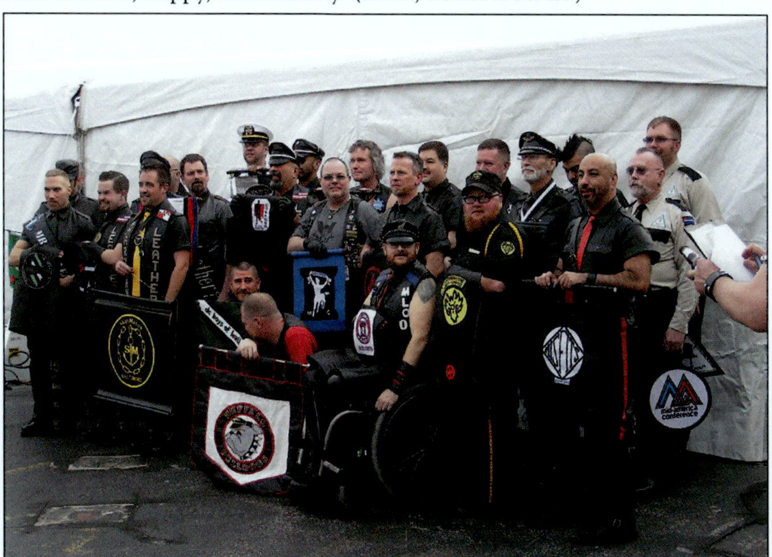

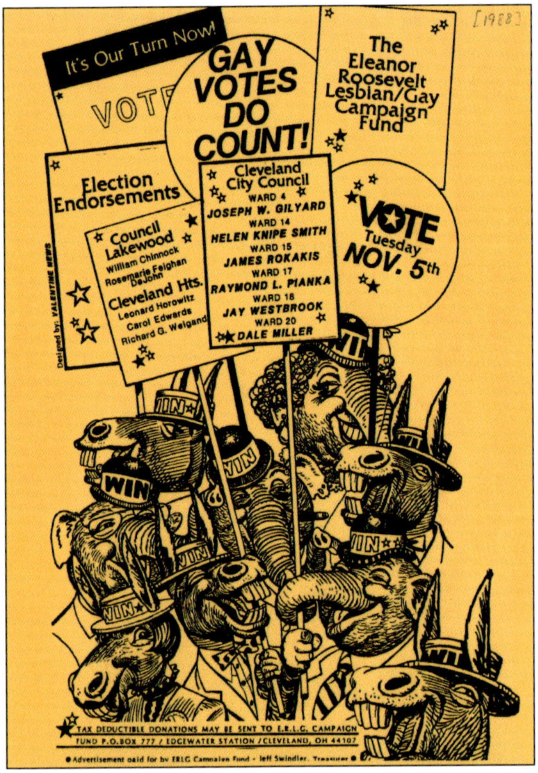

Throughout the 1980s, the Eleanor Roosevelt Gay Political Club was a place for politically-minded individuals to research and disseminate information on candidates and legislative issues important to the LGBTQ community. They also raised funds for candidates who would support the LGBTQ community in the fight for civil rights. Their last major endorsement was of Jesse Jackson in the 1988 presidential Democratic primary. (Western Reserve Historical Society.)

The Cleveland Stonewall Democrats were established in 2000 to educate, endorse, elect, and hold accountable pro-LGBTQ Democrats across Greater Cleveland. They are devoted to securing equal rights for all people, regardless of sexual orientation or gender identity, through advocating public policy, engaging voters to elect Democratic candidates, and energizing the LGBTQ community to provide financial and volunteer support for LGBTQ and LGBTQ-supportive Democratic candidates. (Robert Rivera.)

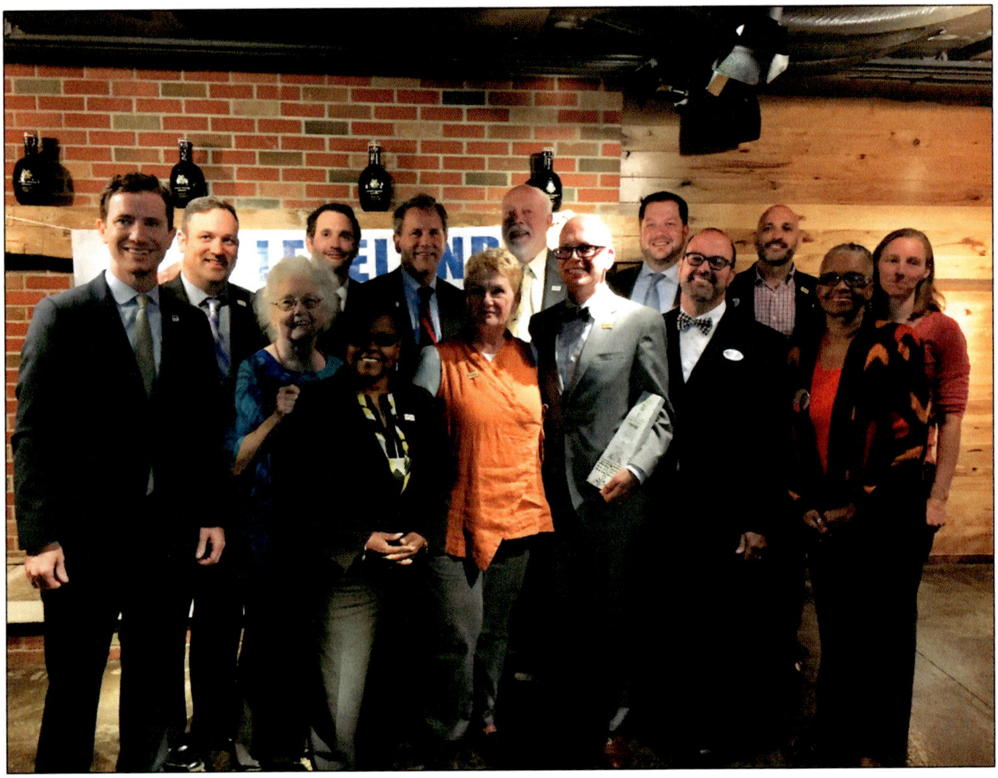

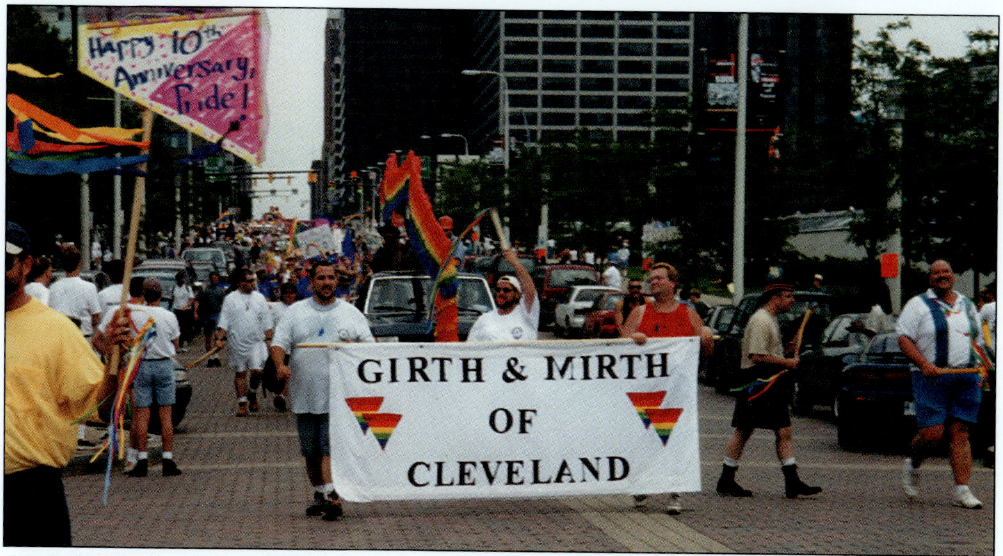

Girth & Mirth of Cleveland was a social club "for gay/bisexual chubby men and their male admirers." The group was also dedicated to educating, promoting, and aiding in the welfare of the gay community. Their meetings on the first Saturday of the month featured a variety of activities including a Monte Carlo night, a chili cook-off, and a heck of a lot of buffets and picnics. (Brynna Fish.)

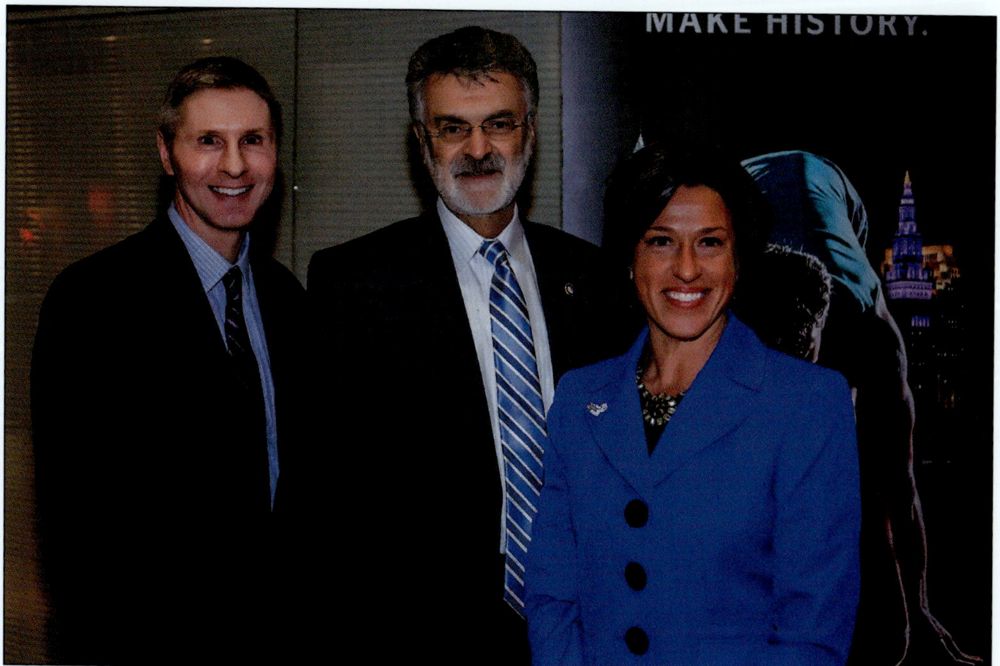

Making its debut as a nonprofit in 2006, Plexus is the region's LGBTQ chamber of commerce. Plexus provides the only network for LGBTQ and allied business owners and professionals by hosting events (including an annual meeting pictured here with Mayor Frank Jackson in 2011); educating on cultural competency, business certification, and Employee Resource Groups; advocating for workplace equality; promoting LGBTQ business development; and serving as a lead community partner in the 2014 Gay Games. (Linda Ford.)

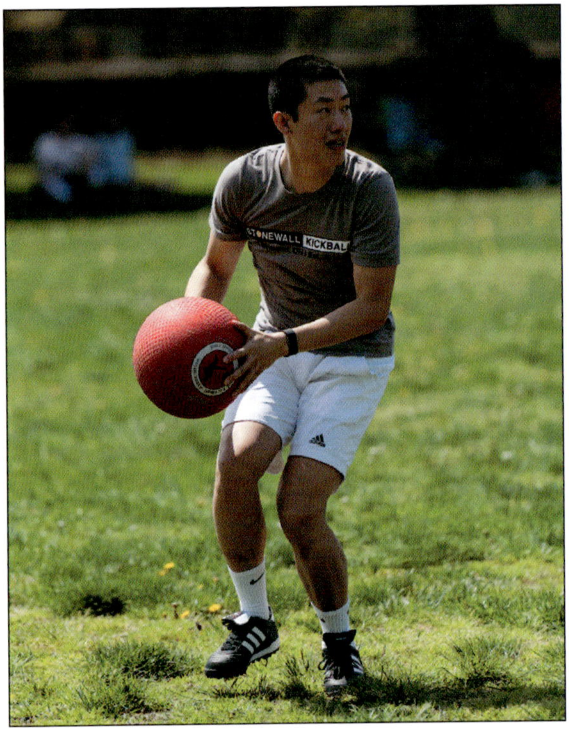

Stonewall Sports was founded in Washington, DC, in 2010 as an LGBTQ & ally community-based, nonprofit sports organization with a philanthropic aim of raising funds for local nonprofit organizations through organized sports. In 2015, Cleveland became the ninth expansion city of the league with the introduction of a wildly popular kickball league. A dodgeball league followed in 2016, and bocce ball hit the grass of Edgewater Park in the summer of 2017. Only a few short years after the launch of Cleveland Stonewall Sports, the league boasts a roster of hundreds of players, has raised tens of thousands of dollars for Cleveland organizations, and continues to create a safe, inclusive, and welcoming environment where individuals are comfortable being themselves while taking part in a fun sport. (Both, Dave Nash.)

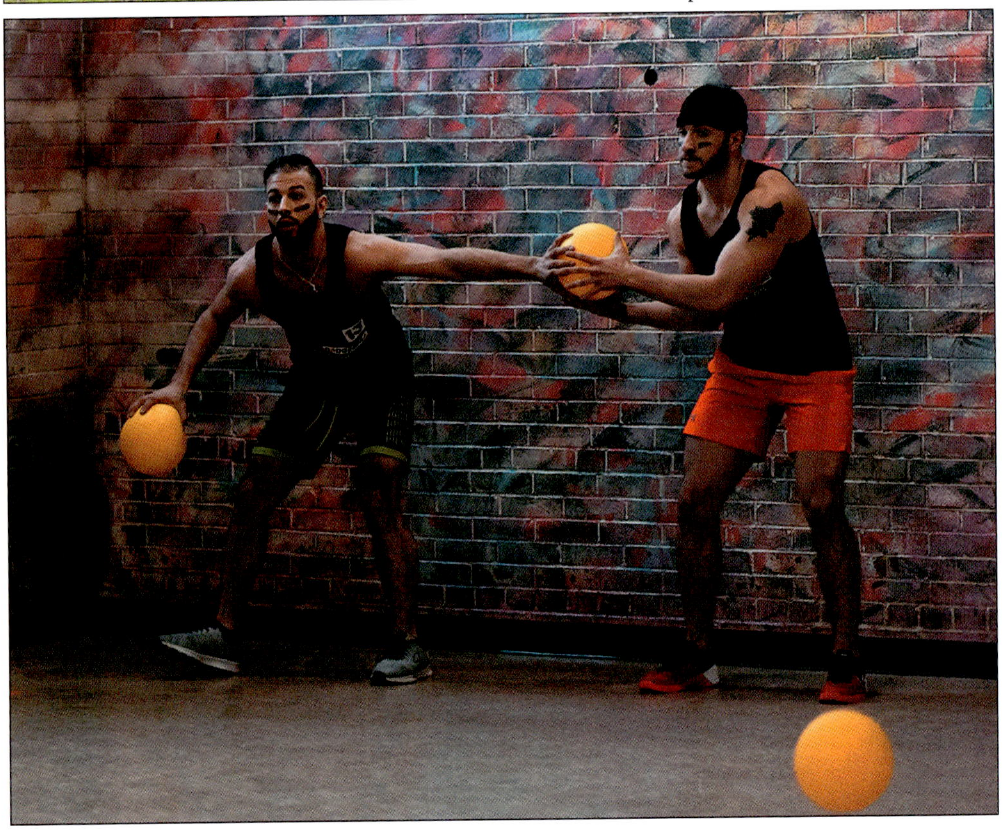

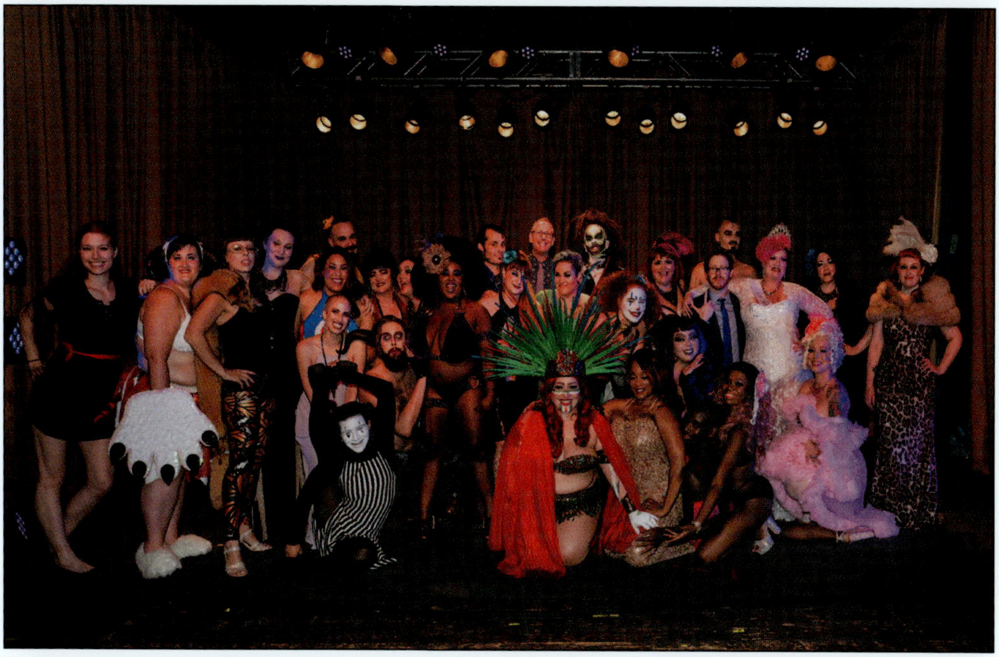

Le Femme Mystique Burlesque was founded by Bella Sin in 2004 and has become the longest running burlesque show in Ohio. The troupe is committed to featuring performers regardless of shape, size, sexual orientation, or gender expression/identity. Le Femme Mystique hosts the Ohio International Burlesque Festival and has been recognized for its philanthropy by both the Cleveland City Council and the Ohio House of Representatives. (Bob Perkoski.)

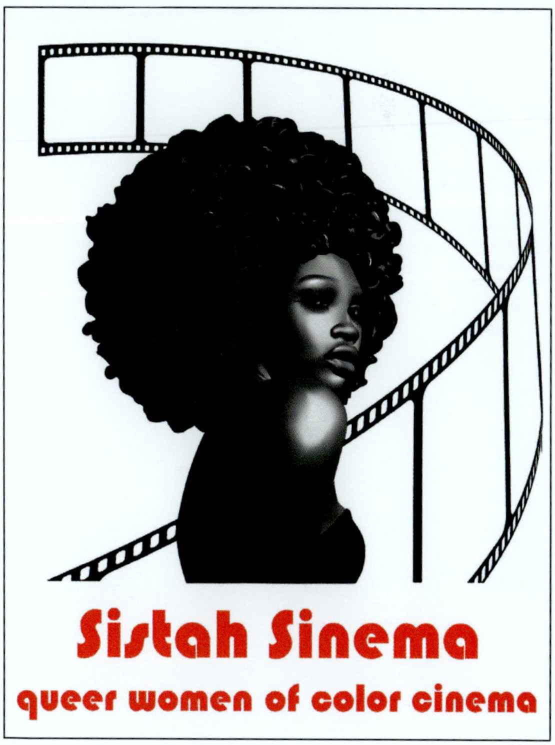

In 2012, Deidre McPherson launched the Cleveland chapter of Sistah Sinema, a monthly film series created to showcase the nuances of queer women of color culture, screening dozens of films at various nonprofit arts venues all over Cleveland. Sistah Sinema got its start in Seattle in 2011 with the hope that these movies would serve as a vehicle to foster honest dialogue on struggles and opportunities unique to queer women of color. (Andrew Warren.)

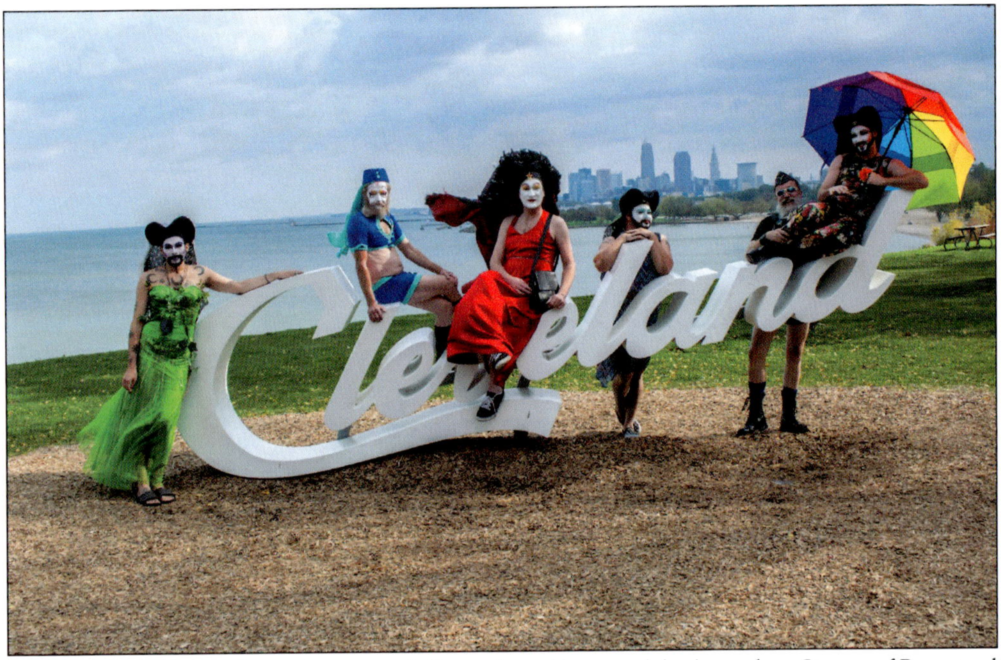

The Rock n Roll City Sisters became a fully professed house of the legendary Sisters of Perpetual Indulgence in 2013. Formed in San Francisco in the late 1970s, the original Sisters quickly became known for their creative activism and ability to raise much-needed funds in some truly dire times. They organized the first AIDS Candelight Vigil in 1983 and, over the years, have inspired the installation of more than 50 houses around the world practicing their "ministry of presence." With their roots firmly planted in this "sistory," the Cleveland chapter works toward the elimination of hate, stigma, prejudice, ridicule, and discrimination through outreach, education, awareness, and direct action. (Both, Ian Argo.)

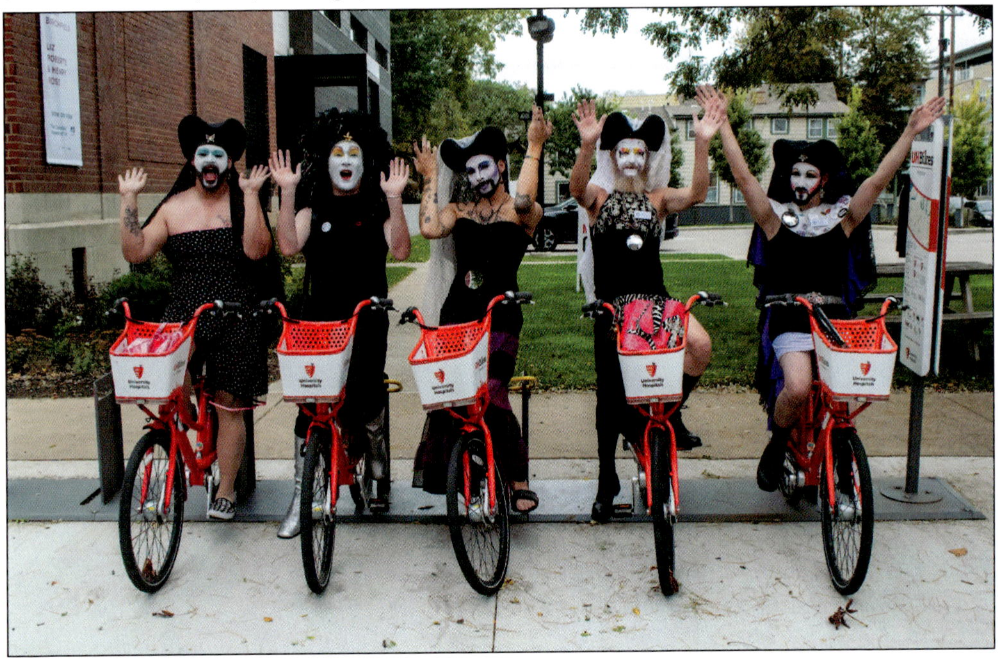

Two

We Gather
Events and Spaces

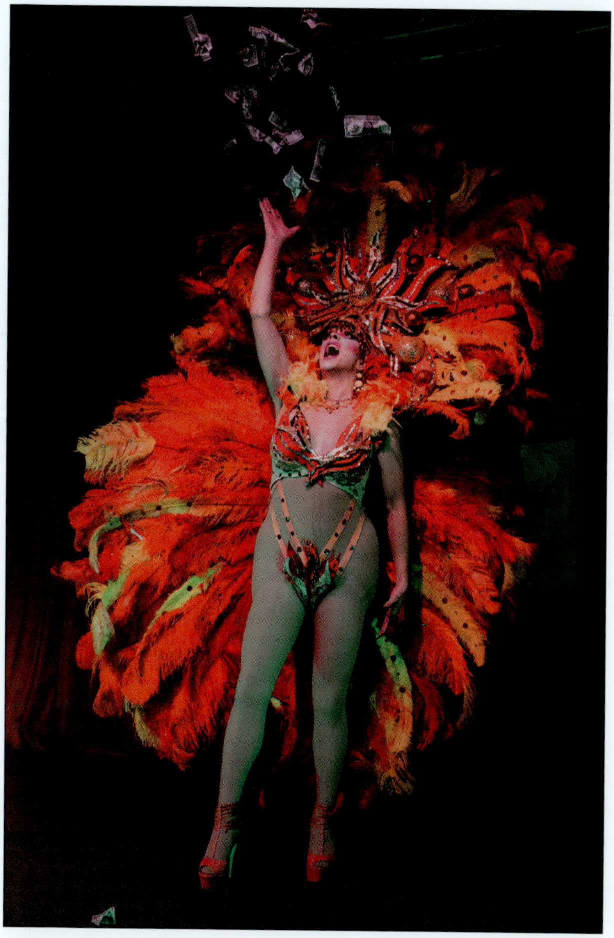

The Cleveland LGBTQ community has physically come together in a broad range of ways. Whether a raucous crowd appreciating the talents in a variety show, a gay figure skater performing against competitors from around the world, or a committed group of citizens simply walking together to raise much-needed funds, these events and spaces provide a vivid illustration of the sheer power of strength in numbers. (Bob Perkoski.)

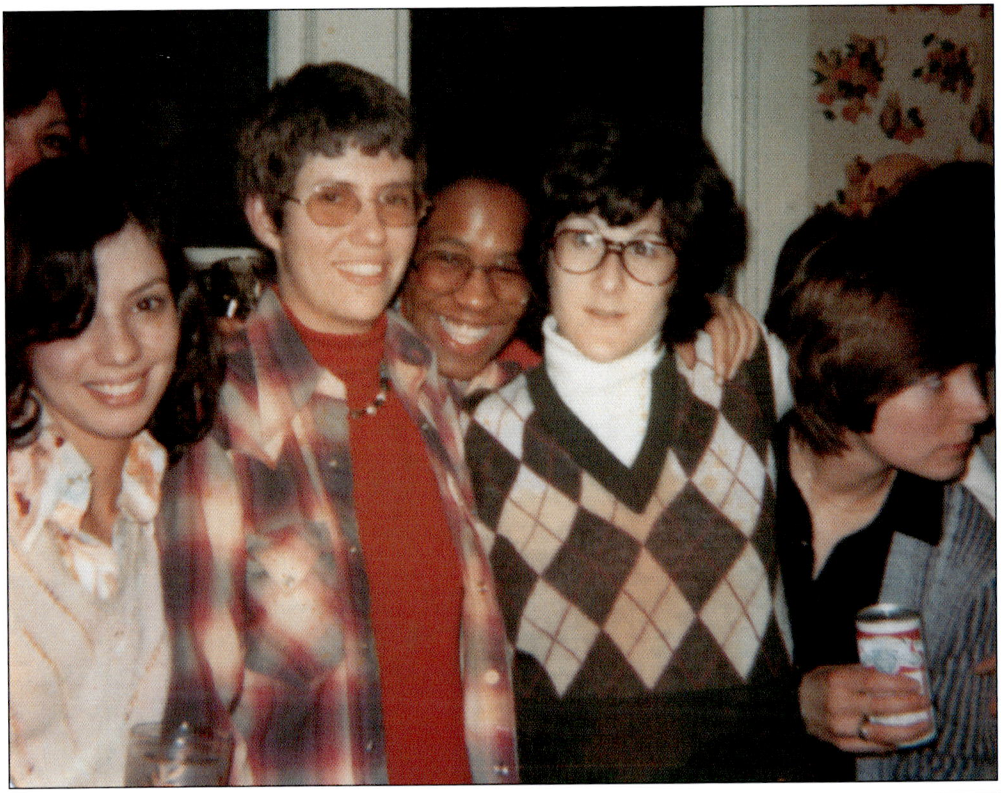

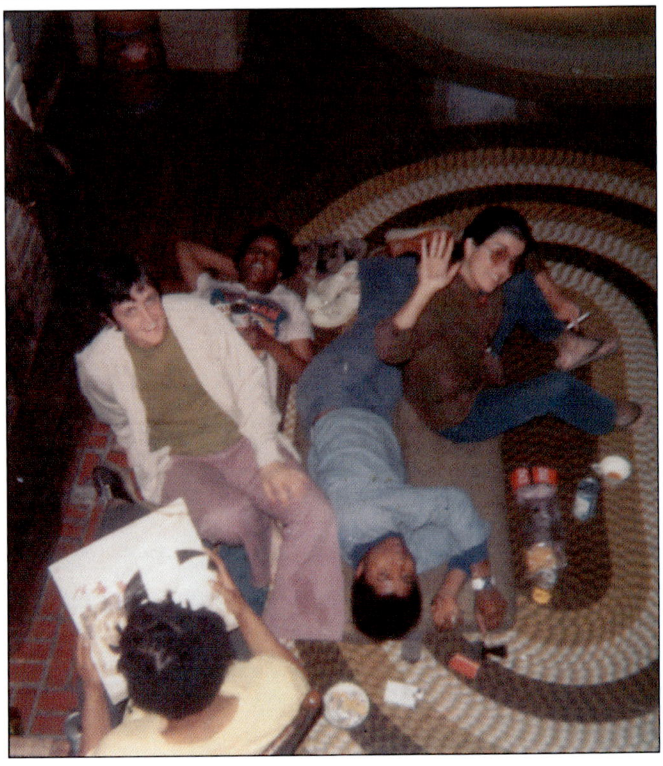

In the mid- to late 1970s, women regularly gathered in a house in Cleveland Heights owned by Sally Tatnall. While some called the space "Berkshire House" (after the street on which the structure was situated), many affectionately referred to it as "Hag House." The space was whatever these women needed it to be: an activist collective, a social gathering spot, a political discourse roundtable, a potluck emporium, and even a roller rink when the women needed to practice their skating routine for the Womyn's Variety Show. Above all else, it was a house where lesbians and their allies could gather together, tap into the spirit of the community, and just be their authentic selves. (Both, Sally Tatnall.)

In the 1970s, a group of lesbians in Cleveland decided that they needed a space where they could acquire, hold, and manage land and other property for the social and recreational use and enjoyment of their members; conserve and preserve natural habitats; and pursue the vision that women and girls have a physical space and the resources to reach their full potential. In 1979, these women bought the first piece of property in what was to become the Land Project: 42 acres situated 100 miles east of Cleveland right outside of Edinboro, Pennsylvania. These Cleveland women trek to the Land Project on the weekends to make it everything they need it to be: physically working the land, building a sweat lodge, hosting a feminist summer camp for girls, and always—always—drawing strength from being in a space owned and run by women. (Both, Sally Tatnall.)

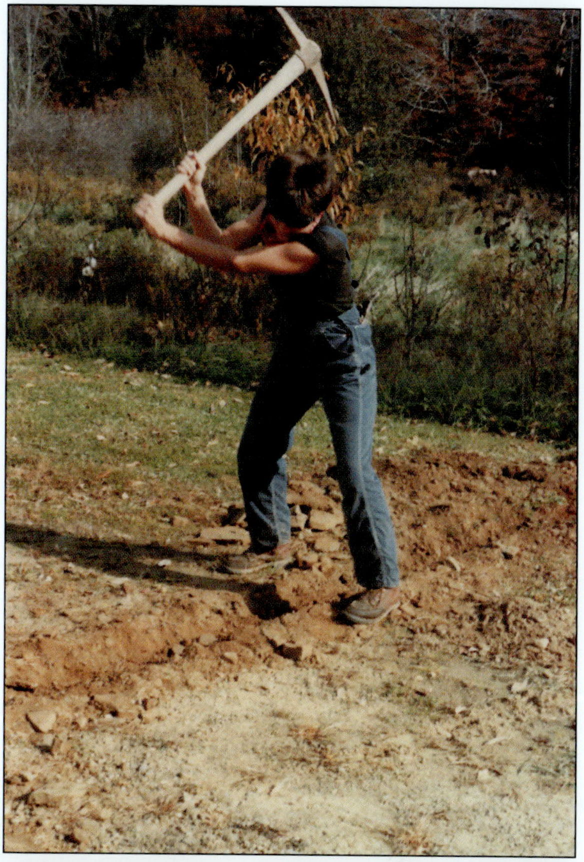

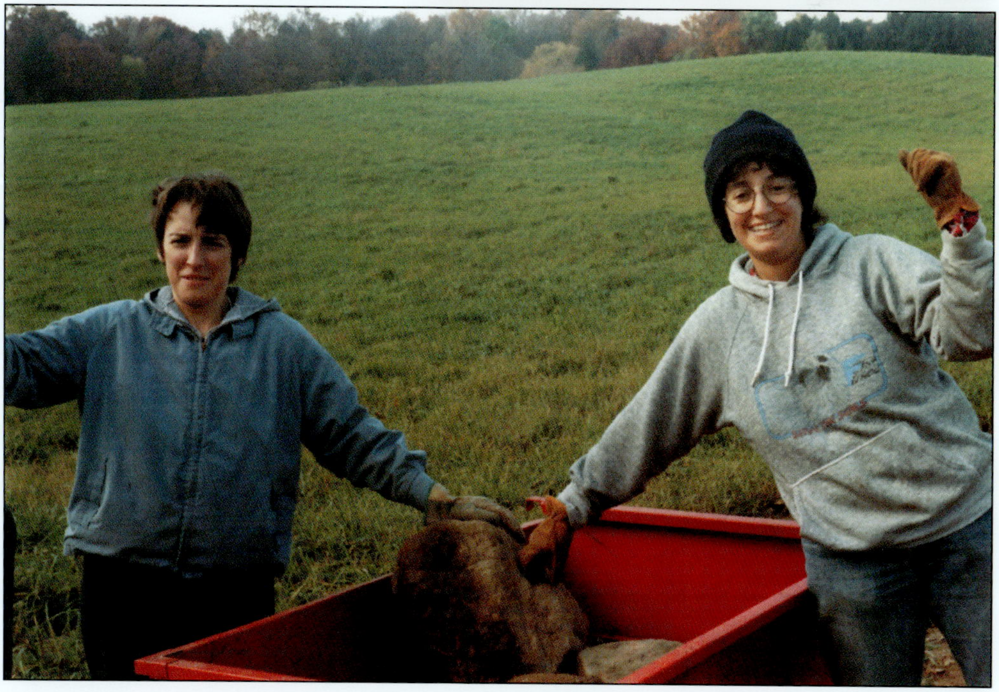

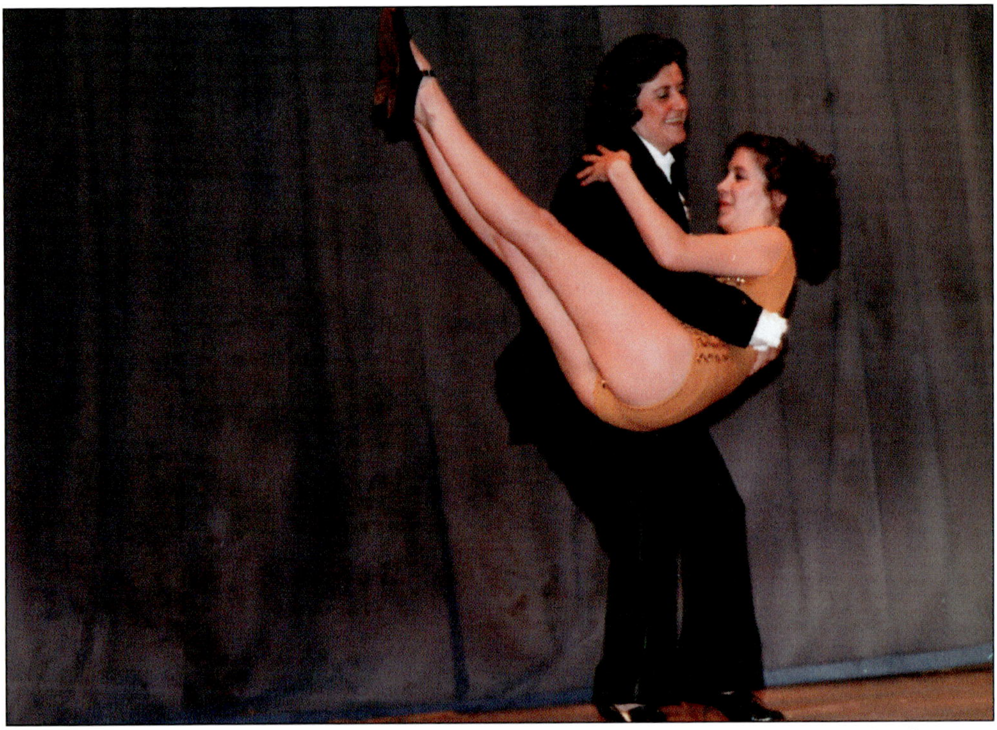

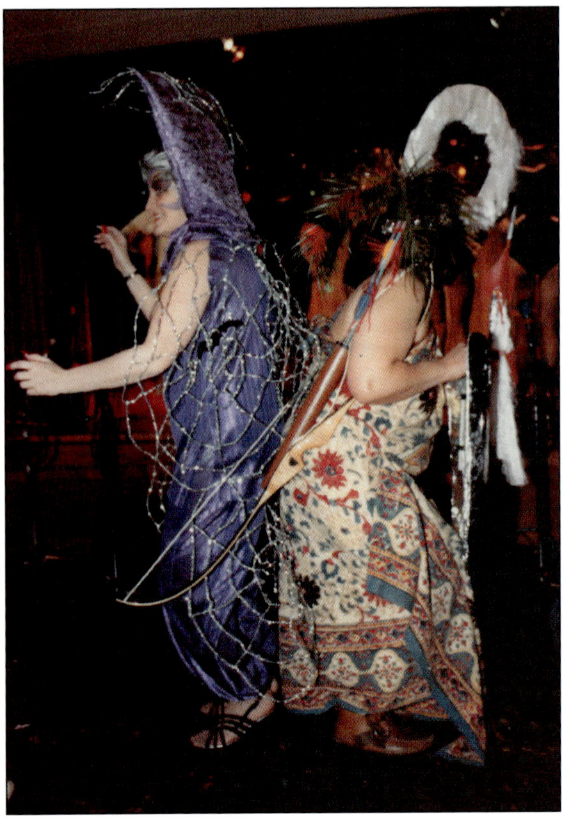

A highlight of every Cleveland calendar is Oven Productions' Womyn's Variety Show. Dating back to 1975, the show began as a small showcase in a church basement and quickly became a packed-house event. Over the years, it has moved to different spaces including the Civic, a former temple in Cleveland Heights, Grays Armory downtown, Temple Tifereth Israel in University Circle, and for many years now, the Park Synagogue. Musical acts, comedy, dancing (including the mother-daughter duo pictured above), and political satire could all be found on stage. But be sure not to call it a "talent show," or risk being swiftly corrected by an organizer. These evenings are characterized by that key word, "variety"—myriad voices put forth in whatever form they choose to best express themselves. (Both, Sally Tatnall.)

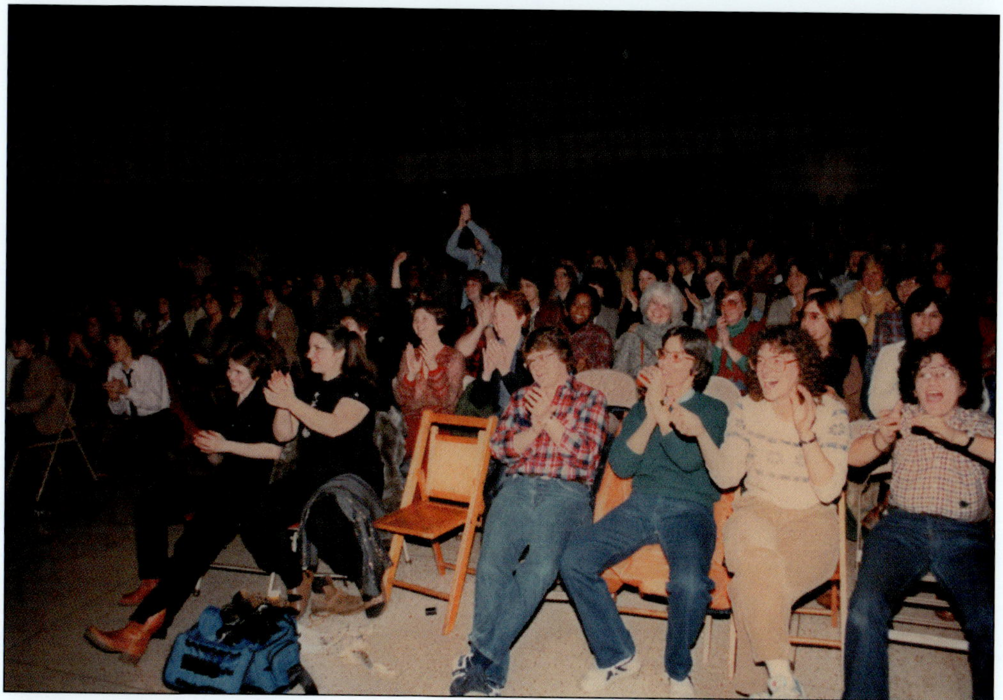

The line between performers and audience was often blurred at the Womyn's Variety Show. As frequent participant Sally Tatnall noted, "They were always an appreciative and vocal crowd. When they liked you, they let you know it." Not every act was instantly approved for performance; one notable exception was a political sketch in 1979 referencing Jim Jones and the mass suicides in Guyana. Though the audience never witnessed that particular content, the very idea of its creation points to how much some performers wanted to generate thoughtful pauses with the assembled crowd. The Womyn's Variety Show celebrated its 40th year in 2015 and (thankfully) shows no signs of slowing down. (Both, Sally Tatnall.)

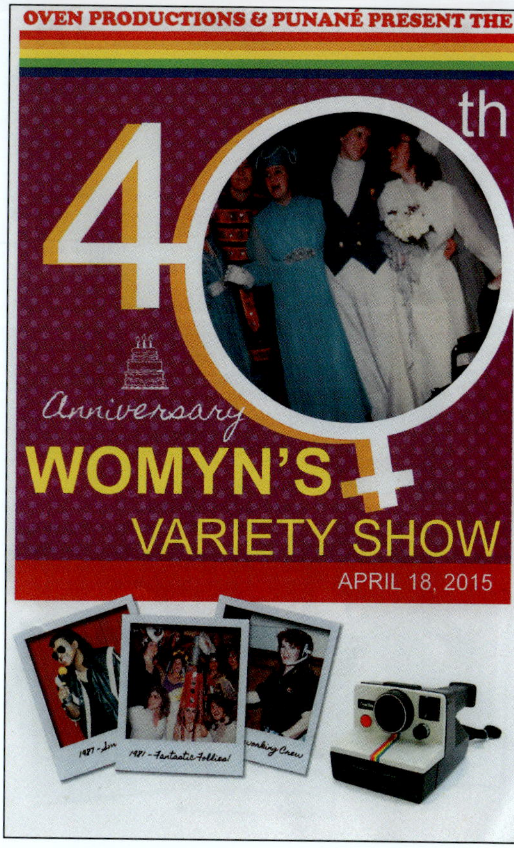

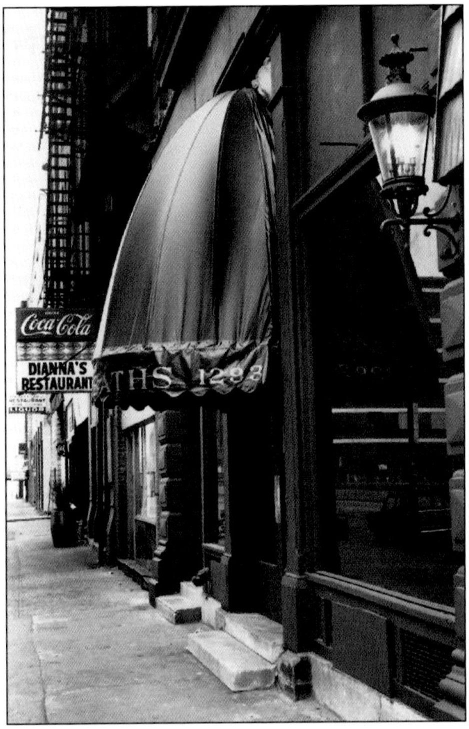

Throughout the decades, Cleveland has been the site of numerous gay bathhouses: Cleveland Depo Baths on St. Clair Avenue (which offered free brunch every Sunday until 3:00 p.m.), the Club Cleveland on West Thirty-Second Street (featuring a television room, Jacuzzi, and, yes, a free buffet), and the West Ninth Street Club Baths (pictured). Modern times saw the introduction of Flex Spas into the site of the former Art Deco Greyhound Building, a historic building constructed in 1939, but transformed in 2006 into one of the largest private alternative men's clubs in the world offering amenities from a steam maze to a free buffet. (Both, Western Reserve Historical Society.)

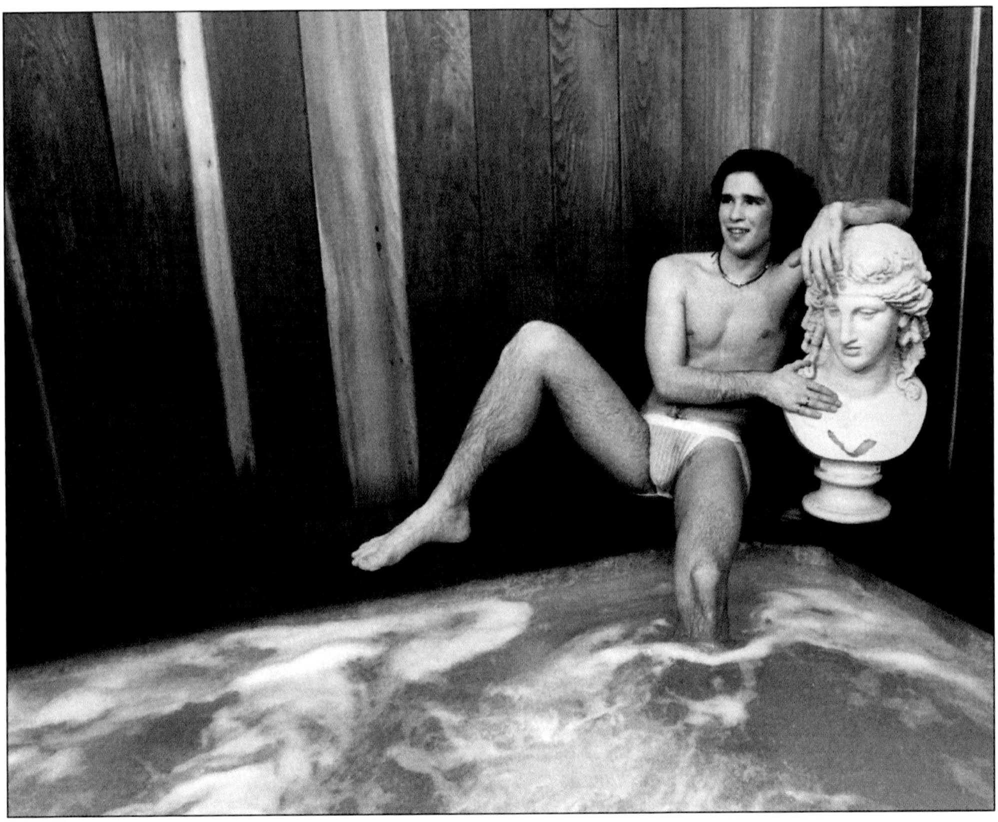

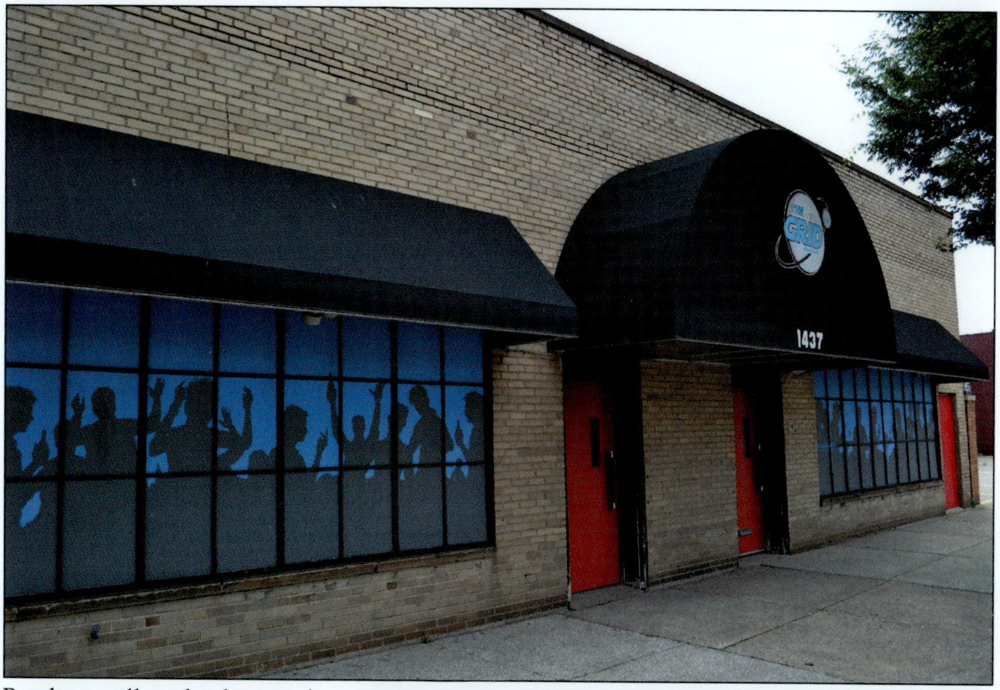

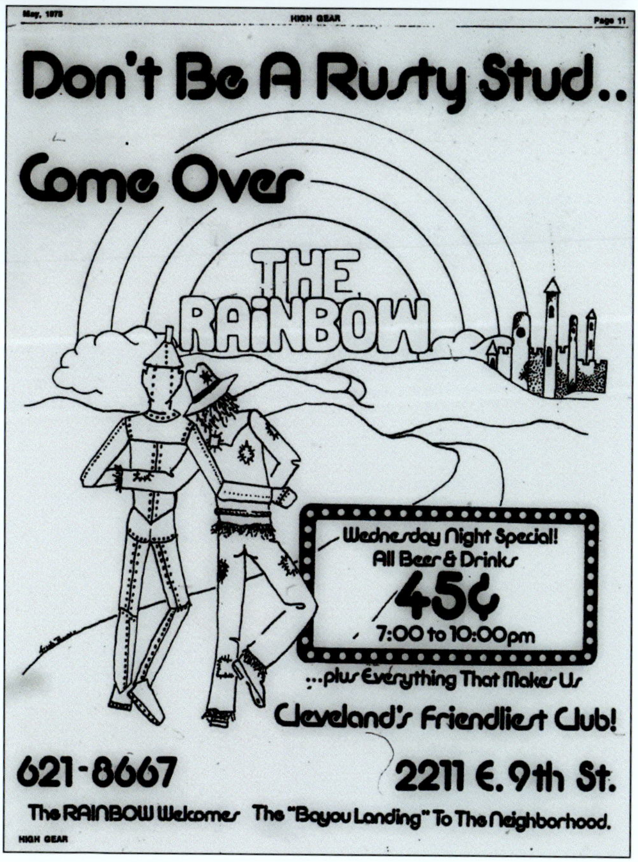

Reading really is fundamental, and one can learn their ABC's just by studying a list of all of the gay bars that have come and gone in Cleveland over the years. Adam's Row, After Midnight, Attraxxions, A Man's World, The Bayou Landing, Bounce, the Club Cleveland, Dirty Sally's, the Equinox—and that is just the first five letters. The Leather Stallion holds the record for longevity, having opened its doors in 1970. And lest one think that the literacy bar crawl wouldn't stroll through the entire alphabet, the Zanzibar, formerly located on Payne Avenue, has readers and revelers covered. (Above, Matthew Chojnacki; right, Western Reserve Historical Society.)

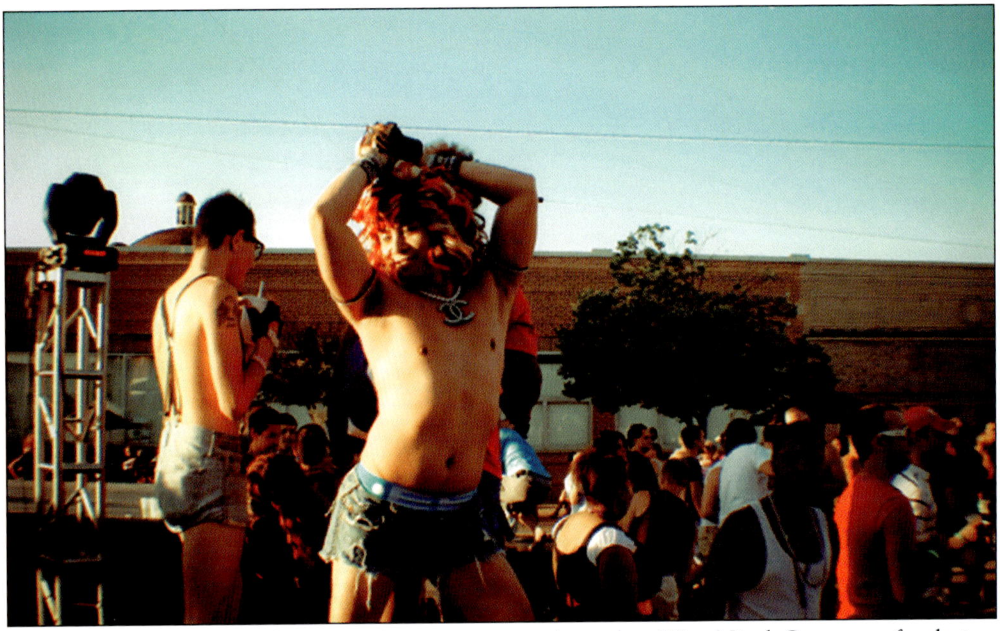

Born in 1984, Dancing in the Streets began as a street festival on West Ninth Street as a fundraiser for Health Issues Task Force (which later became the AIDS Task Force of Greater Cleveland) to raise money for services for those living with HIV/AIDS as well as serving a space to remember and honor those who lived through the darkest days of the disease. The event expanded over the years and was held in venues like the Nautica Stage and Tower City Amphitheater. The fundraiser had to be canceled for a year due to flagging attendance, but it was revived in the mid-2000s on Clifton Boulevard between West 116th and West 117th Streets. Tragedy struck the event in 2012 when a drunk driver plowed through the barricade, killing one attendee and injuring four others. The event celebrated its 30th year in 2014 in the Gay Games Festival Village. (Both, Zoë Renee Lapin.)

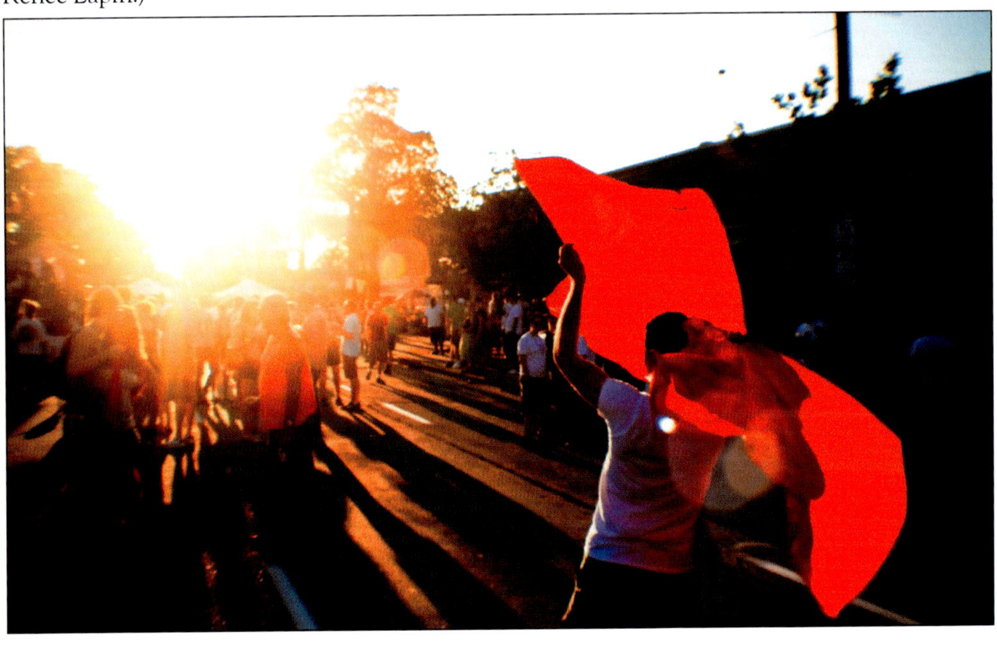

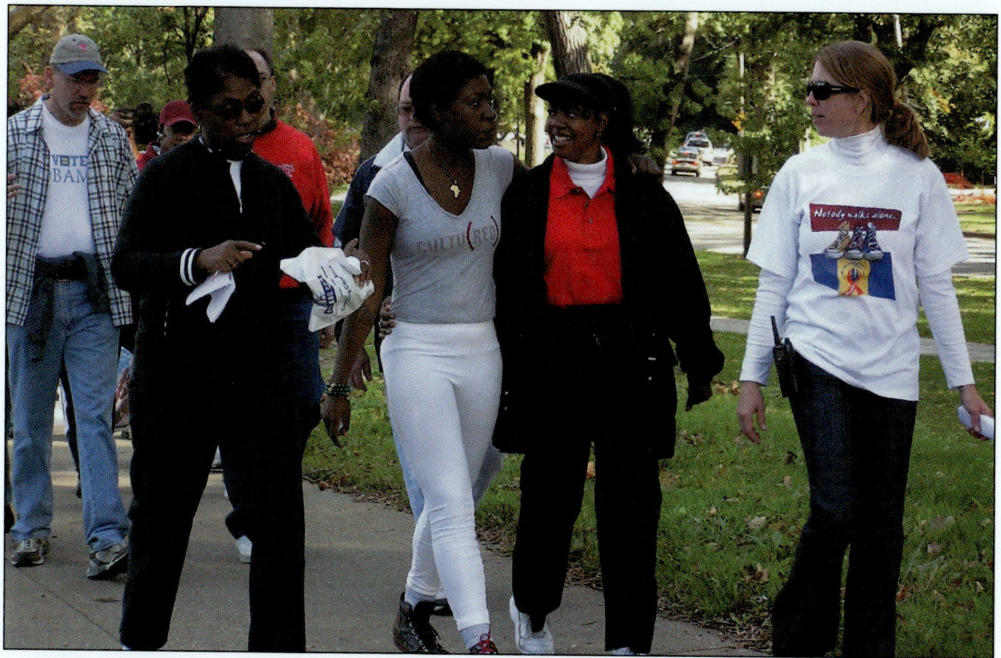

In 1992, Juliann Fausel and Jeff Swindler organized the first Cleveland AIDS Walk to raise awareness and funds for programs providing critical HIV/AIDS services to residents of Northeast Ohio. At the time, there were a little over 1,000 cases in all of Ohio. As the number of affected lives grew, so too did the number of both AIDS Walk participants and funds raised. The walk was later renamed the Dr. John T. Carey Memorial AIDS Walk to honor Dr. Carey's life as an excellent Cleveland physician and HIV educator. As with similar events in many cities across the country, the AIDS Walk was discontinued due to lower participation and, in many peoples' opinions, a declining sense of urgency. The final Dr. John T. Carey Memorial AIDS Walk was held in 2009. (Both, Brian DeWitt.)

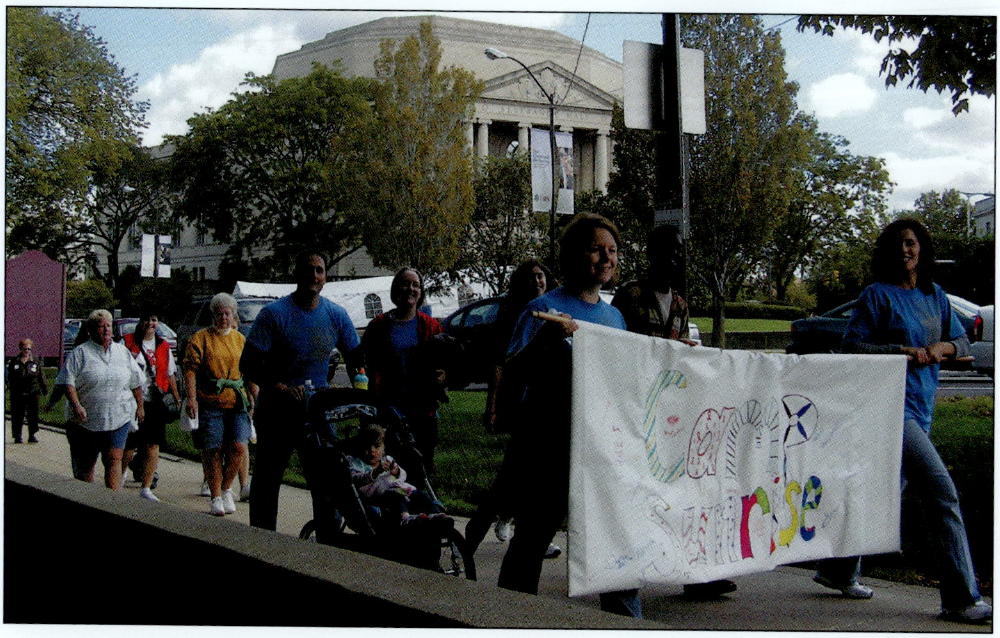

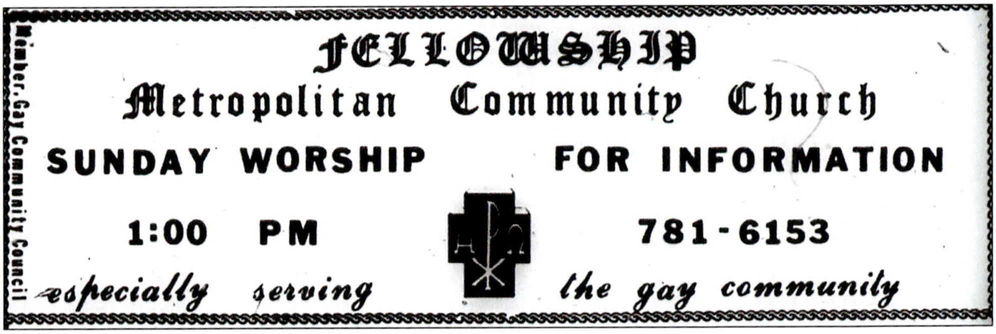

Various Cleveland houses of worship have been present from the very start of the modern gay rights movement as havens for the LGBTQ community. The Metropolitan Community Church advertised itself as "especially serving the gay community" and was instrumental in planning the early Pride celebrations in the mid-1970s. Plymouth Church of Shaker Heights regularly hosted LGBTQ-affirming events for decades and was declared an "Open and Affirming Congregation" in 2005. Cleveland even houses the national headquarters of the United Church of Christ, a denomination that endorsed marriage equality in 2006, far before other churches and nine years before it became the law of the land. (Above, Western Reserve Historical Society; below, Brian DeWitt.)

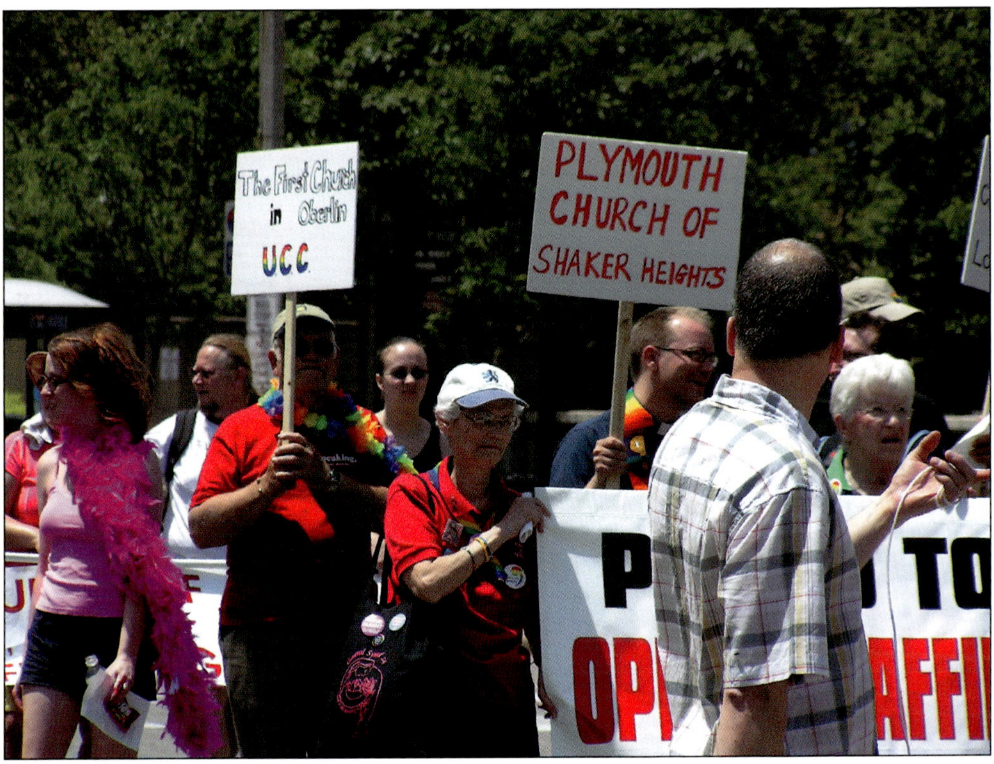

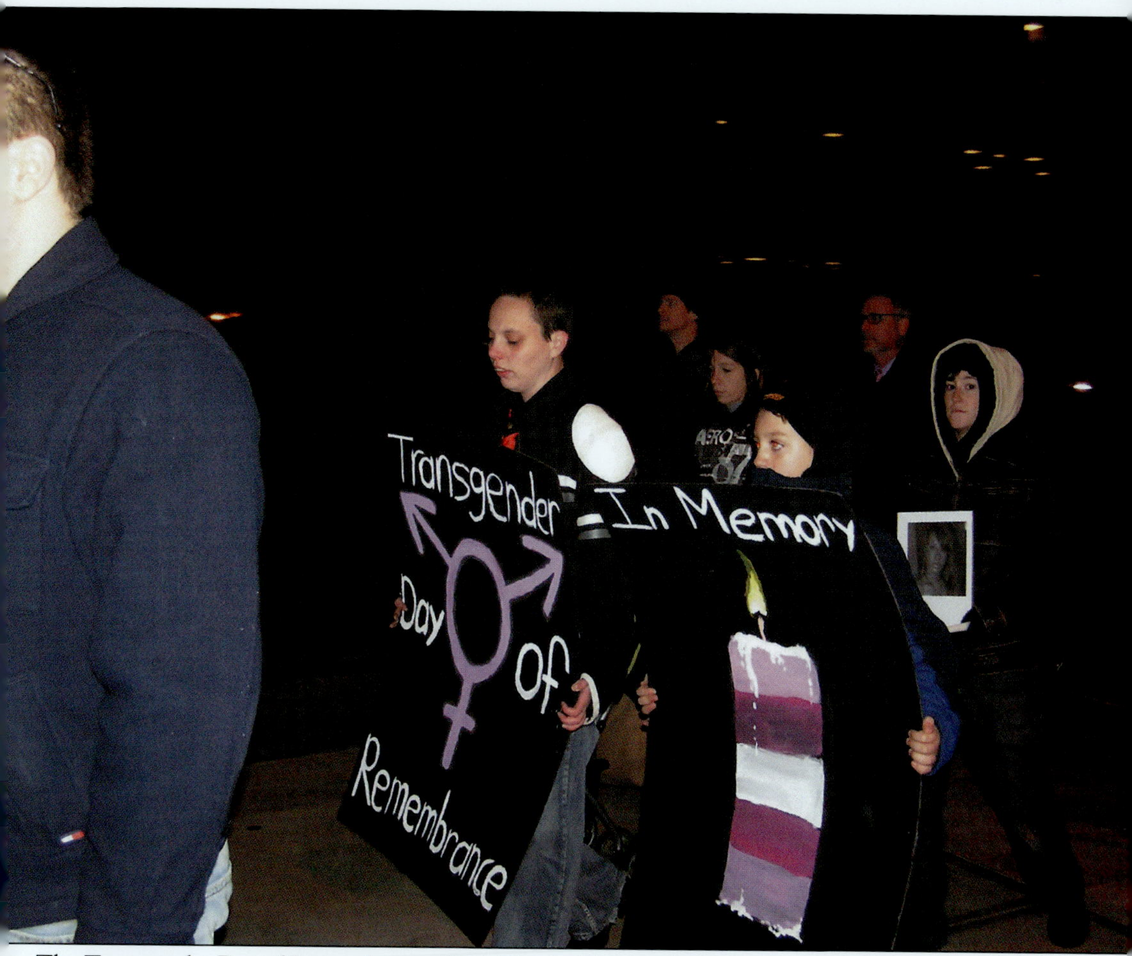

The Transgender Day of Remembrance (TDoR) is held annually as a memorial to trans-identified and gender-variant individuals who are murdered each year due to hate, transphobia, and society's strict adherence to the gender binary. The event takes place in November to honor Rita Hester, whose murder on November 28, 1998, kicked off the "Remembering Our Dead" web project and a San Francisco candlelight vigil in 1999. The Cleveland observance of TDoR began in 2002 in the home of Karen and Bob Gross and consisted of a small group gathered together to light a candle and share a moment of silence. Subsequent years featured candlelight vigils, readings of the names of those murdered in the previous year, and the presentation of the Illumination Awards recognizing individuals in the community who use their voice to protect all of our siblings. (Brian DeWitt.)

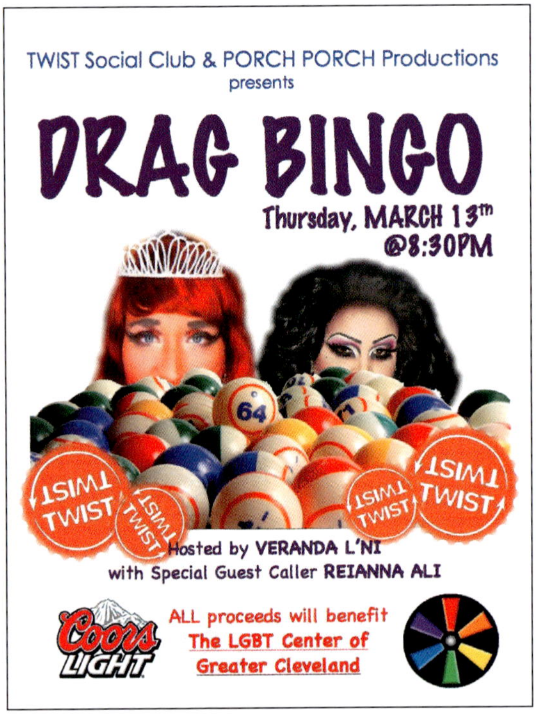

"O-69" was first called at Drag Bingo in 2010 at Twist Social Club, hosted by Veranda L'ni (pictured) and Bunny Beretta. The goal was to raise money for smaller nonprofits that needed additional funds to keep their programs running. Drag Bingo has averaged close to $10,000 a year, with all of the proceeds going directly to the nonprofits; not a single dollar is kept by the bar or the entertainers. (Shamus Dickinson.)

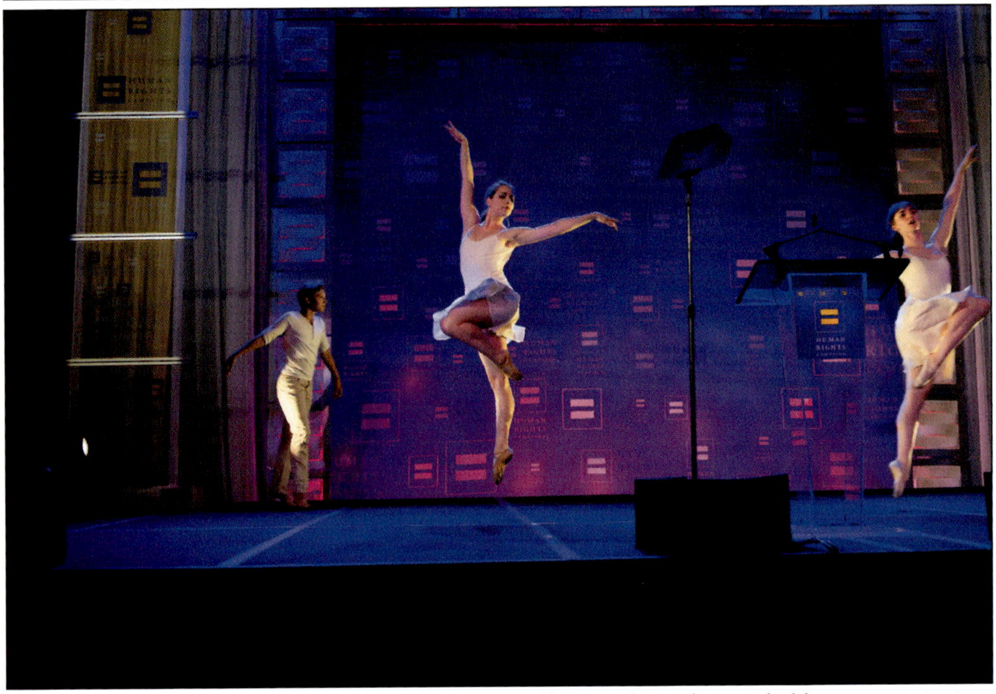

When you see the Cleveland LGBTQ community all gussied up, that probably means it is time for the Cleveland Human Rights Campaign (HRC) Annual Gala. Dating to 1994, this black-tie fundraiser honors the progress the Human Rights Campaign continues to make toward achieving equality and diversity for everyone in the LGBT community and the individuals who were integral in helping move the needle forward. (Melanie Falls.)

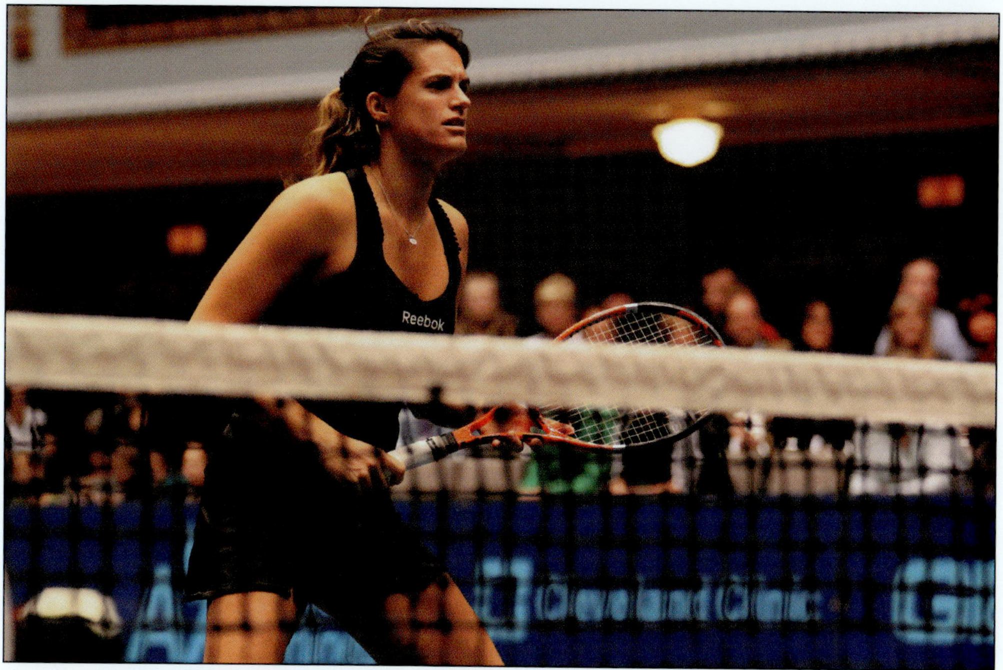

On October 27, 2011, the Cleveland community was treated to an all-star display of athletics and entertainment when legendary rocker Elton John and tennis icon Billie Jean King (both at center below) brought their World Team Tennis Smash Hits tournament to Public Hall (in the Public Auditorium). The heroic activists brought with them a slew of top-tier tennis players including out legends Amélie Mauresmo (above, and second from left below) and Martina Navratilova (far right below). The event raised over a half a million dollars, almost doubling the total of the same event held the year before in the Baltimore-Washington area. $180,000 of the money raised stayed in Cleveland, donated to the AIDS Task Force of Greater Cleveland to support its mission to provide a compassionate and collaborative response to the needs of people infected, affected, and at risk of HIV/AIDS. (Both, Janet Macoska.)

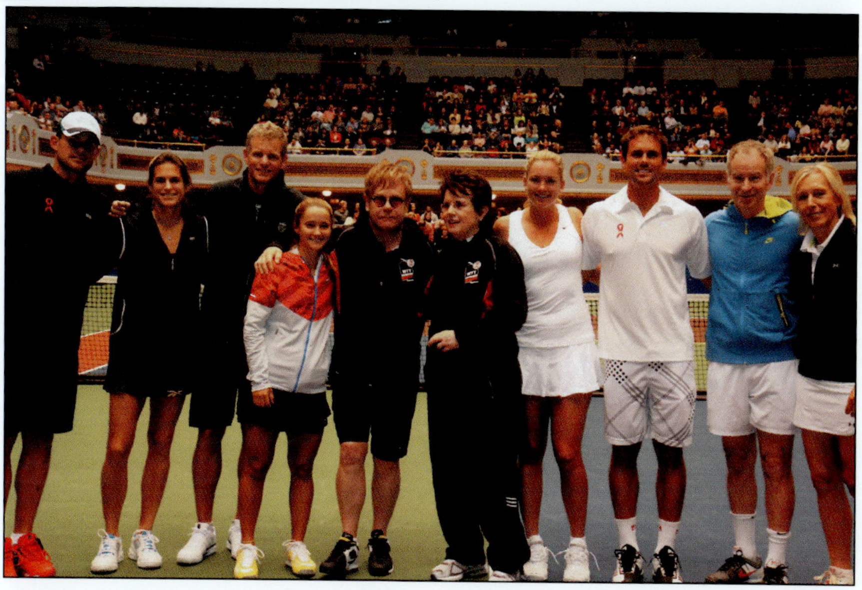

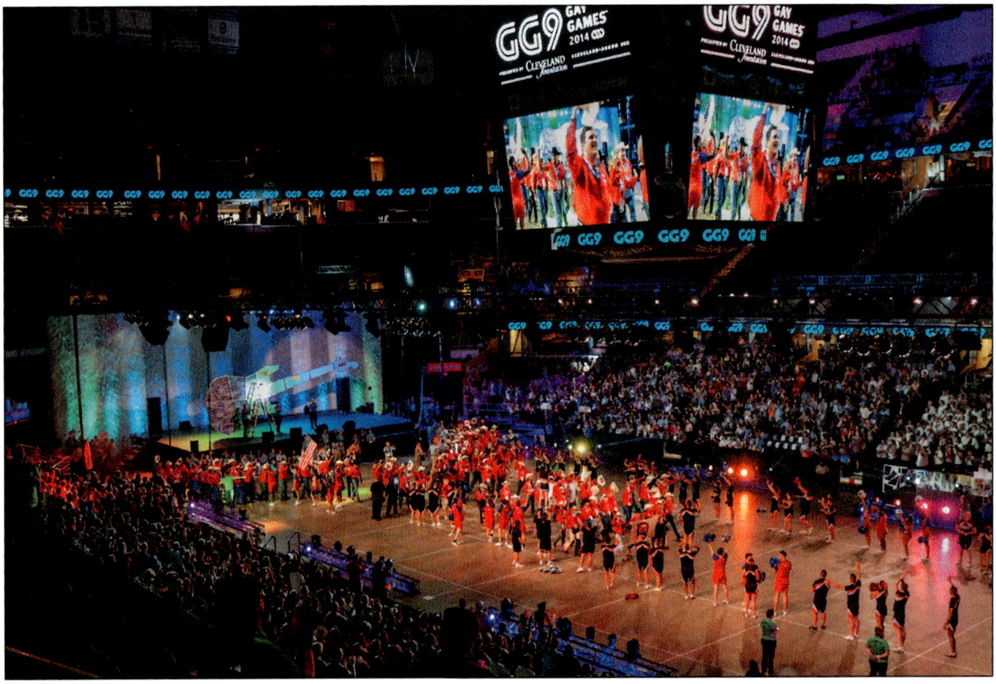

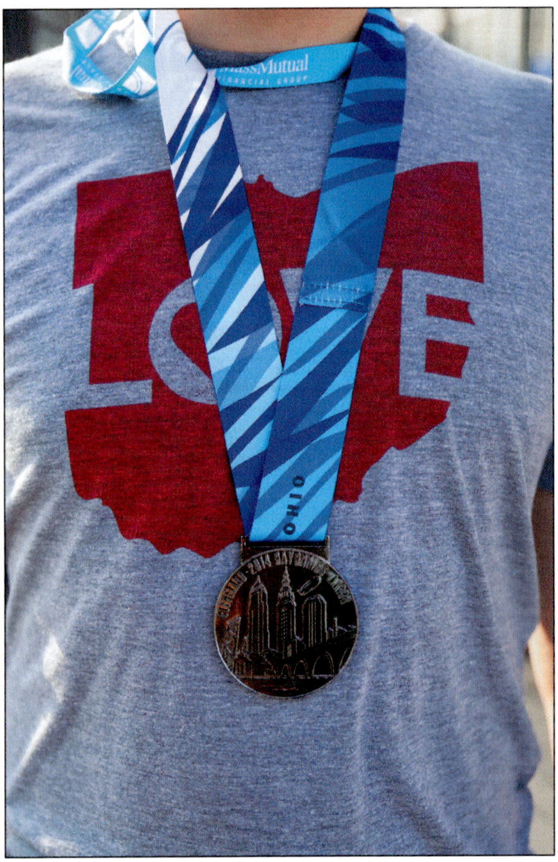

In August 2014, Cleveland/Akron hosted Gay Games 9, becoming the smallest ever region to host the international-level sporting event and the first two-city host. Over 6,000 attendees witnessed the opening ceremonies. Pres. Barack Obama's video welcome to the participants represented the first time the president of the host country had addressed attendees. The economic impact of the games was estimated to be $52.1 million to the region, with $20.6 million in additional job income. Over 3,000 volunteers and 130 community partners came together to staff the events and the bustling Festival Village. The extensive media coverage even broke into primetime with the first-ever broadcast commercial advertising the Gay Games debuting during the 2014 Winter Olympics. (Both, Bob Perkoski.)

From badminton to martial arts, figure skating to water polo, the participants competed in 36 sports and 2 cultural events at 40 different venues. They hailed from 48 states and 50 countries with delegations ranging from the United States' envoy of thousands of athletes to countries with one sole (but proud) participant. Competitors themselves represented the entire age spectrum, from 18-year-old tennis players to 99-year-old Ida Keeling, who became the first person in the 95–99 age category to run the 100 meters in an internationally certified race (finishing in 59.8 seconds). At the closing ceremonies, the torch was officially handed off to Paris to host the 2018 Gay Games. (Right, Kevin Yung; below, John Mendel.)

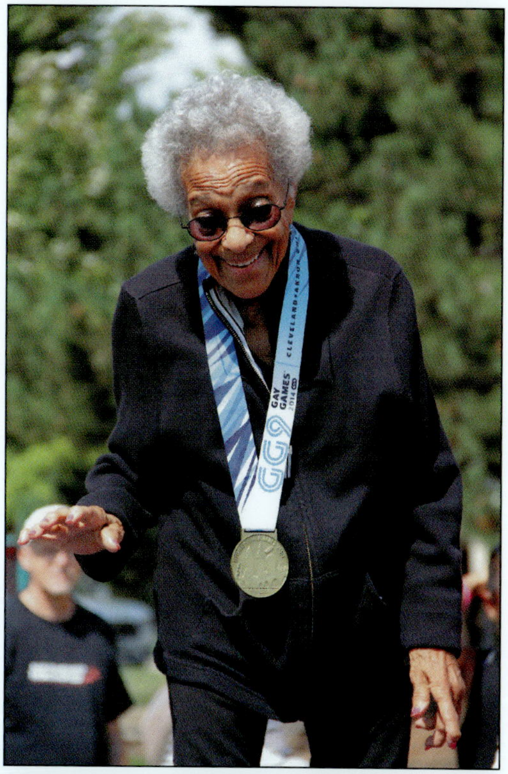

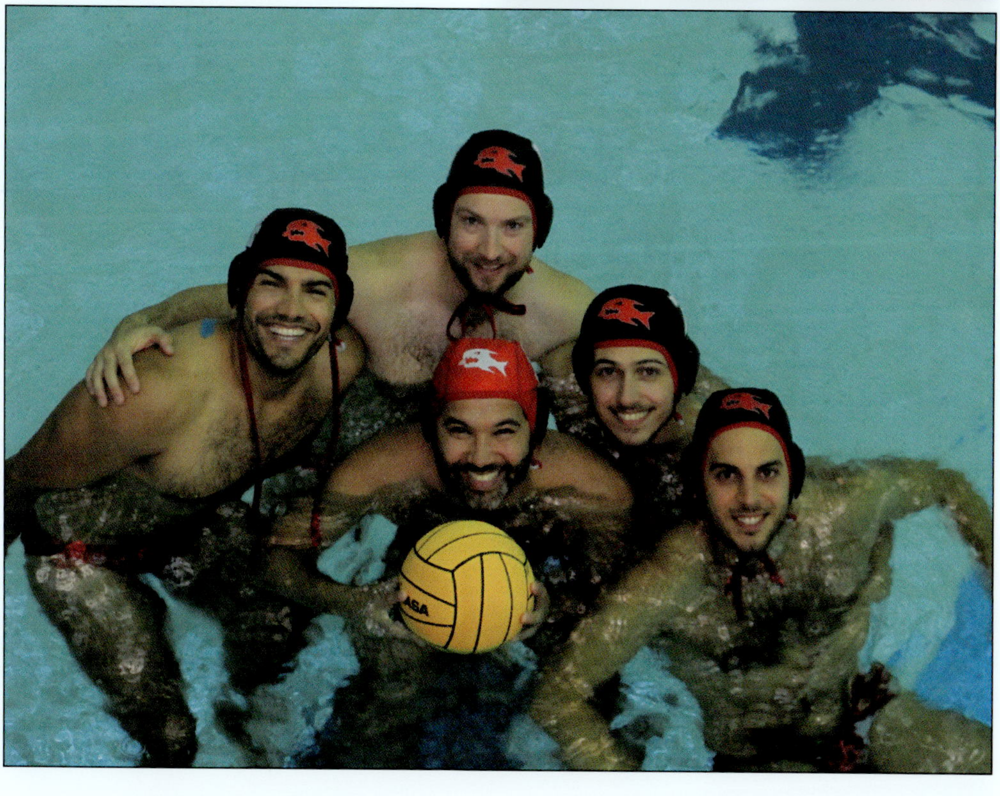

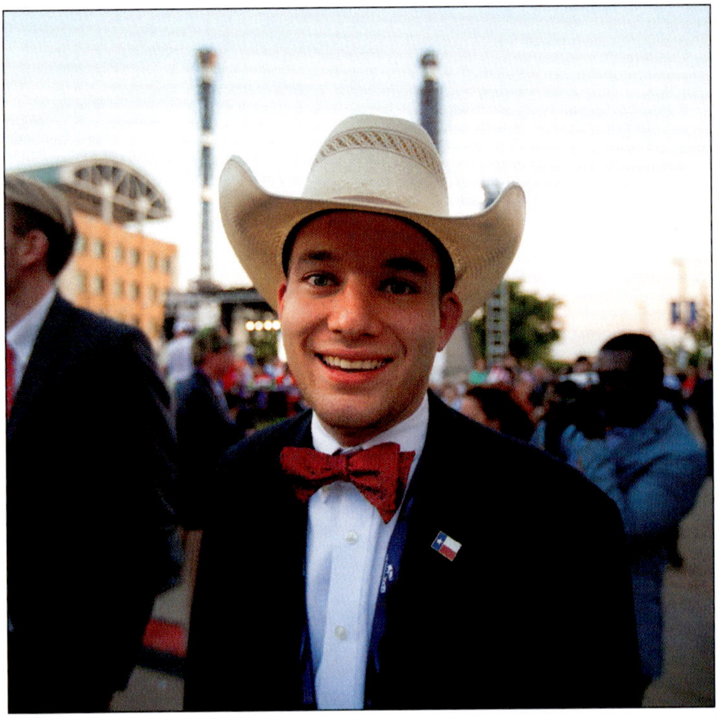

The eyes of the world were on Cleveland in July 2016 as the city hosted the Republican National Convention (RNC). Despite one of the most anti-gay platforms ever written by the GOP, gay Republicans made their presence known, from gay billionaire Peter Thiel, who became the first speaker at an RNC to disclose his sexual orientation, to 21-year-old Texas delegate Colton Buckley (pictured), who gained wide media coverage for his attempts to reconcile his conservative views with his LGBTQ identity. (The Slate Group.)

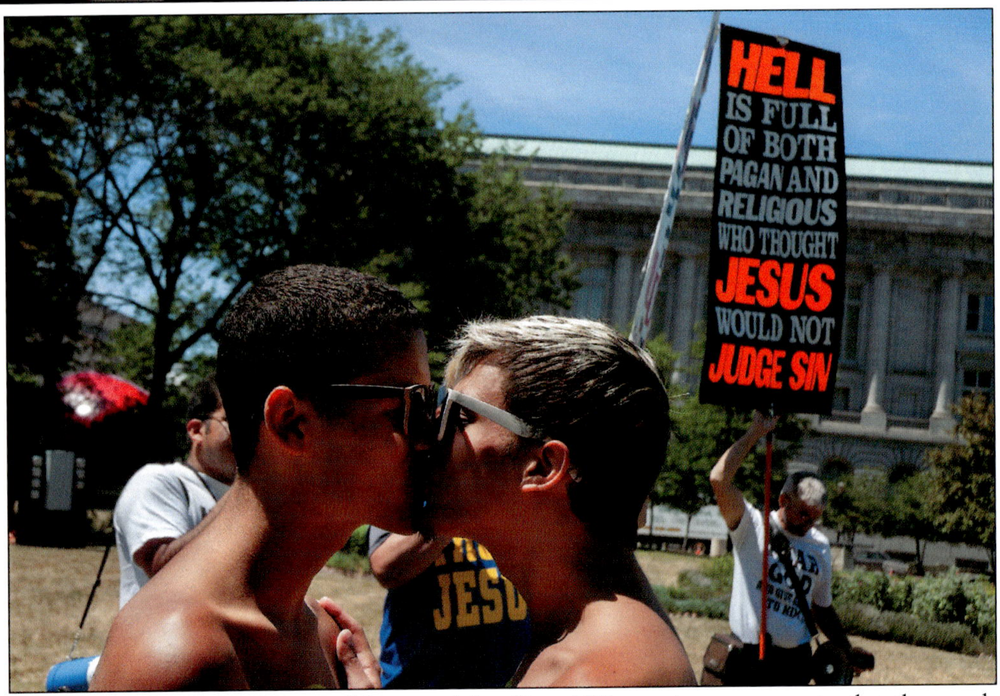

With the deeply polarizing views of then-candidate Donald Trump, it was no surprise that thousands of protesters from every corner of the country descended upon Cleveland to raise their voices in dissent. From immigrants-rights advocates to racial justice change-agents to LGBTQ equality warriors, the entire world bore witness to protests notable for their size, strength of message, and deep commitment to nonviolence. (Bob Perkoski.)

Three

We Groove

Music

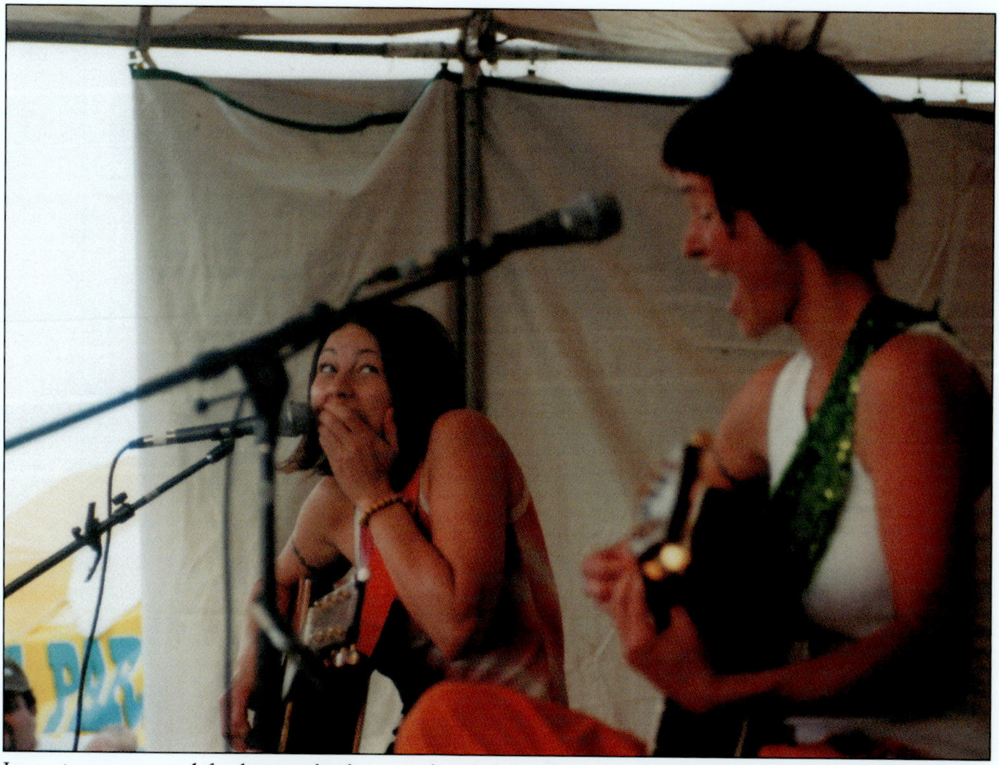

In a city renowned for being the home of rock 'n' roll, it should come as no surprise that music has underscored much of Cleveland's LGBTQ history. Whether it was a superstar LGBTQ artist performing on the main stage of Cleveland Pride or a trans singer/songwriter performing at a tiny house concert benefitting nonprofit organizations, these beats have kept Cleveland moving, grooving, and dancing together. Pictured are the Murmurs at Pride 2000. (Brynna Fish.)

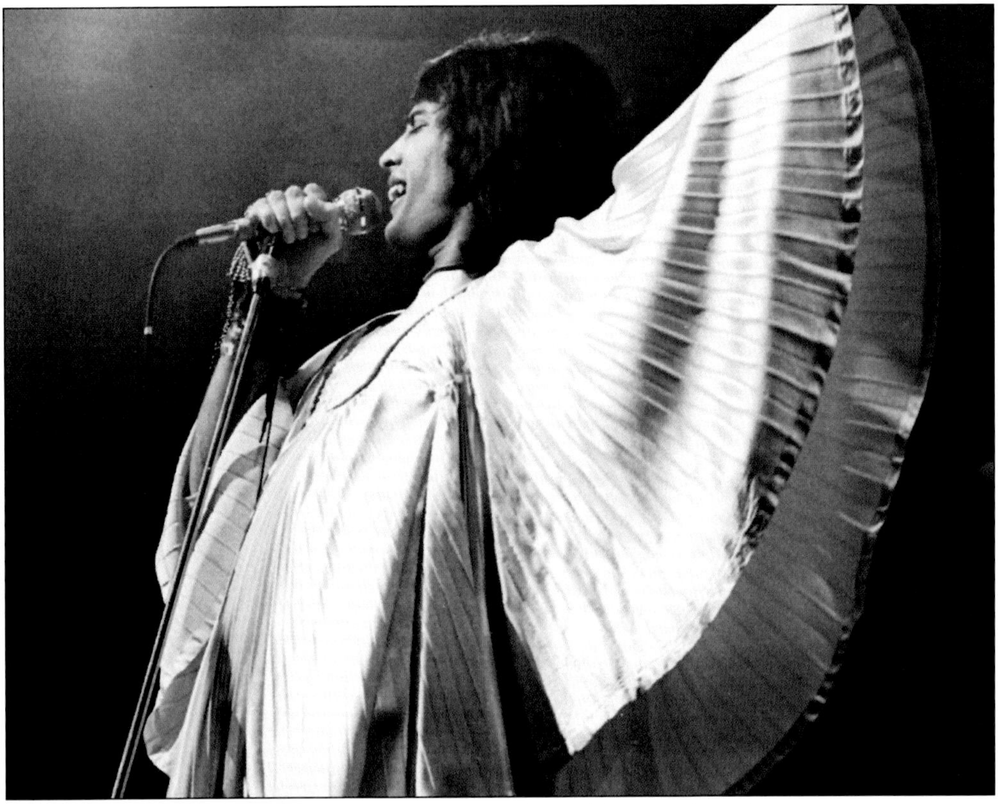

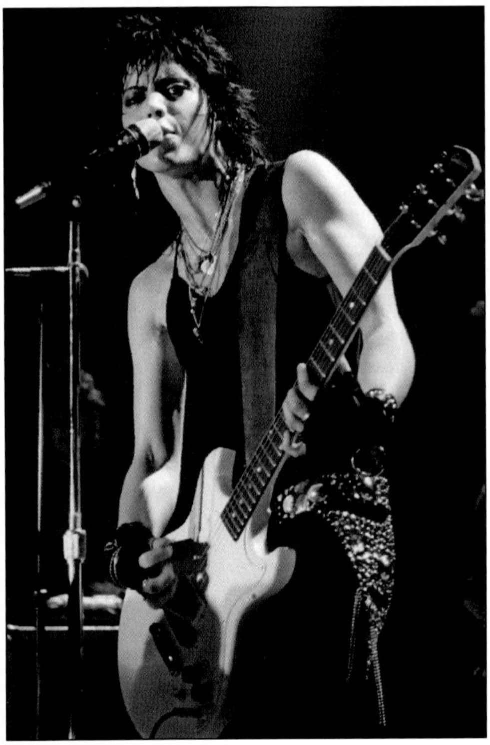

One of the benefits of living in the home of rock 'n' roll is that LGBTQ Clevelanders are perpetually treated to a full schedule of the most legendary LGBTQ and ally musical artists performing on Cleveland stages. From Freddie Mercury and Queen dazzling audiences at the Cleveland Music Hall in 1975 (above) to Bette Midler's long-awaited first live album (*Live At Last*) recorded in 1976, to Joan Jett's legendary set at the Phantasy Nightclub in 1987 while filming *Light of Day* with Michael J. Fox (left), the roster is simply too jaw-dropping and lengthy to fully list. Suffice to say, Cleveland rocks. (Both, Janet Macoska.)

Sometimes talent is booked in Cleveland, and other times, LGBTQ Clevelanders have taken a far more active role in bringing big musical names to Northeast Ohio. In 1984, famed singer-songwriters, feminists, and activists Ronnie Gilbert and Holly Near (right) were brought to perform at the Civic for an extraordinarily successful benefit raising funds for the Women's Community Fund, an initiative "controlled by women to make grants to women's organizations in order to empower all women." When Olivia Records announced the dates for its 15th anniversary tour in 1988, some Clevelanders were miffed to not see the city's name on the list. In stepped Oven Productions; Brynna Fish contacted Judy Dlugacz, Olivia's cofounder, and Cleveland soon went from not being on the list to being the first stop on the tour. The result was a sold-out performance featuring Nancy Vogl, Diane Davidson, and Cris Williamson. (Right, Western Reserve Historical Society; below, Linda Malicki.)

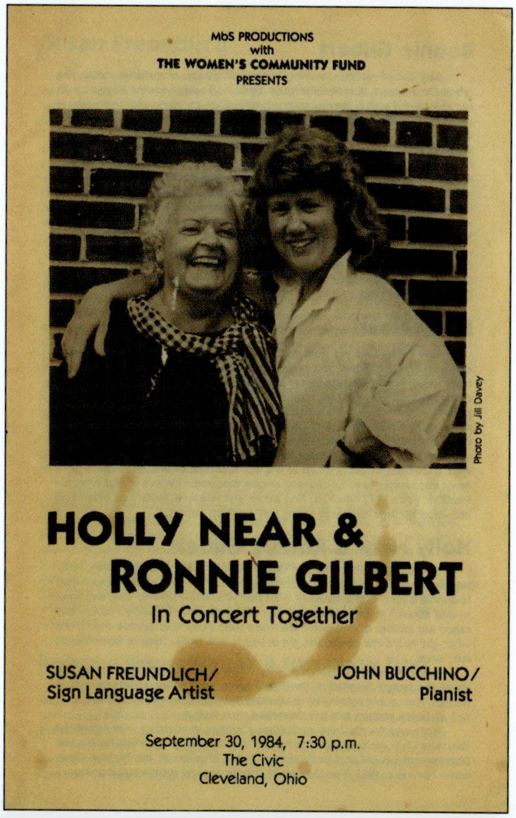
MbS PRODUCTIONS
with
THE WOMEN'S COMMUNITY FUND
PRESENTS

Photo by Jill Davey

HOLLY NEAR &
RONNIE GILBERT
In Concert Together

SUSAN FREUNDLICH/
Sign Language Artist

JOHN BUCCHINO/
Pianist

September 30, 1984, 7:30 p.m.
The Civic
Cleveland, Ohio

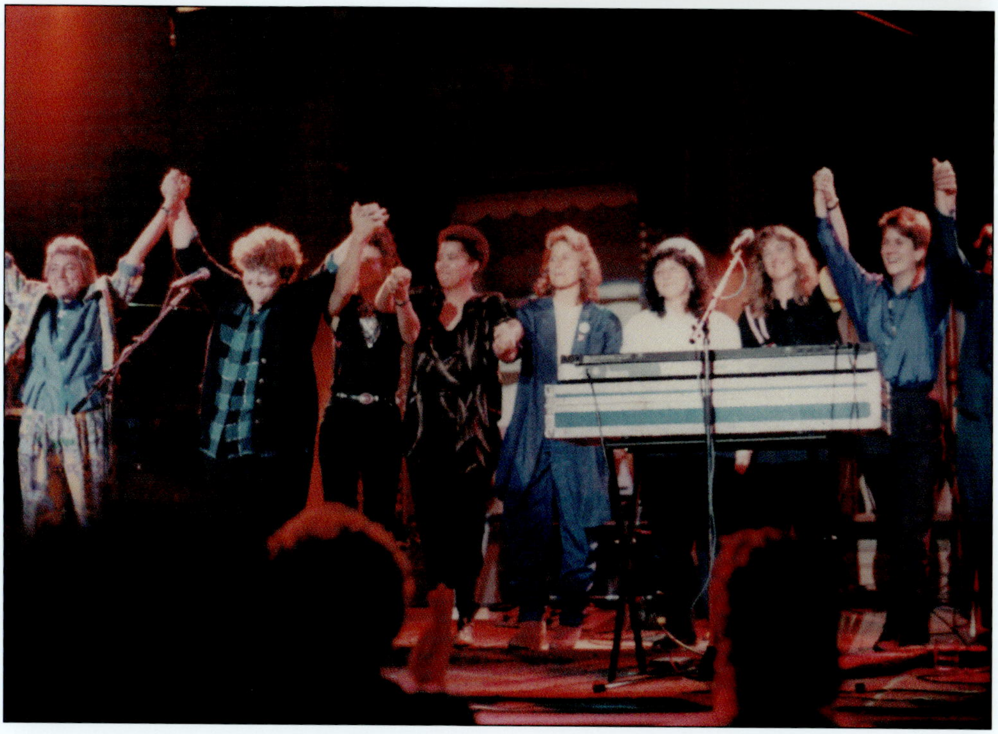

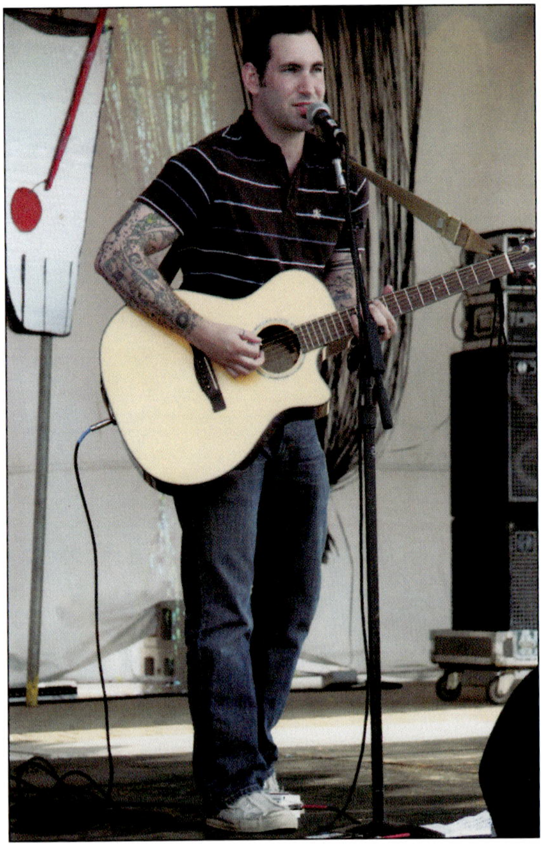

Cleveland Pride often features the wonderful voices of ridiculously talented singer/songwriters who deliver a more acoustic bent to the appreciative ears of those assembled before them. These artists have been heard on both the main stages as well as an acoustic stage set up in some years to feature their music. Award-winning musician Eric Himan (left) brought his distinctive voice (and many tattoos) to the stages of three different Cleveland Pride celebrations as well as the Gay Games' Festival Village. Crowd favorite Girlyman (below) was a huge hit at Cleveland Pride 2004 with their soaring harmonies, infectious spirit, and comical tuning songs. (Both, Brynna Fish.)

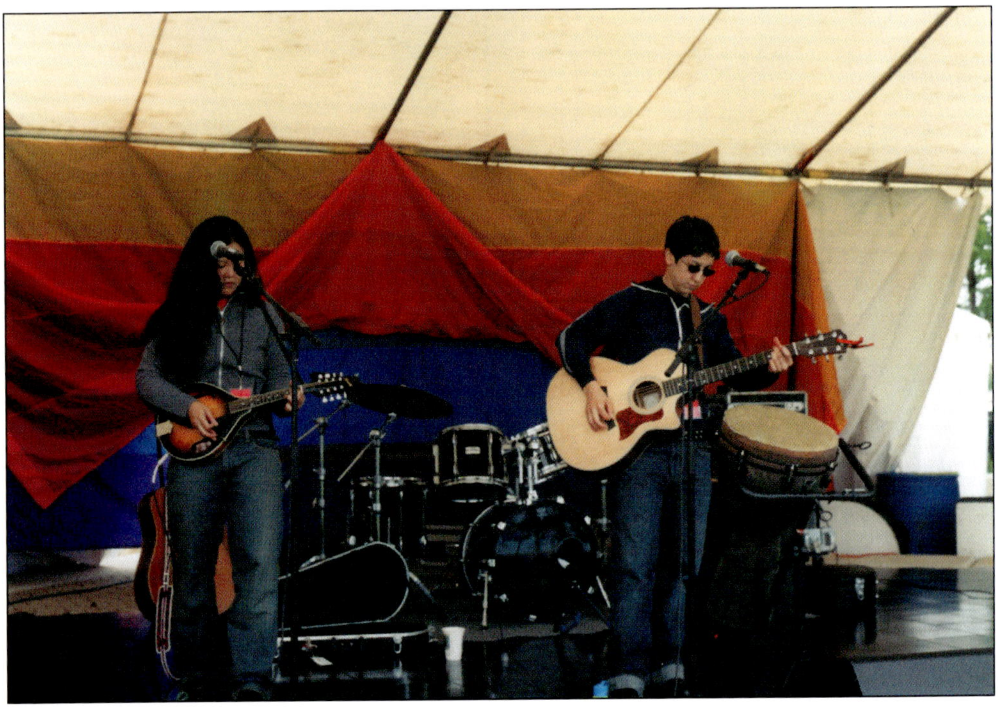

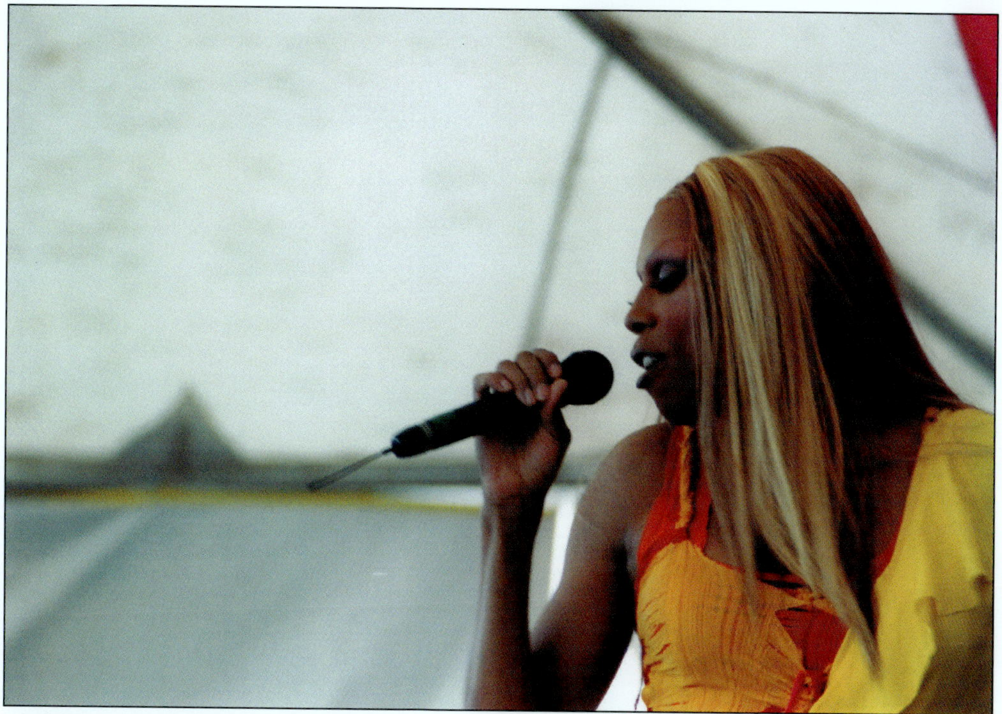

Nothing says "pride" quite like the LGBTQ and ally community dancing together as one. Year after year, Cleveland Pride features recording artists well known for their pulsing beats uniting friends and strangers grooving together as a community on the dancefloor (or, more likely, grass). Five years before *RuPaul's Drag Race* first aired, RuPaul (above) was already a legend, and she lived up to that status at Cleveland Pride 2004. In 2002, even heavy rains could not keep the crowd from dancing up a storm as Kristine W (right), the queen of dance music, provided "One More Try" for the sun to shine down on the assembled joyous masses. (Both, Brynna Fish.)

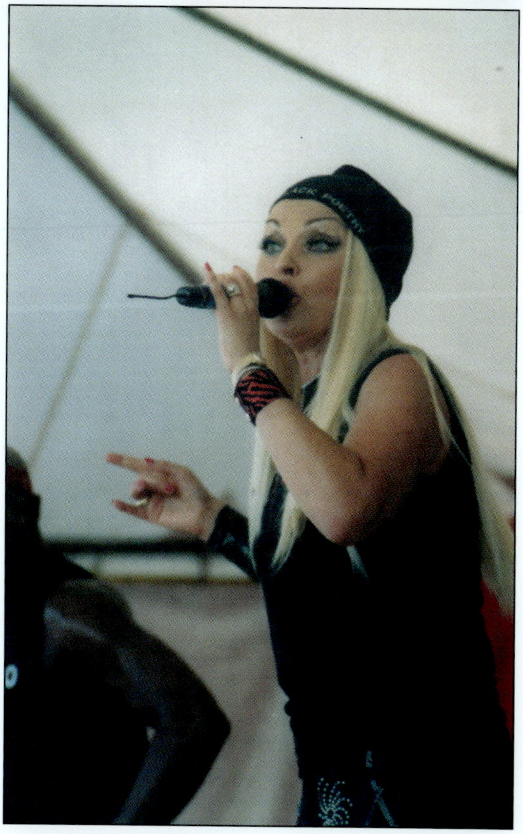

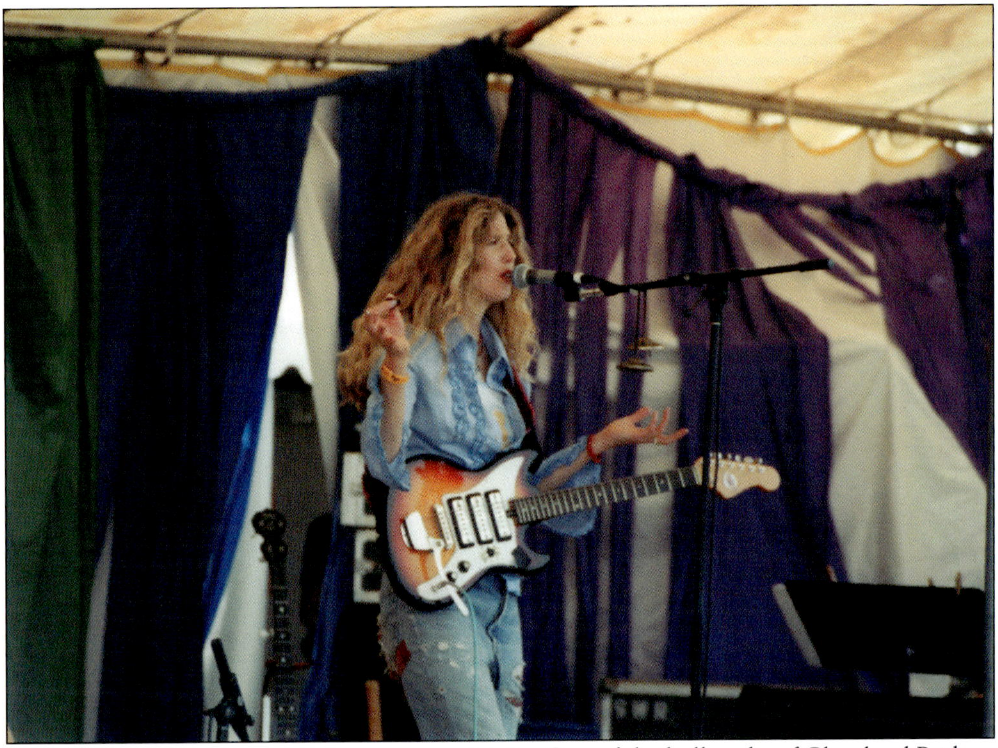

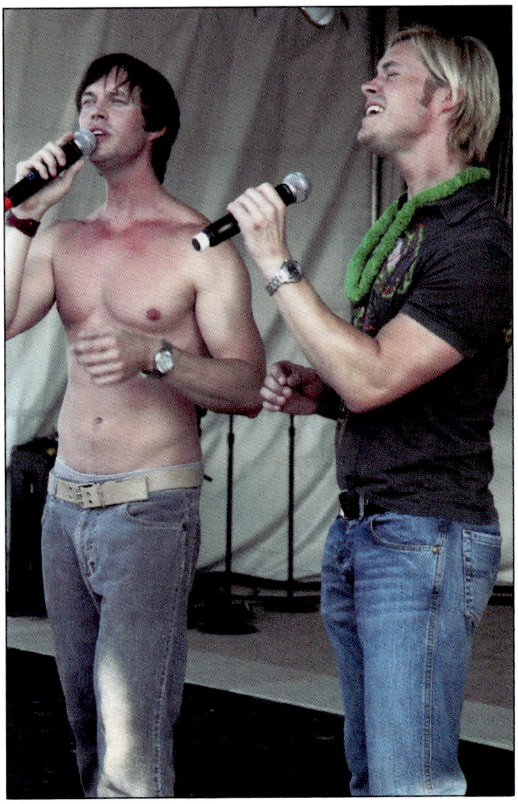

One of the hallmarks of Cleveland Pride is the sheer variety of the musical acts that the incredible planning committees bring to the city each and every year. From 1980s superstars Debbie Gibson, Taylor Dayne, and Belinda Carlisle to 1990s diva CeCe Peniston, to Queen of Clubland Martha Wash, every festival features a different flavor and style of music. In 2000, audiences were enthralled by Sophie B. Hawkins leaving everyone saying, "Damn." Then, in 2007, Christian duo and life partners Jason and deMarco brought their unique brand of spirit pop to Cleveland, melding their deep faith with their love of music for all of Cleveland to celebrate. (Both, Brynna Fish.)

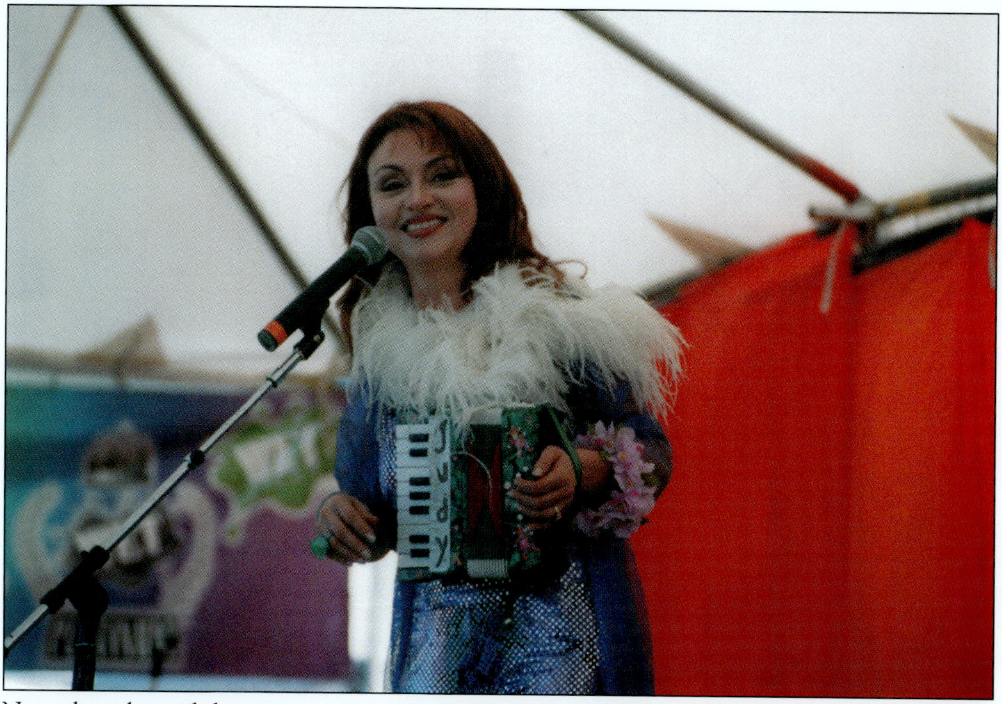

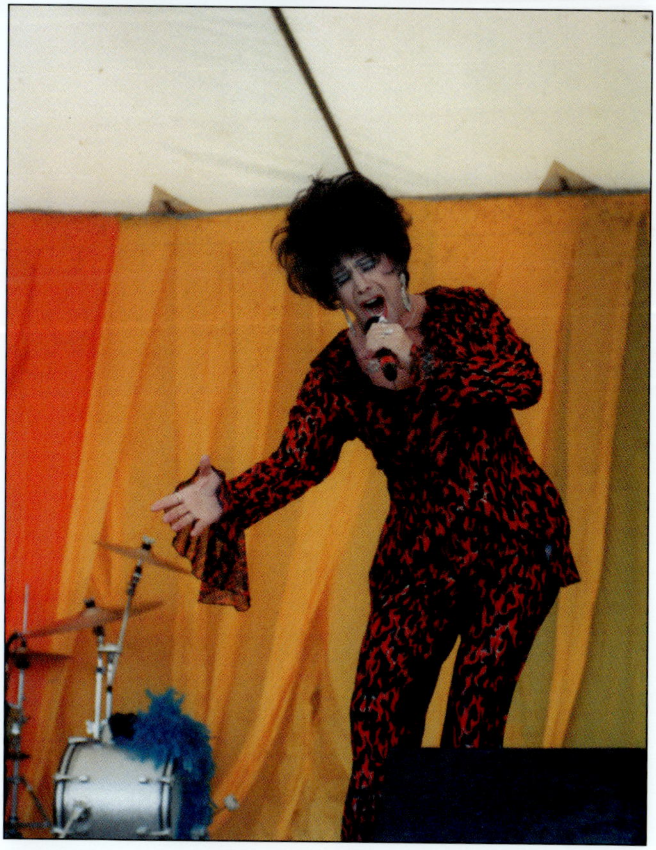

Never let it be said that music and humor are mutually exclusive. Cleveland Pride has found itself at the intersection of tunes and comedy several times in the past, leaving the crowds in stitches. In 2001, Judy Tenuta, the "Love Goddess" herself, brought her accordion and her sharp wit to the stage. Her performance caused one individual to write a letter to the editor of *Gay People's Chronicle* praising Judy's "rather risqué humor and rather stinging remarks about heterosexuals." The following year, drag star Trinity alternated her comedic audience interactions with some powerhouse torch songs, showing once again how music and laughter can bring an audience of Pride-goers together. (Both, Brynna Fish.)

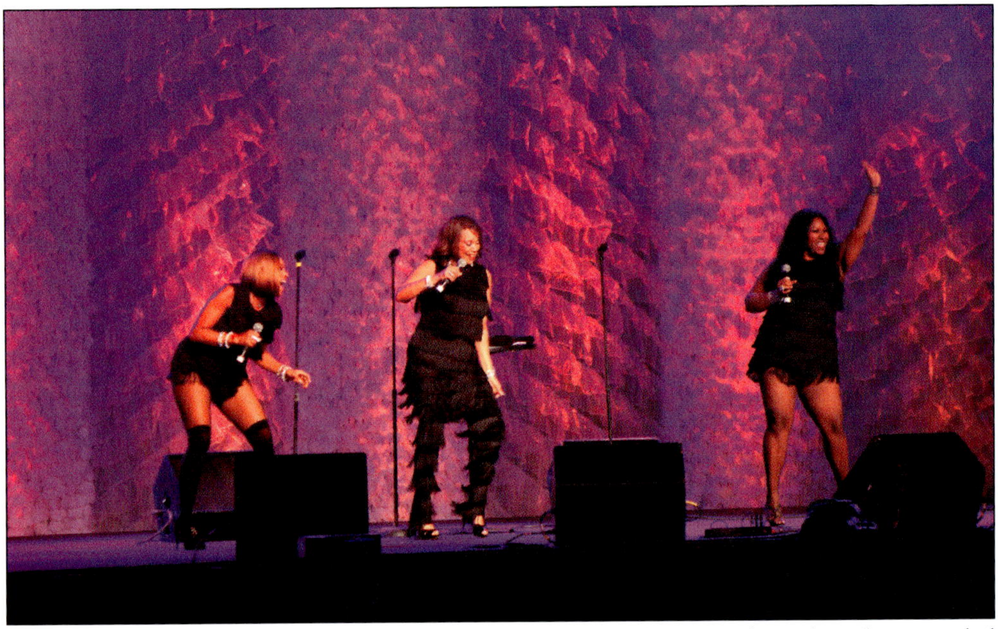

The Gay Games were not only a source of competition and camaraderie, but also provided audiences with some incredible musical moments. The opening ceremonies were a star-studded affair featuring appearances by Lance Bass, the Pointer Sisters (above) getting everyone to jump, Alex Newell of *Glee* fame, and Broadway star Andrea McArdle (below) joining the Gay Games Chorus to lift up the entire Q Arena in a song of welcome. The stage of the Festival Village featured live entertainment around the clock, including Cleveland's own JD Samson & MEN and the Scissor Sisters' Ana Matronic, with Pandora Boxx of *RuPaul's Drag Race* serving as emcee. (Both, Matt Cordish.)

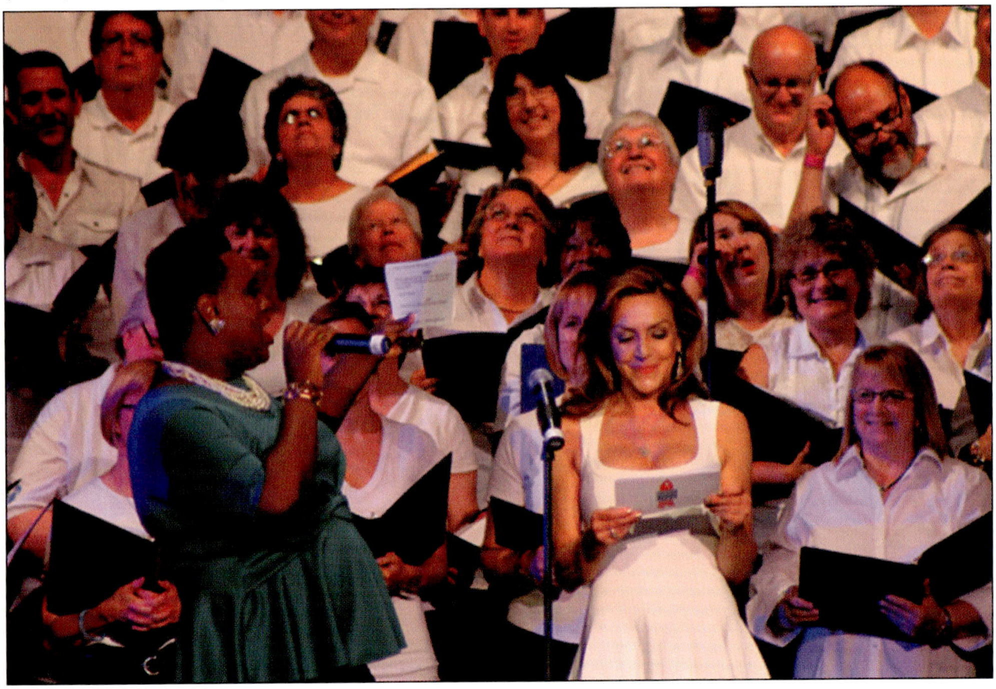

Four

We March
Pride Celebrations

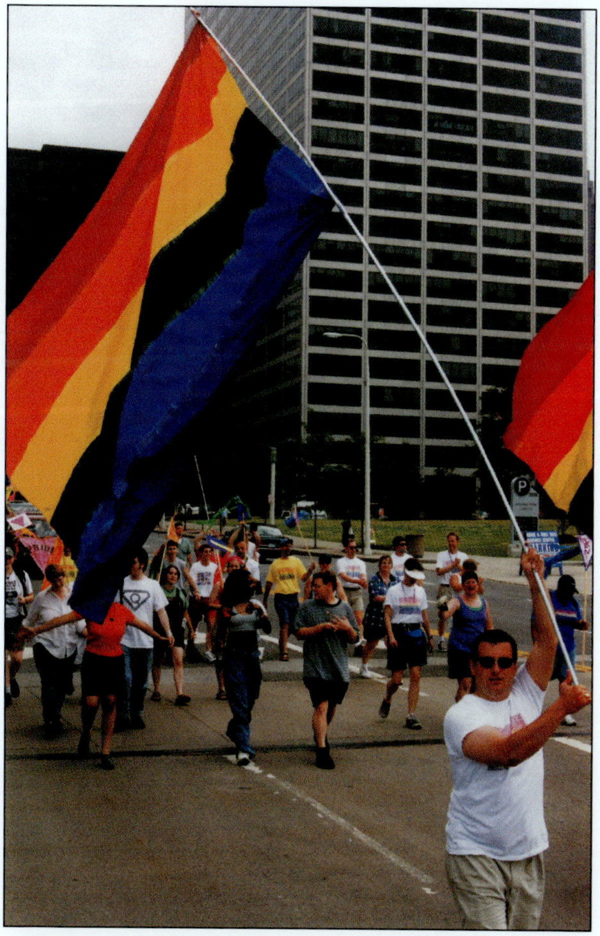

The history of Pride in Cleveland is a tale of love, drama, fortitude, bravery, and resilience. From a small group loudly singing "We Shall Overcome" at the second annual Gay Pride Celebration in 1974 in Edgewater Park, to the trailblazing and historic festivities in 1989, to the heroic (and successful) efforts to save Pride in 2016, the narrative thread of a community standing together is apparent for all to see. (Brynna Fish.)

Page 4

****

Gay Pride Synopsis

Art MacDonald

Cleveland's second annual Gay Pride Celebration was a quiet success. While nothing was done inthe way of a parade, or mass meetings in Public Square, a very successful Friday night Coffeehouse, and a Gay Pride Picnic at, where else? Edgewater Park! Unfortunately, the Seminars that were scheduled for the KIVA at Cleveland State University had to be cancelled, because of last minute withdrawals by the guest speakers. All in all, however, a good step forward for the newly- emerging political gay community.

The Coffeehouse featured entertainment from Miami, to replace a locally scheduled singer. Roy was a terrific fill-in, and surprised the Coffeehouse managementby agreeing to perform at the last minute at no cost. THE ALTERNATIVE, the Coffeehouse that sponsored the program, is a Youth Outreach of the Metropolitan Community Church here in Cleveland, and is in its' second month of providing an alternative (hence the name)for the under 21 community, and those who do not like the bar scene.

The picnic on Sunday afternoon had to be considered a success, although there was little cooperation in the local community in promoting it. Most of the bars would not post the special Gay Pride posters that the GEAR Foundation had printed for the occassion, nor would they distribute the Gay Pride brochures that were printed. One establishment referred to the posters and brochures as litter, and another simply took the materials and later threw them away. Despite the non-cooperation, about one hundred people attended the Picnic held at the Edgewater Park Pavilion, the majority of them members of the MCCs in Akron and Cleveland. An MCC Worship Service in the Park was held later in the afternoon, with Stan Roberts, the Worship Coordinator from the Akron group delivering a "challenge" to the people present. Following the message, Mr. Roberts, and Art MacDonald,the Worship Coordinator from the MCC in Cleveland, concelebrated a communion service, followed by a loud singing of "We Shall Overcome".

The attitude among the participants in the Gay Pride festivities were enthusiastic, happy, and unlike previous years, even Proud! Although threatening telephone calls were recieved by the MCC Hotline during the week preceding the Gay Pride activities, no actual incidents occurred during the weekend. There were uniformed officers present during the coffeehouse, and the picnic, both volunteer security officers from within the gay community.

The first "official" Pride celebration was held in 1974, but it went largely under the radar for many members of the LGBTQ and greater Cleveland community. The second Pride in 1975 featured a "coffeehouse" and a picnic in Edgewater Park attended by 100 people, a majority of whom were members of the Metropolitan Community Church (MCC). In 1976, the celebration featured another picnic and "gay workshops" on topics from the media to legal rights to meditation. Then, in 1977, the remarkable happened: Cleveland held two Pride marches. The first, on June 22, was sponsored by Gay Caucus of Youth Against War and Fascism and attracted nearly 2,250 people, many of them from other towns in Northeast Ohio. The second, on July 9, was sponsored by the Cleveland MCC and featured around 200 marchers walking two to three abreast chanting, "Hey, hey, ho, ho, Anita Bryant's got to go!" (Western Reserve Historical Society.)

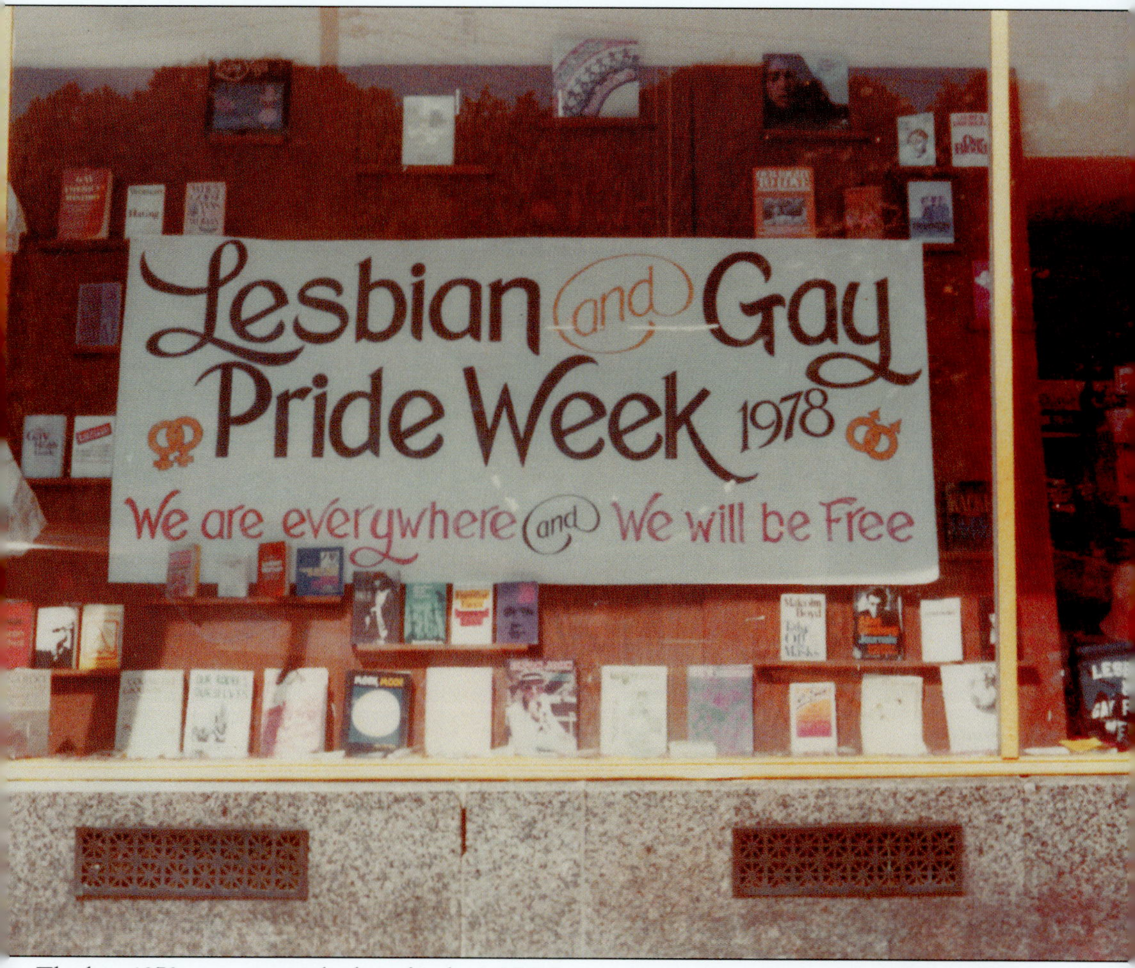

The late 1970s was a watershed era for the LGBTQ community. It was the time of Harvey Milk, Anita Bryant, the birth of the rainbow flag, and gay rights ordinances being both passed and repealed all over the country. Coverage of gay issues and people regularly hit the news and firmly broke into pop culture consciousness with Billy Crystal's portrayal of Jodie Dallas on the hit television show *Soap*. The idea had never been stronger of an actual "community" bonded together by their yearning for positive representation and fundamental equality in the face of vocal opposition to their rights and very existence. As this bold sign in Coventry Books proclaims, Pride in the late 1970s was as much about a declaration of presence and yearning for freedom as it was a chance to celebrate individual and collective identities, both in Cleveland and in the world at large. (Brian DeWitt.)

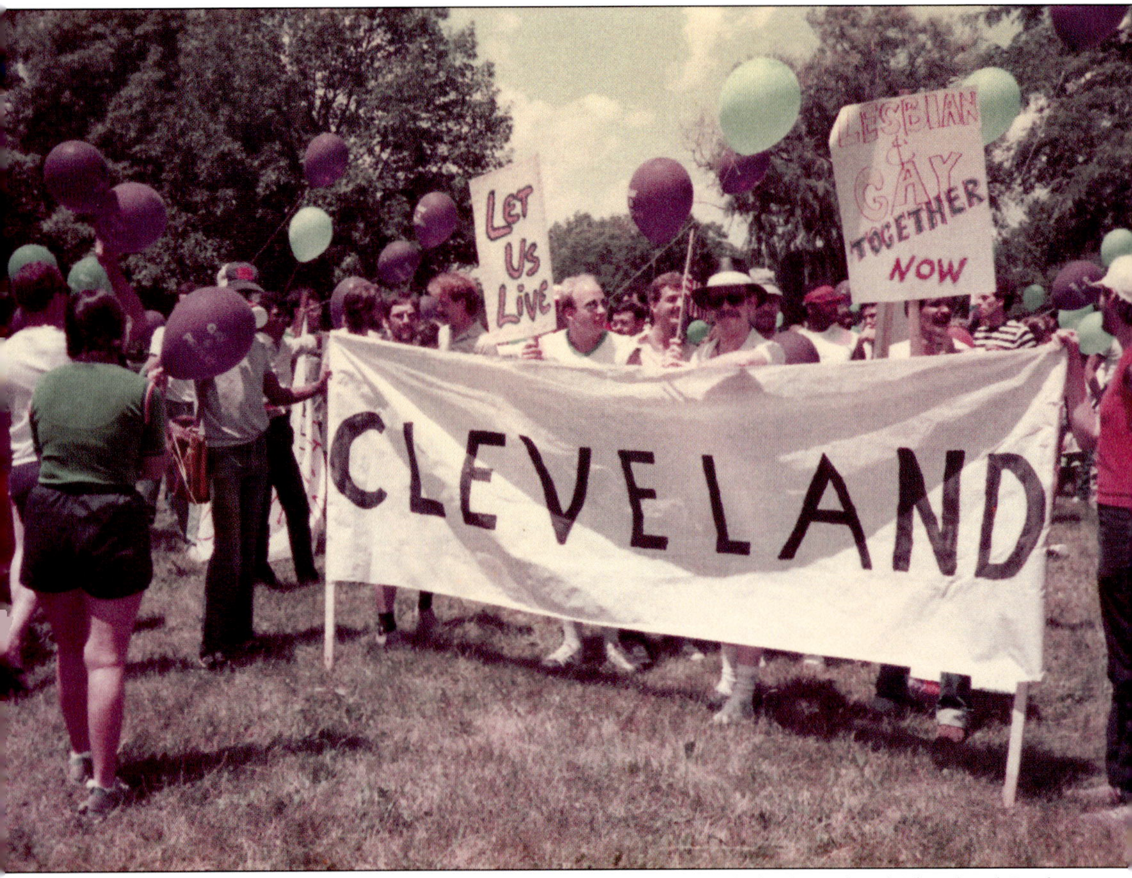

Between the early Prides held in Cleveland in the 1970s and the launch of Cleveland Pride in 1989, contingents of LGBTQ Clevelanders would regularly travel together to Columbus, the state capital 142 miles to the southwest. The Stonewall Columbus Pride Festival began in 1981 and, over time, became the second largest Pride event in the Midwest. Attending Columbus Pride provided LGBTQ Clevelanders with the opportunity to openly walk down the street holding a partner's hand, something many did not feel comfortable doing in Cleveland for fear of their identity being revealed to loved ones or employers. The Cleveland revelers pictured here were gathered to celebrate the 1982 Columbus festivities, displaying pride in their lives, their unity, and of course, their home city. Seven years later, citizens of Columbus were finally able to return the favor by traveling northeast to attend Pride 89, the rebirth of Pride celebrations in Cleveland. (Robert Downing.)

In 1988, Stonewall Columbus sponsored the March on the Midwest in the Ohio capital. In a letter urging participation, organizers wrote, "For the seventh year in a row, lesbians, gays, and their supporters will take to the streets of Columbus, Ohio demanding what is rightfully ours—civil rights. We would like to invite you, your organization or group to march with us to demonstrate the collective power of the Midwestern Lesbian/gay community. . . . Remember, we must stand together as one united force that demands to be recognized." Clevelanders not only attended the march in droves as participants and volunteers, but were also given top billing as Gene Witts of the Eleanor Roosevelt Gay Democratic Club delivered remarks and the Cleveland City Country Dancers entertained the assembled masses. (Both, Special Collections, Michael Schwartz Library at Cleveland State University.)

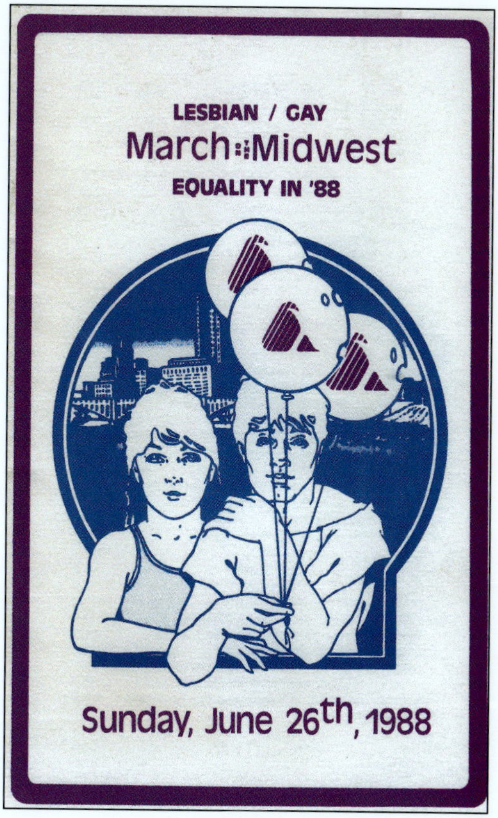

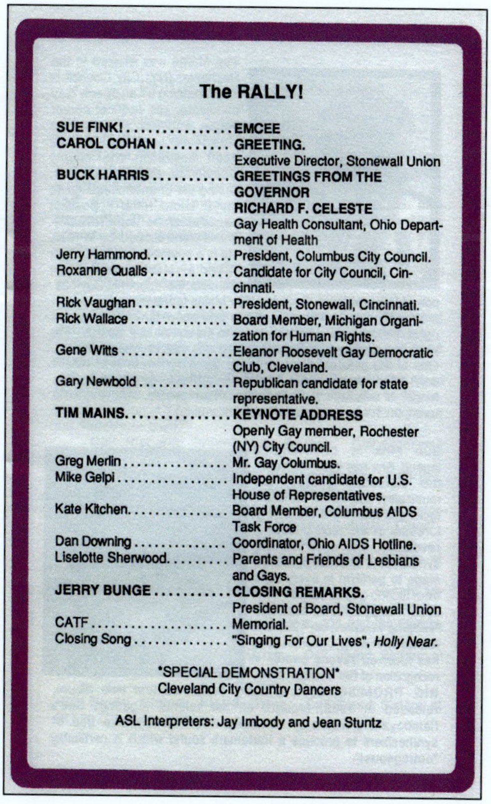

The RALLY!

SUE FINK!	**EMCEE**
CAROL COHAN	**GREETING.** Executive Director, Stonewall Union
BUCK HARRIS	**GREETINGS FROM THE GOVERNOR RICHARD F. CELESTE** Gay Health Consultant, Ohio Department of Health
Jerry Hammond	President, Columbus City Council.
Roxanne Qualls	Candidate for City Council, Cincinnati.
Rick Vaughan	President, Stonewall, Cincinnati.
Rick Wallace	Board Member, Michigan Organization for Human Rights.
Gene Witts	Eleanor Roosevelt Gay Democratic Club, Cleveland.
Gary Newbold	Republican candidate for state representative.
TIM MAINS	**KEYNOTE ADDRESS** Openly Gay member, Rochester (NY) City Council.
Greg Merlin	Mr. Gay Columbus.
Mike Gelpi	Independent candidate for U.S. House of Representatives.
Kate Kitchen	Board Member, Columbus AIDS Task Force
Dan Downing	Coordinator, Ohio AIDS Hotline.
Liselotte Sherwood	Parents and Friends of Lesbians and Gays.
JERRY BUNGE	**CLOSING REMARKS.** President of Board, Stonewall Union
CATF	Memorial.
Closing Song	"Singing For Our Lives", *Holly Near.*

SPECIAL DEMONSTRATION
Cleveland City Country Dancers

ASL Interpreters: Jay Imbody and Jean Stuntz

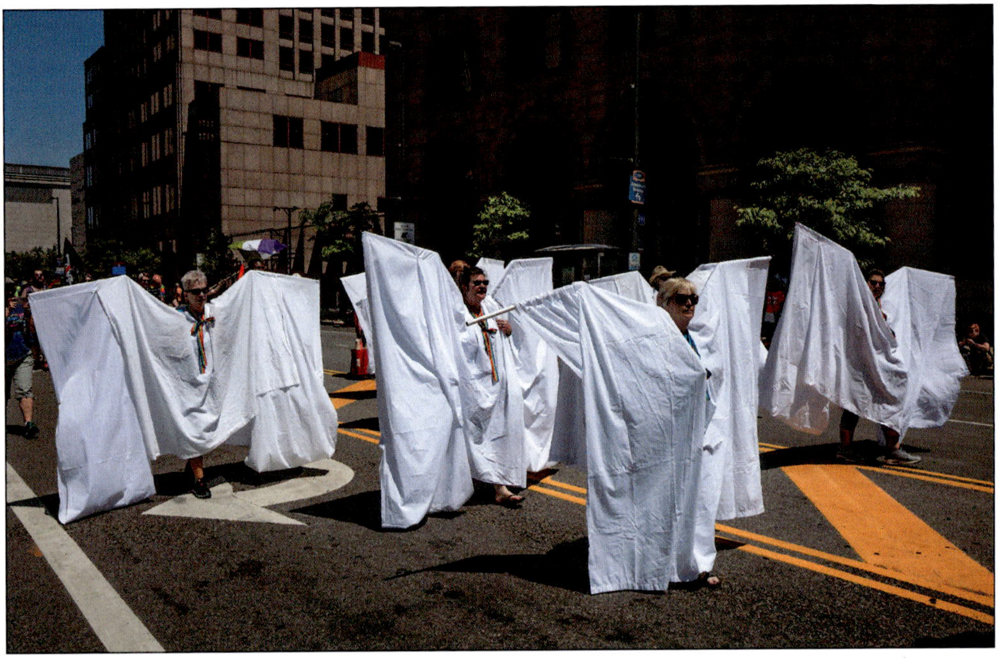

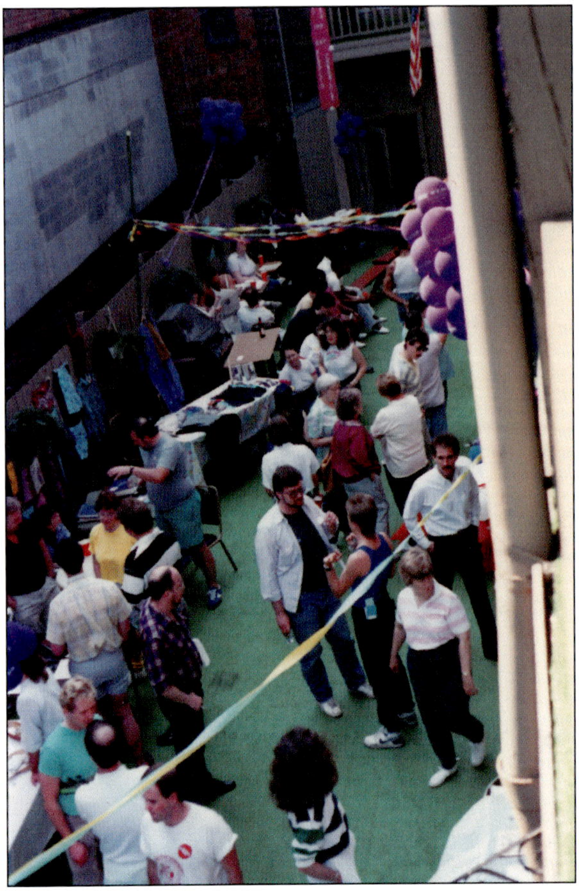

It sometimes comes to pass that a tiny handful of demonstrators show up to voice their meager opposition to the festivities. Inspired by the "Angel Action" first organized by Romaine Patterson to block the sight of the Westboro Baptist Church at the funeral of Matthew Shepard, here members of the West Shore Unitarian Universalist Church raise their heavenly arms to form a barrier between the scant protestors and the overwhelming number of individuals celebrating pride. (Bob Perkoski.)

The year before Pride 89 was organized, a precursor of what was to come took place on May 24, 1988. The Lesbian/Gay Community Service Center organized a Gay Community Fair, held in the space behind the center on Twenty-Ninth Street. Gay-friendly businesses, nonprofit organizations, and individual vendors gathered together for a sense of what a united community could accomplish, setting the stage for what would happen barely a year later. (Linda Malicki.)

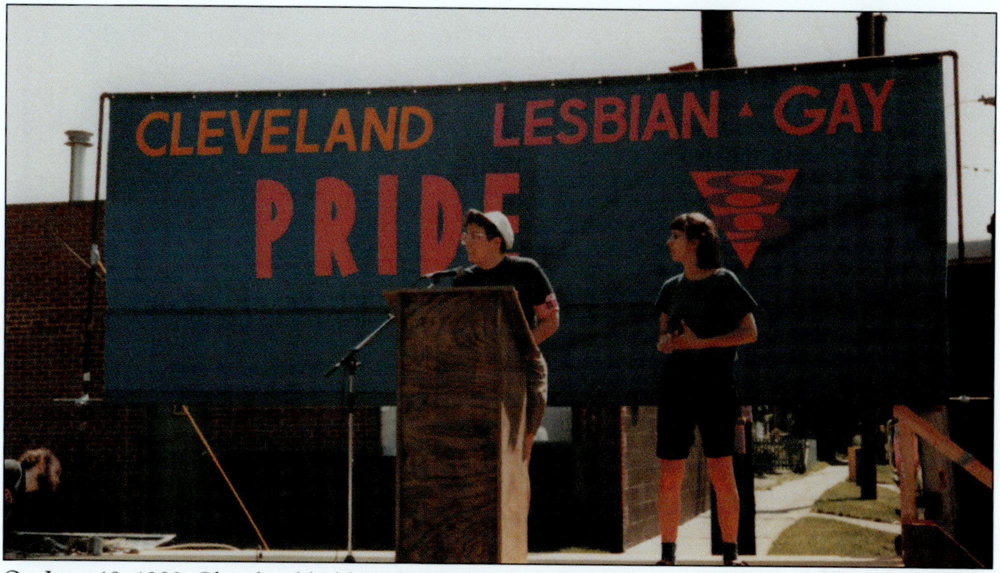

On June 18, 1989, Cleveland held Pride 89: An Out of the Closet Experience, a full-scale Pride celebration after a many years' absence. Held outside the Lesbian/Gay Community Service Center on West Twenty-Ninth Street and Detroit Avenue, the event was a true grassroots effort by volunteers and was co-chaired by Drew Cari and Martha Pontoni. In addition to local speakers, the program featured keynote speeches by Renee McCoy of the National Coalition of Black Lesbians and Gays and Craig Davidson of the Gay and Lesbian Alliance Against Defamation. North Coast Freedom Band and the Cleveland City Country Dancers provided the entertainment. In the welcome letter to Pride 89, the organizers wrote, "The idea to have a Pride celebration in Cleveland was not a new one. What was new this year was the willingness of the entire community to participate and make the day a success." (Above, Robert Downing; below, Brian DeWitt.)

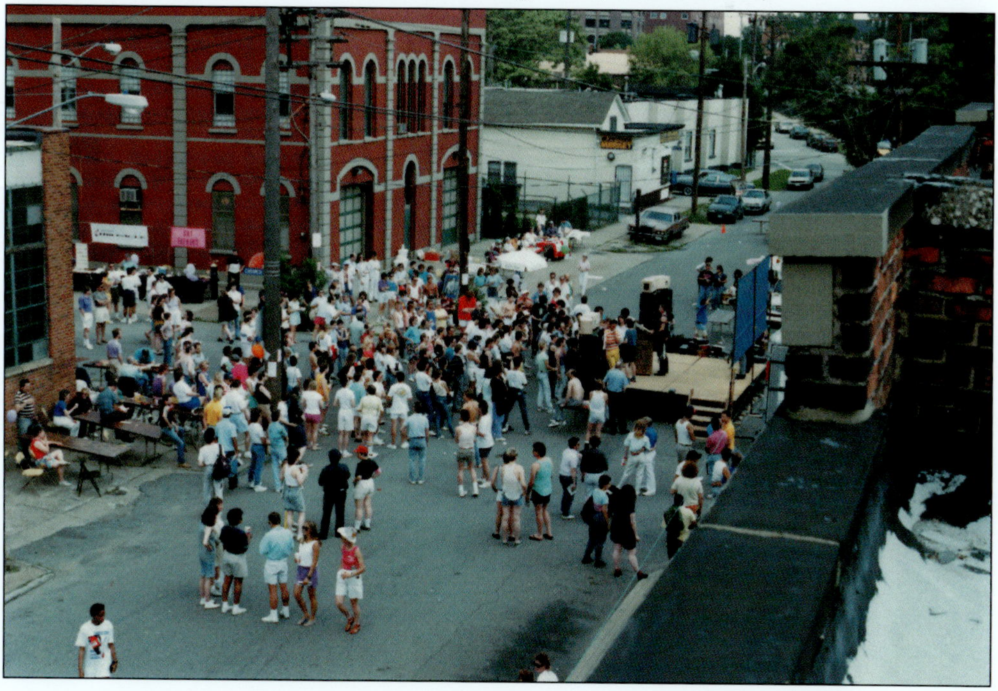

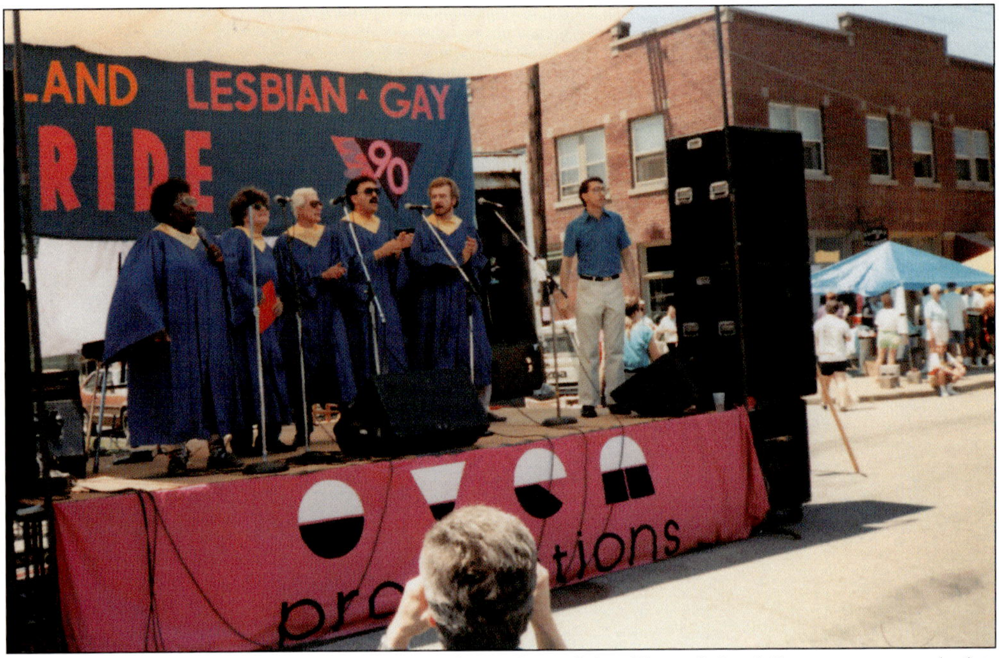

While the message for Pride 89 was centered on "Out of the Closet," the following year took this one step further by adding "Into the Streets." Officially, the theme was "Look to the Future," but clearly, the way to get there was through movement. Cleveland Pride 1990 added a march or parade (the correct word really does depend on who you ask) to the festival, walking from Public Square in downtown Cleveland, over the Detroit-Superior Bridge, to the site of the festival, which was situated again outside of the Lesbian/Gay Community Service Center on West Twenty-Ninth Street. Estimates of attendance vary, but most agree that the crowd was at least double the size of the year before. (Both, Robert Downing.)

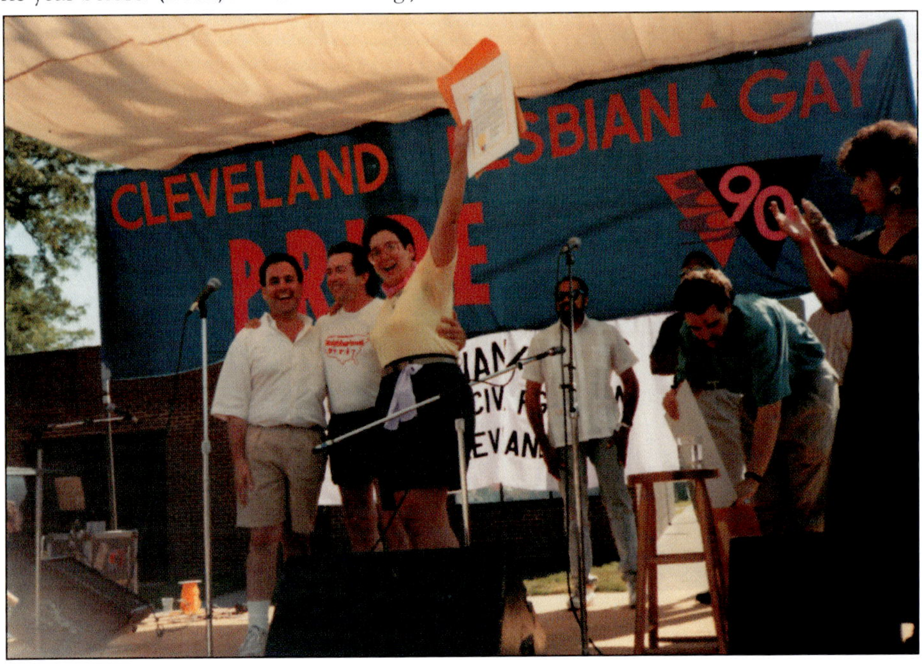

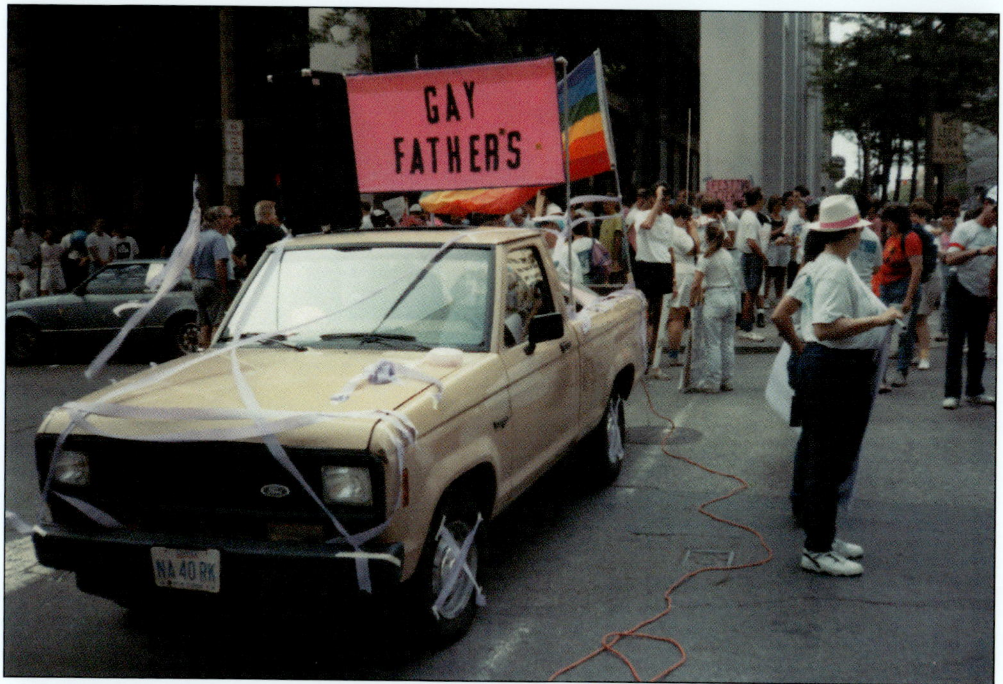

Video footage of the Cleveland Pride 90 march/parade shows hundreds of enthusiastic people walking closely together as one big group. Chants of "Come out, come out, wherever you are," and "What do we want? Gay rights! When do we want them? Now!" were interspersed with a rousing chorus of "When the Gays Go Marching In." The signs and banners were barely visible for lack of space between participants, but they ranged from homemade placards reading, "Silence=Death," and "Lesbian and Proud," to the more professionally printed advertisements for local bars and organizations. Onlookers were few, but they were never the focus; the crowd was moving forward to move forward together. (Above, Bob Downing; below, Brian DeWitt.)

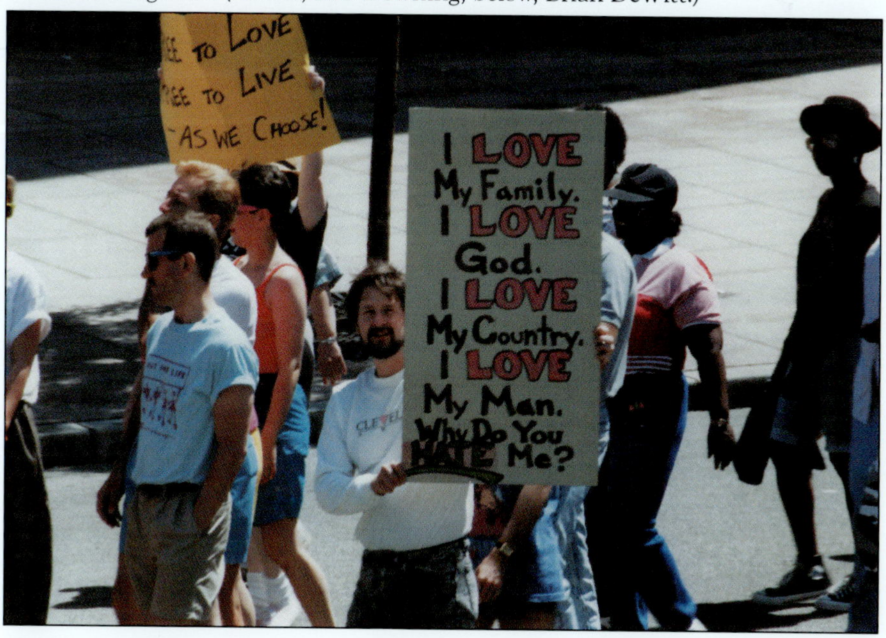

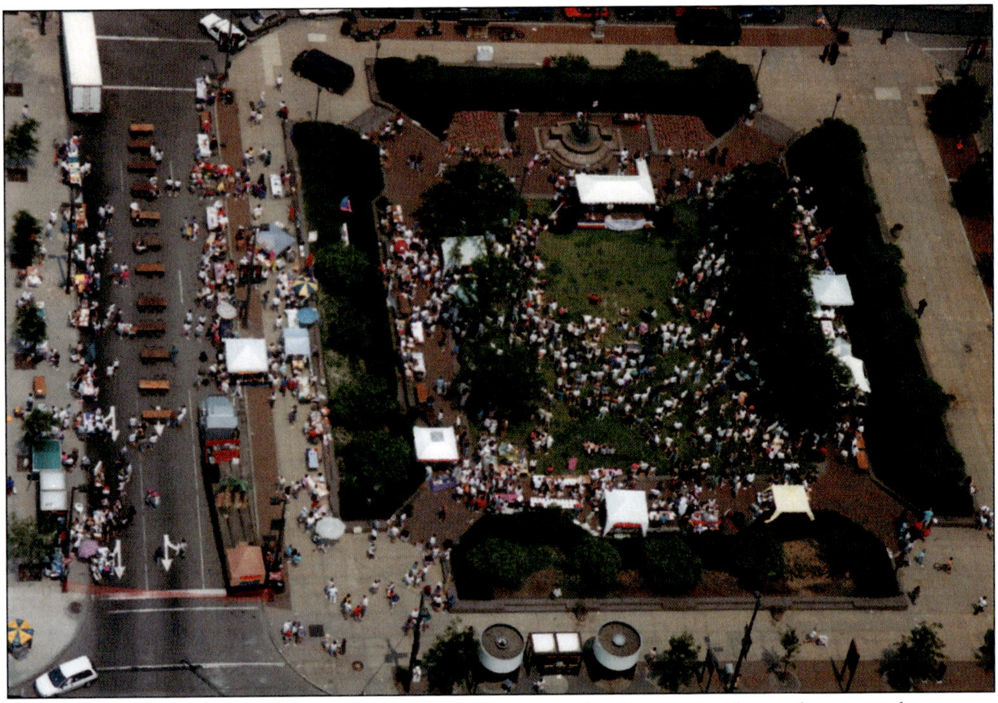

In 1994, Cleveland Pride took a bold step by moving the festivities from the immediate area surrounding the LGBT Center on Twenty-Ninth Street to Public Square in downtown Cleveland. The slogan for the celebration that year was, appropriately, "Community of Pride." Coordinated by Brynna Fish and Izzy Schachner, there was a huge uptick in both attendance and visibility as Pride moved to the very heart of the city. (Brian DeWitt.)

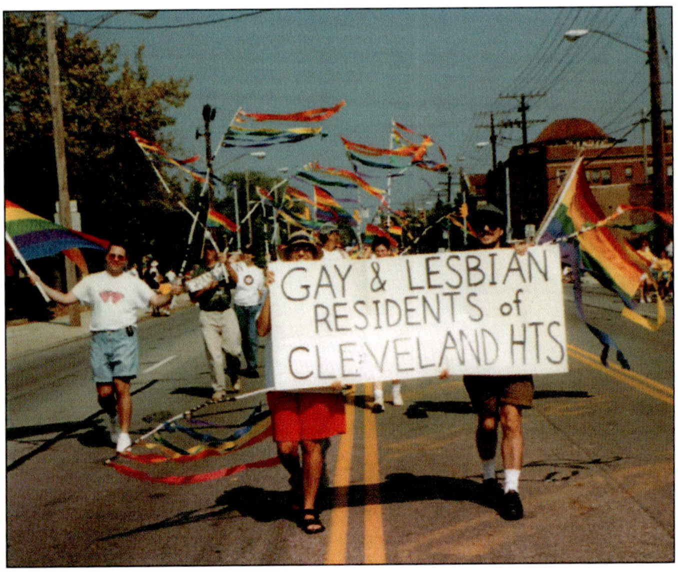

The LBGTQ community does not always need a Pride parade to break out the rainbow flag and march together. In this example, gay and lesbian residents of Cleveland Heights united behind a banner to walk proudly down Mayfield Road in the Cleveland Heights 75th anniversary celebration in 1996. Each resident carried with them a placard indicating the street on which they lived, proclaiming to all present that they were indeed "here and queer." (Brian DeWitt.)

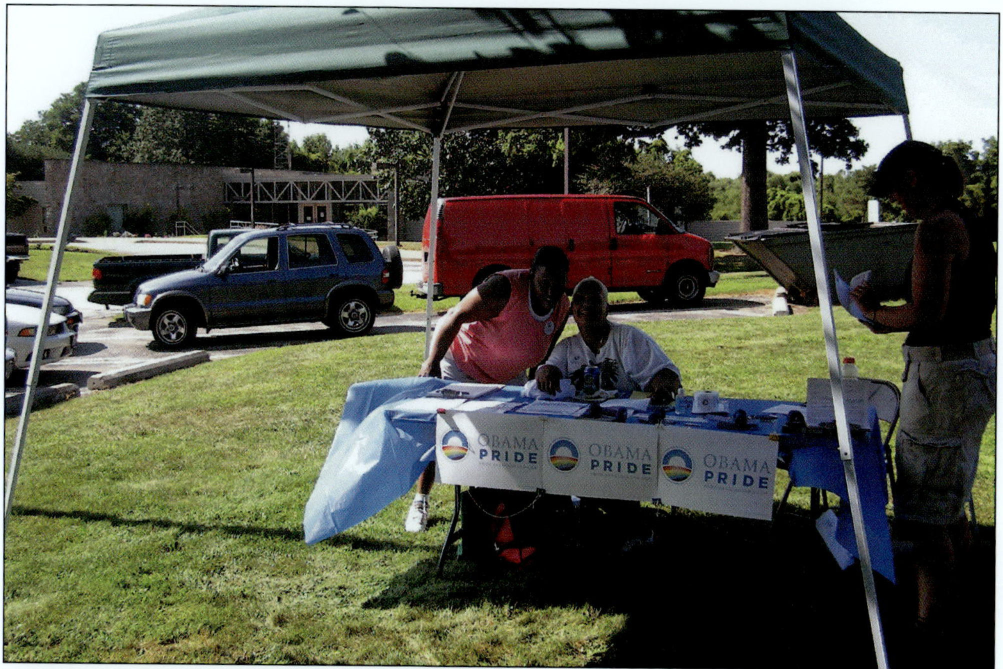

Though it had been informally taking place for many years, 1997 marked the first official Black Gay Pride from August 15 to 17. Activist/change-agent Mandy Carter provided the keynote address, and Isis Tiffany Soul served as the emcee of a celebration that featured live entertainment, impassioned speeches, a picnic, and voter registration. The event received an official commendation from the Ohio House of Representatives, noting that the event was "unprecedented in the Cleveland area" and highlighting that "Cleveland Black Pride Inc. merits praise for encouraging not only camaraderie, but civic commitment as well." The official program for the celebration emphatically declared, "If we as Black lesbians, gay men, bisexuals, and transgender people remember from where we've come and take Pride in ourselves as individuals and as a people, our possibilities are endless. We can do and be anything and anyone we choose." (Both, Brian DeWitt.)

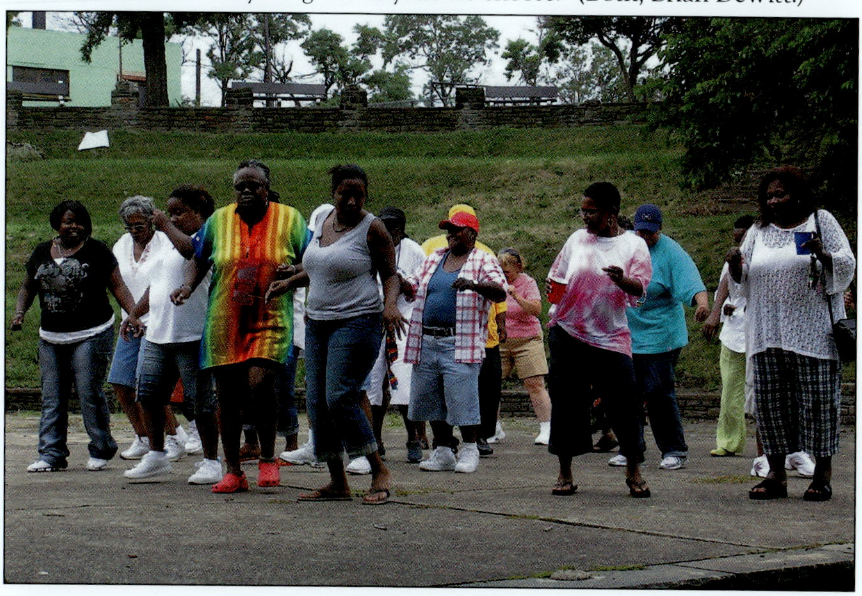

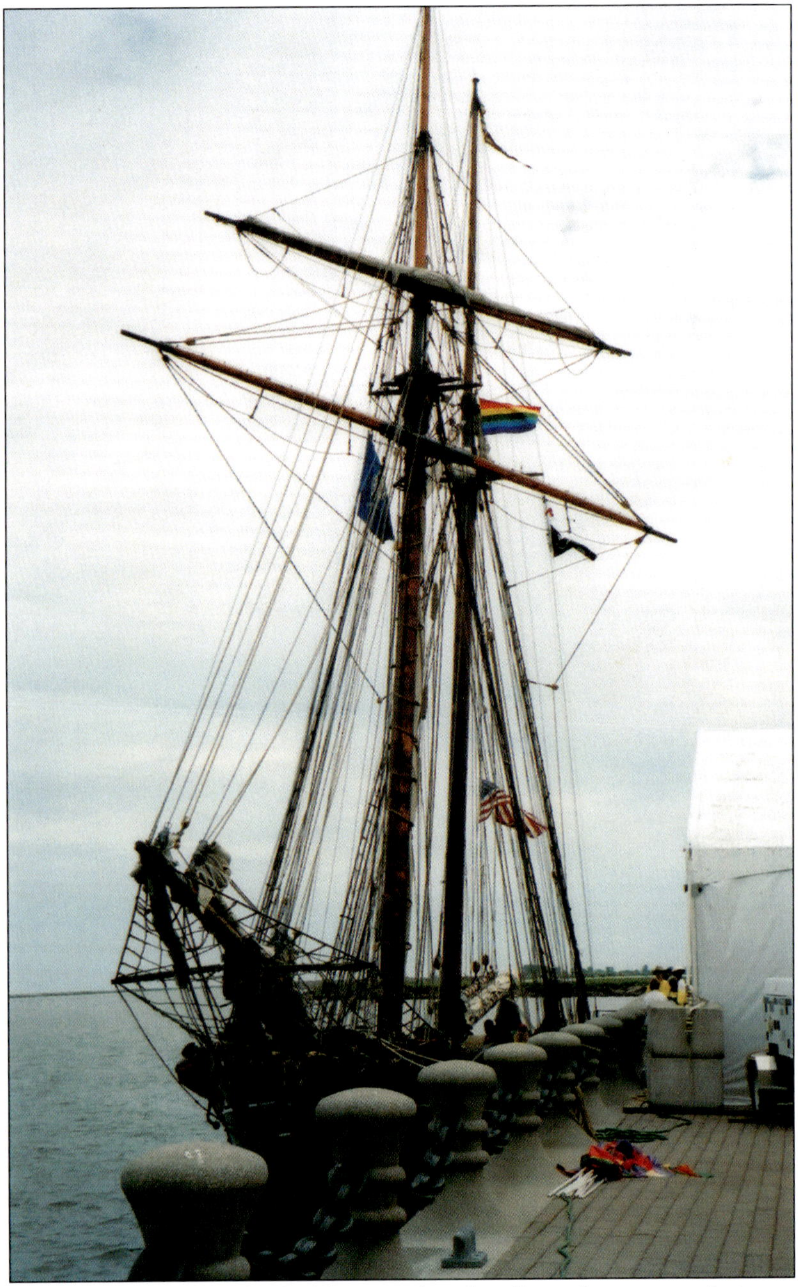

In July 1889, captive Africans who had been enslaved in Sierra Leone were being transported from Cuba to their owners' plantations abroad *La Amistad*. The slaves seized control of the two-masted schooner and demanded that the ship return them to Africa, killing some of the crew before being captured off the coast of Long Island. This uprising resulted in a Supreme Court case affirming the freedom of the captives and became a key symbol in the fight to end slavery. When the *Freedom Schooner Amistad*, a wooden re-creation of *La Amistad*, visited Cleveland during Pride in 2003, Cleveland Pride organizers petitioned the crew to fly a rainbow flag high atop the mast. The crew readily agreed, thus uniting these two symbols of unity and the human struggle for freedom for all of Cleveland to see. (Brynna Fish.)

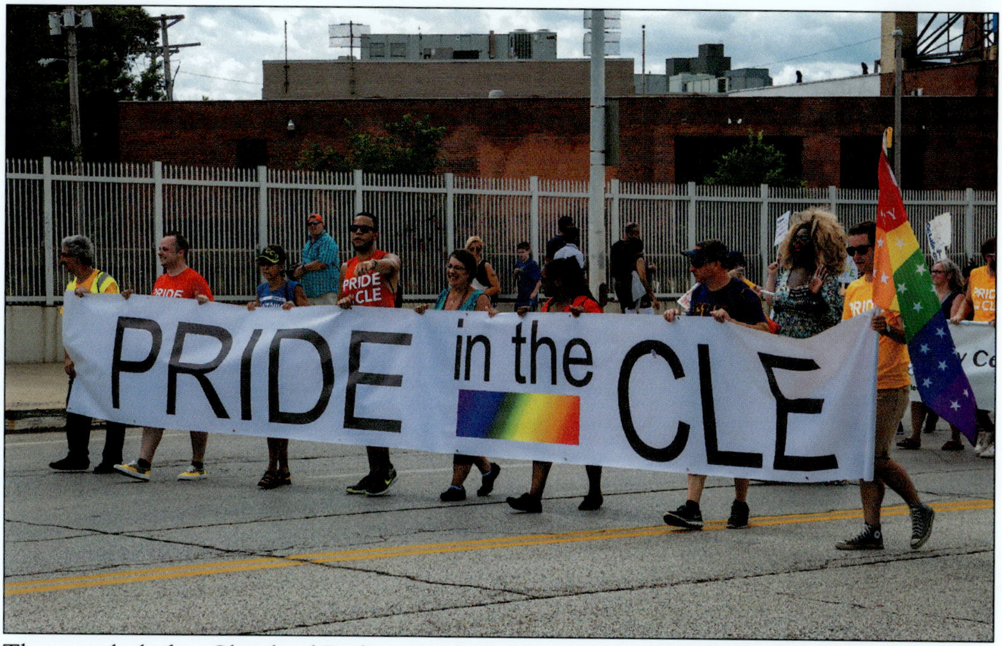

Three weeks before Cleveland Pride was to be held in August 2016 (pushed back from June that year due to the Republican National Convention in Cleveland), a press release announced that the event had been canceled due to "the changing social climate," a vague phrase and even more intangible reason for cancelation. The LGBT Center of Greater Cleveland sprang into action and led community organizations, elected officials, and volunteers to the creation of "Pride in the CLE," a march across the Detroit/Superior Bridge into a festival of performers in the newly renovated Public Square in downtown Cleveland. The forecast called for downpours early in the day, but the positive energy of a city that wanted its Pride was able to successfully banish the clouds. Both Cleveland Pride and Pride in the CLE returned in 2017. (Both, Bob Perkoski.)

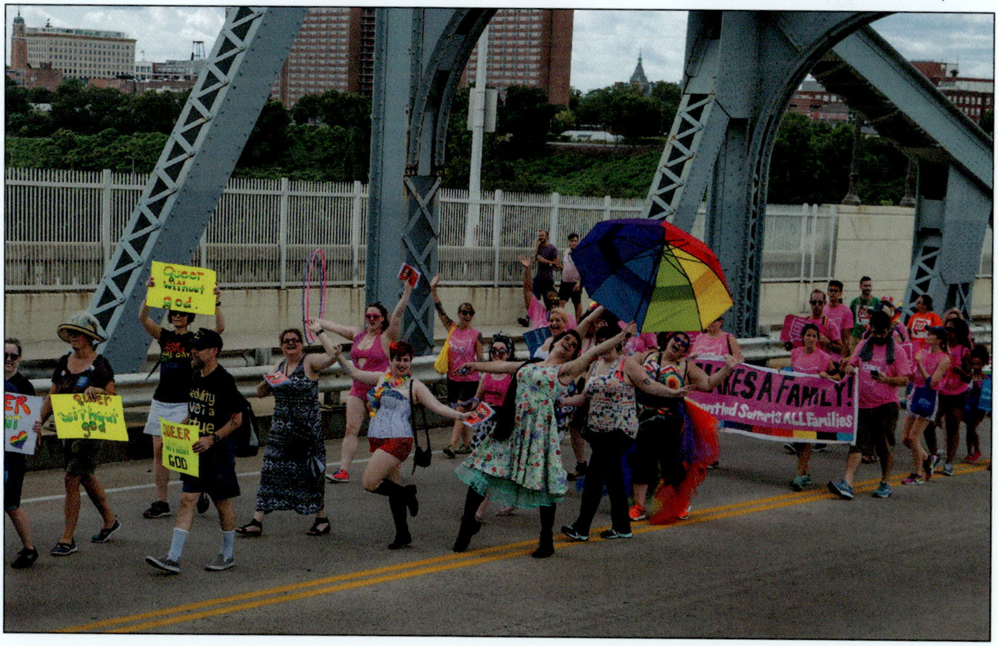

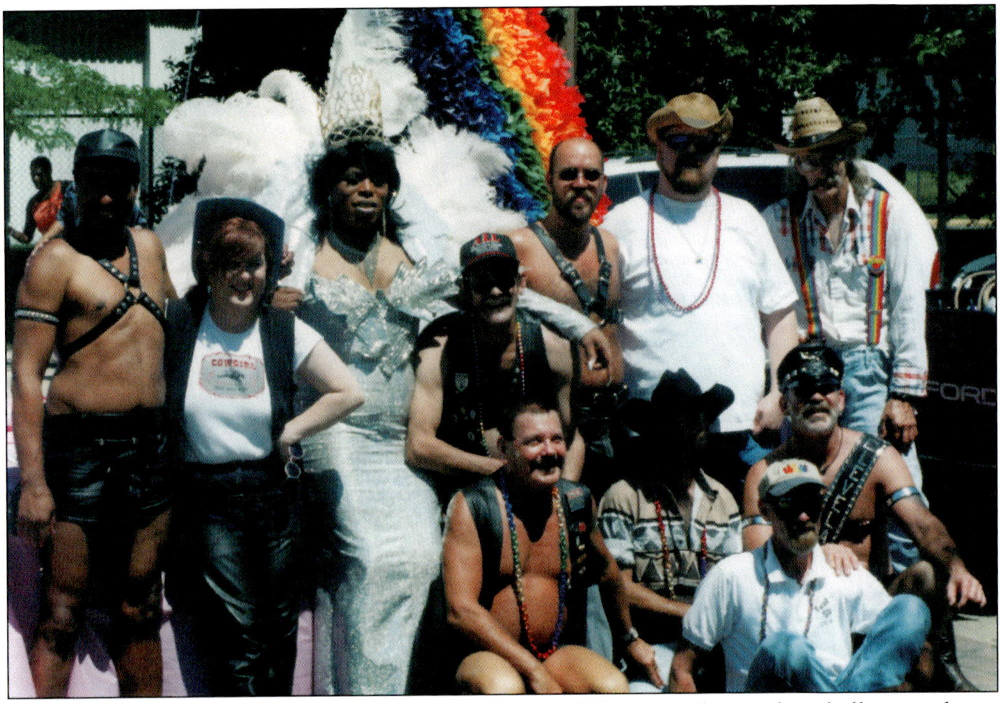

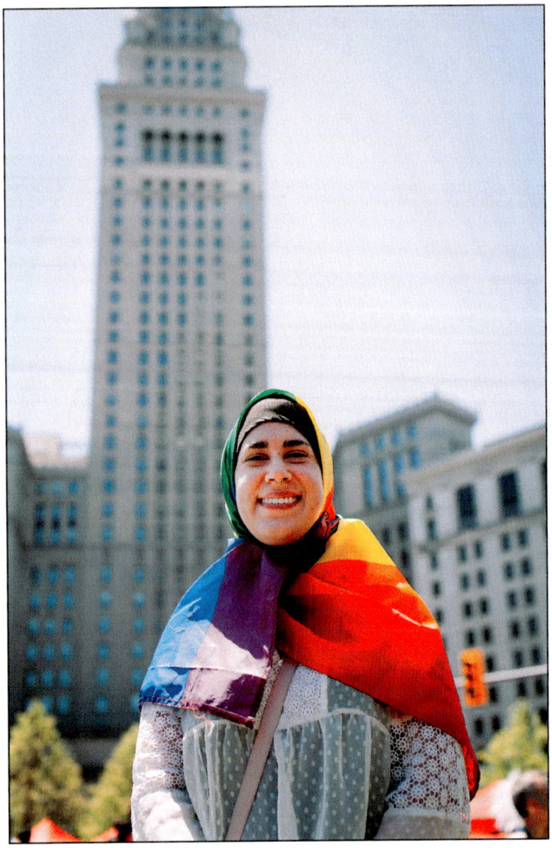

Take away the rainbow balloon arch. Subtract both the stage and Taylor Dayne performing on top of it. Get rid of the vendors, the beer tent, and the free merchandise from the corporate sponsors. What's left are the people, and the people alone will always be enough to constitute Cleveland Pride. Over the years, Cleveland Pride has seen its share of drama, from hostile planning committee takeovers, to marches in the face of antigay threats, to a last-minute cancellation about which the community may never get the full story. Through it all, LGBTQ Clevelanders have shown up in force: as individuals expressing their authentic selves and as a community that stands (and dances) stronger together. (Above, Brynna Fish; left, Molly Castle.)

Five

WE ORGANIZE
ACTIVISM & ISSUES

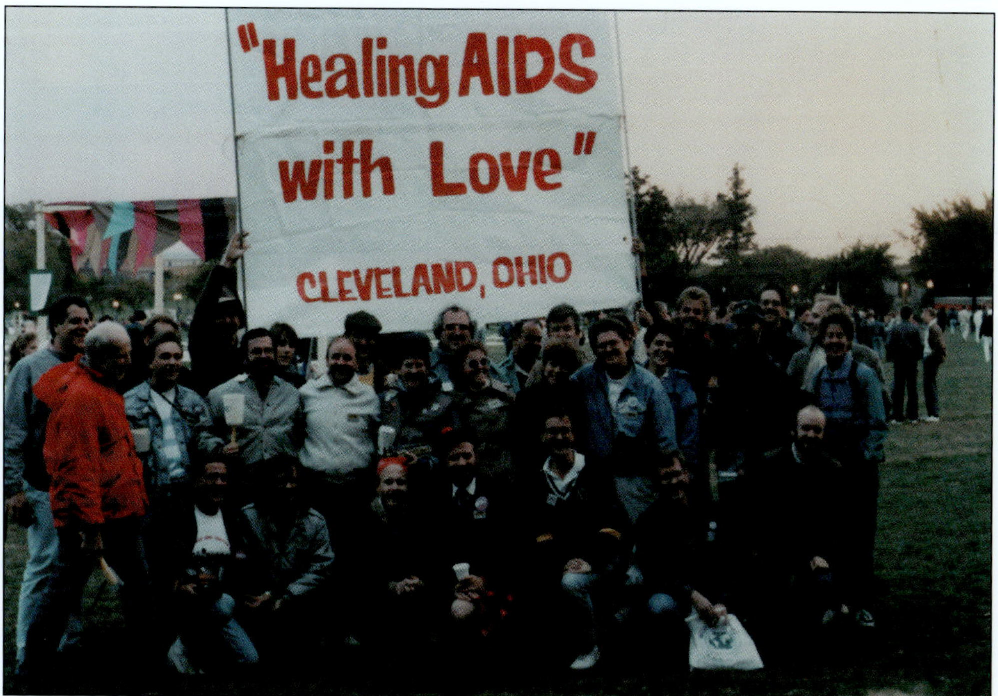

Whether responding to national events or phenomena that were distinctly more Cleveland-ish, the LGBTQ community banded together countless times over the years to protest discriminatory actions, draw attention to a lack of equality, and demand change when rights were at stake. When a unified voice was needed, differences were put aside, and Cleveland did what needed to be done to fight and be heard. (Brian DeWitt.)

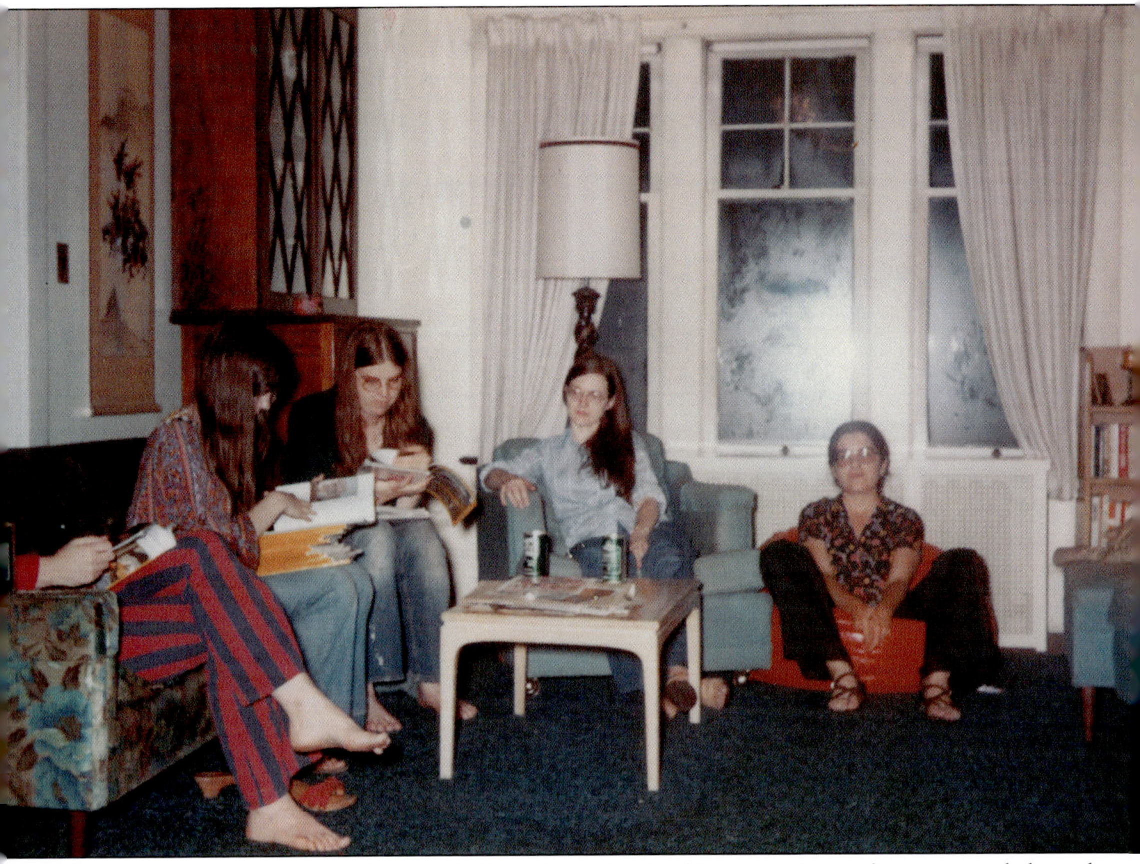

Women came together in the early 1970s to form Cleveland Women's Counseling, a group dedicated to informing women of their options with regard to reproductive options, connecting women to vetted providers, and supporting them throughout the process. As abortion was not legal at the time, a subgroup of Cleveland Women's Counseling traveled to New York City and Washington, DC, to research viable options for women and then presented the results of their findings to other groups in Cleveland dedicated to women's health. Cleveland Women's Counseling also raised money to help women pay for some of these services. The energy around these efforts (along with some of the very same women directly involved) led to the creation of Preterm, one of Ohio's most trusted providers of abortion and sexual health care, including birth control, STD testing and treatment, and wellness care. (Sally Tatnall.)

AIDS Panics Indianapolis Officials

By SEBASTIAN MELMOTH

Cleveland health officials, Council President George Forbes, and the Plain Dealer have sharply criticized the panic-stricken behavior of Indianapolis offiials who rushed an AIDS victim here on a one-way bus ticket.

The man they deported was arrested by Indianapolis police who suspected him of stealing a bicycle. At the Marion County jail he told Deputy Sheriff Terry A. Dale that he had been diagnosed as having AIDS in Houston, where he had received treatment. He had come to Indianapolis because two sisters lived there.

Apparently unaware of the precise mechanisms involved in the transmission of AIDS, the deputies who booked him wore rubber gloves and gauze masks, and destroyed the pens he used to sign documents. They threatened bodily harm if he were to cough at them.

Fearful that he would spread AIDS throughout the county jail, the Marion County sheriff passed word of the man's condition on to Municipal Judge John D. Downer.

Equally fearful that he might contaminate court personnel, the judge decided not to press charges against him. Rejecting all the other alternatives open to him, Judge Downer ordered the man to leave Indianapolis and placed him in the custody of two deputy sheriffs with orders to take him to the bus station and buy him a one-way ticket to Cleveland, his original home.

The Indianapolis officials felt that these actions discharged all their responsibilities. They did not contact Cleveland health officials.

His treatment in Cleveland, which enjoys the advantages of more sophisticated legal and medical establishments, was very different. Through the Health Issues Task Force and the American Red Cross, housing was found for him. He was directed to the AIDS Clinic at University Hospitals.

Dr. V. Diana Richardson, Cleveland Commissioner of Health and Chairwoman of the city AIDS Task Force, expressed further anger because the Associated Press released the victim's name over the wire services, violating the general practice of not naming someone who has not been formally charged with an offense.

Further evidence of the value of Ohio's state program for AIDS education is provided by a New York Times story from Kokomo, Indiana, where officials have barred a 13-year-old hemophiliac with AIDS from attending school, fearing he will infect his fellow students.

Panic, chaos, plague, terror, and death: AIDS brought with it an absolute onslaught of debilitating words and overwhelming emotions to the public at large. Though individuals and organizations in Cleveland were doing heroic work to combat the crisis, there was absolutely no way to control the devastating fear of the unknown. In a jaw-dropping example as unfathomable today as it was de rigeuer in 1985, a man was arrested for bike theft in Indianapolis and revealed to the deputy sheriff that he had been diagnosed with AIDS. Fearful that he might contaminate court personnel, the judge bypassed pressing charges and instead ordered that the man be taken to the bus station with a one-way bus ticket to Cleveland, his childhood home. Note the final paragraph in the article about the breaking news of an unnamed 13-year-old hemophiliac with AIDS who was barred from attending his school in Kokomo, Indiana. That boy's name would soon be known by the whole country, as Ryan White's story was about to captivate the nation. (Western Reserve Historical Society.)

Page 4 Gay Peoples Chronicle

gay peoples CHRONICLE

Publisher
Cleveland Gay Peoples Press Associates, Inc.

Editor-in-Chief
Charles Callender

Business Manager
Bob Reynolds

DON'T TAKE THE TEST

In this issue of The Chronicle, Buck Harris repeats his earlier warnings against taking the HTLV-III blood test. A release from the National Gay Task Force reiterates it. Recently the national gay organizations and publications, like significant parts of the medical community, have advised gay men not to take the test.

First, it is NOT a test for AIDS. Operating with an admitted margin of error, the test at best shows whether you have been exposed to the HTLV-III/LAV virus that many believe to be the cause of AIDS. A positive reaction does not necessarily mean exposure, because other factors may produce this. Even if you have been exposed to the virus, this does not in itself mean that you have AIDS or that you will develop it.

Second, the test's purpose is to screen blood and quiet fears of acquiring AIDS through transfusions. As a high-risk AIDS group, gay men should not donate blood. If they crowd into blood centers to be tested, they will overstrain these facilities without deriving any benefit themselves. The testing program was not instituted to deal with gay men and offers no counselling.

Third, there are no guarantees that test results will remain confidential and will not be made available to employers or insurance companies. The Federal government has shown no concern with this problem.

The NGTF blames much of the current confusion about the test and its purpose on the Department of Health and Human Services, which has issued conflicting statements and show little interest in clarifying the uses or the limits of the test. We agree. The main point, right now, is don't take the test.

"Know Your Status" may be the crucial rallying cry of modern times, but it wasn't always the prevalent sentiment. The sudden assault of HIV/AIDS on the LGBTQ community brought with it a crushing supply of justified trepidation and confusion. In April 1985, *Gay People's Chronicle* urged men to not get tested for a variety of reasons, including a fear of the federal government releasing those results to employers and insurers. (Western Reserve Historical Society.)

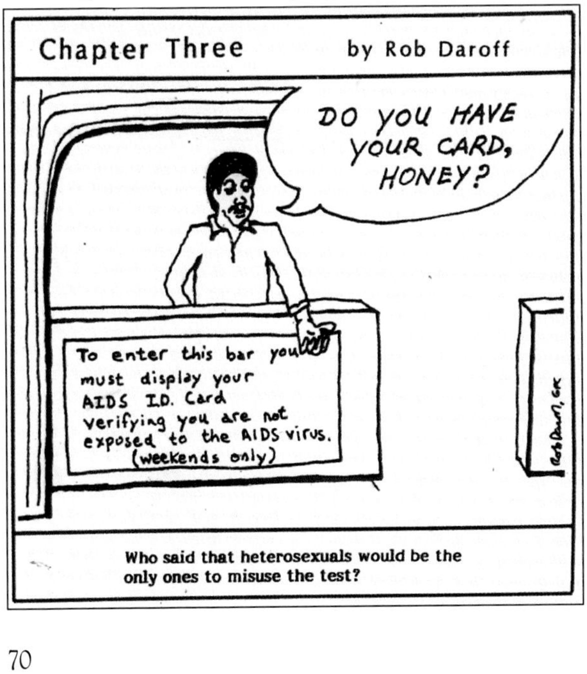

The attack of AIDS could not help but have a profound effect upon the LGBTQ community itself. The unconditional care and compassion of the community coming together to take care of their fallen siblings has been well documented. On the other end of the spectrum, the disease also caused a rift within some segments of the LGBTQ community, notably with the social scene as illustrated in this cartoon in *Gay People's Chronicle* in October 1985. (Western Reserve Historical Society.)

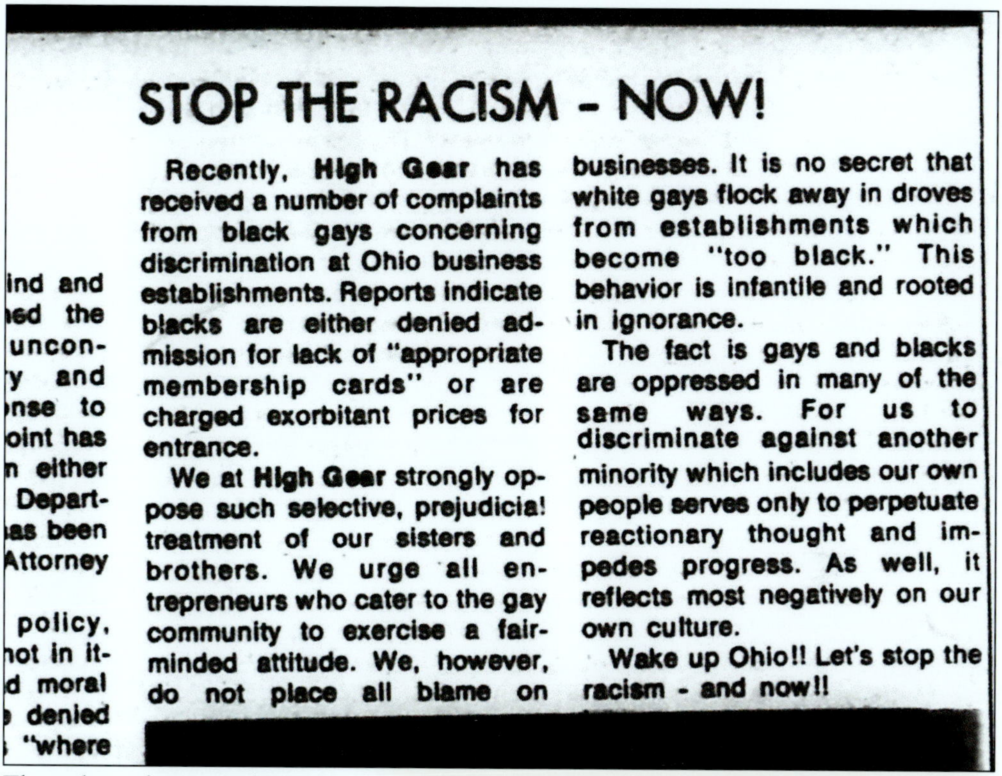

ind and
ed the
uncon-
y and
nse to
oint has
n either
Depart-
as been
Attorney

policy,
not in it-
d moral
denied
"where

STOP THE RACISM - NOW!

Recently, **High Gear** has received a number of complaints from black gays concerning discrimination at Ohio business establishments. Reports indicate blacks are either denied admission for lack of "appropriate membership cards" or are charged exorbitant prices for entrance.

We at **High Gear** strongly oppose such selective, prejudicial treatment of our sisters and brothers. We urge all entrepreneurs who cater to the gay community to exercise a fair-minded attitude. We, however, do not place all blame on businesses. It is no secret that white gays flock away in droves from establishments which become "too black." This behavior is infantile and rooted in ignorance.

The fact is gays and blacks are oppressed in many of the same ways. For us to discriminate against another minority which includes our own people serves only to perpetuate reactionary thought and impedes progress. As well, it reflects most negatively on our own culture.

Wake up Ohio!! Let's stop the racism - and now!!

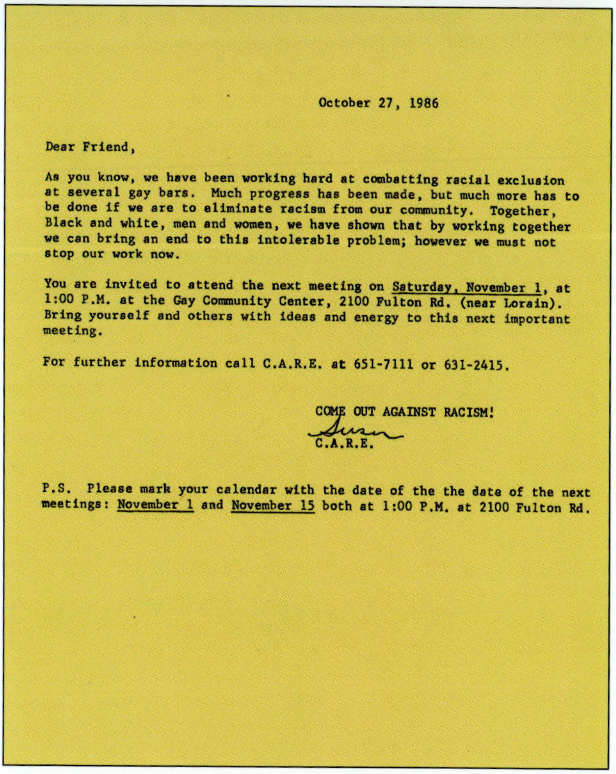

October 27, 1986

Dear Friend,

As you know, we have been working hard at combatting racial exclusion at several gay bars. Much progress has been made, but much more has to be done if we are to eliminate racism from our community. Together, Black and white, men and women, we have shown that by working together we can bring an end to this intolerable problem; however we must not stop our work now.

You are invited to attend the next meeting on Saturday, November 1, at 1:00 P.M. at the Gay Community Center, 2100 Fulton Rd. (near Lorain). Bring yourself and others with ideas and energy to this next important meeting.

For further information call C.A.R.E. at 651-7111 or 631-2415.

COME OUT AGAINST RACISM!
Susan
C.A.R.E.

P.S. Please mark your calendar with the date of the the date of the next meetings: November 1 and November 15 both at 1:00 P.M. at 2100 Fulton Rd.

Throughout the years, the intersection of race and the LGBTQ community has been fraught in Cleveland, and one of the prime battleground locales was in the nightlife. Though these two messages were written 10 years apart, the circumstances read like they have been separated by mere seconds. In 1976, numerous black gay people wrote to *High Gear* complaining of discriminatory practices at local establishments, inspiring the editorial above exhorting business owners and white gay people to "stop the racism." A decade and only a few weeks later, the same race-based exclusion at gay bars was reported to the Gay Community Center, prompting the letter at right urging individuals to show up with their ideas and energy to an upcoming meeting. (Both, Western Reserve Historical Society.)

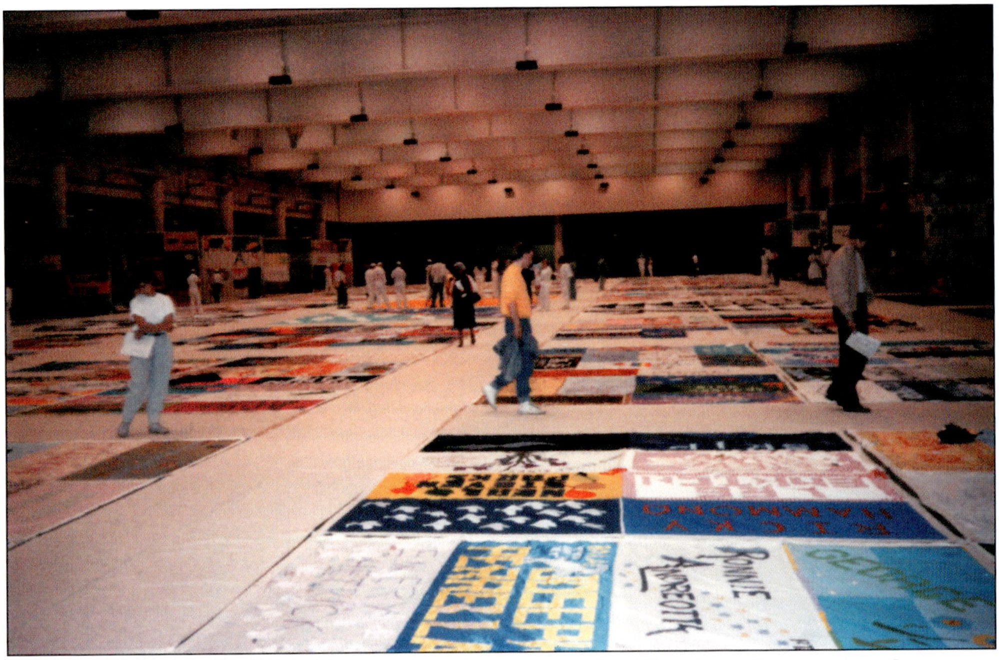

The NAMES Project AIDS Memorial Quilt came to the Cleveland Convention Center on Lakeside Drive in June 1988 (above). Cleve Jones, who addressed the Case Western Reserve University Lesbian and Gay Conference earlier in March 1988, organized the creation of the quilt as a memorial for those who had died of AIDS. He called it "a gift from the hands and hearts of thousands of Americans who have not despaired." Also in 1988, a contingent of Clevelanders traveled together to Washington, DC, to participate in the candlelight march honoring the quilt being shown in its entirety (below). The last display of the full quilt in 1996 covered the entire National Mall in Washington. (Above, Robert Downing; below, Brian Dewitt.)

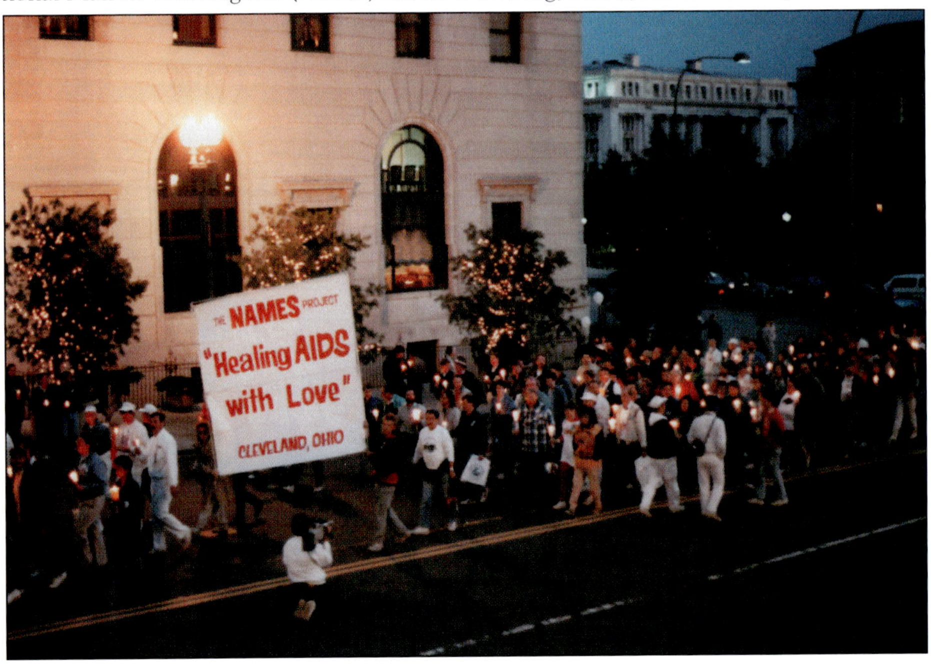

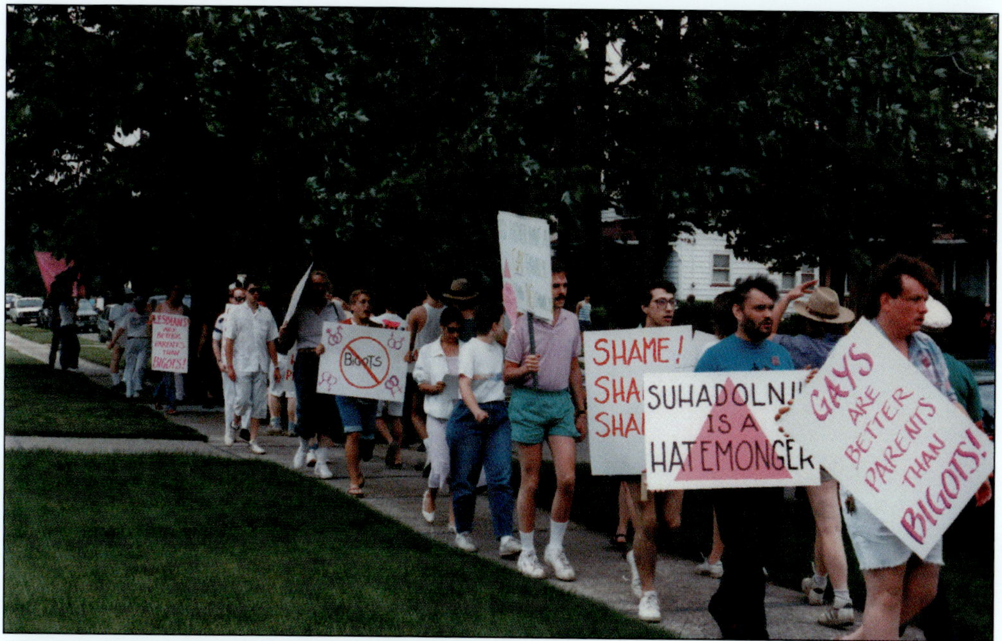

Ohio state senator Gary Suhadolnik, a Republican from Parma Heights, was no friend to the LGBTQ community. In 1989, he (unsuccessfully) tried to shut down the Gay, Lesbian and Bisexual Student Services office at Ohio State University. A year earlier, he threatened to introduce legislation to ban lesbian and gay people from adopting or serving as foster parents. This led to an action affectionately called "Picket the Bigot," with over a hundred marchers making their voices heard through signs and presence as they made their way to Senator Suhadolnik's house. They were careful to stay on the sidewalk so as not to trespass on anyone's property. Senator Suhadolnik's discriminatory bill never made it out of committee. (Both, Brian DeWitt.)

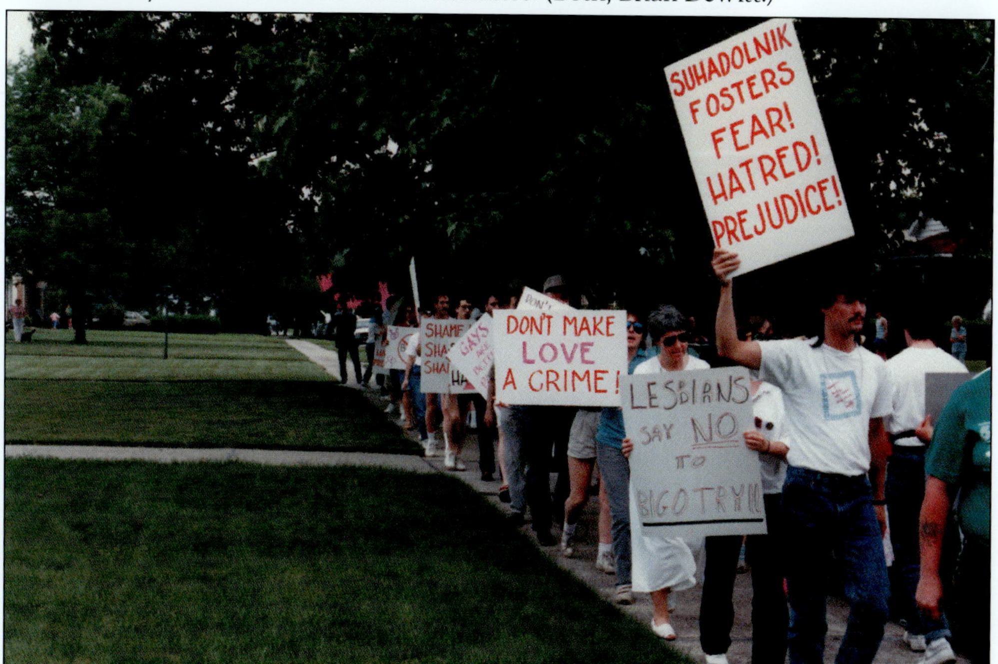

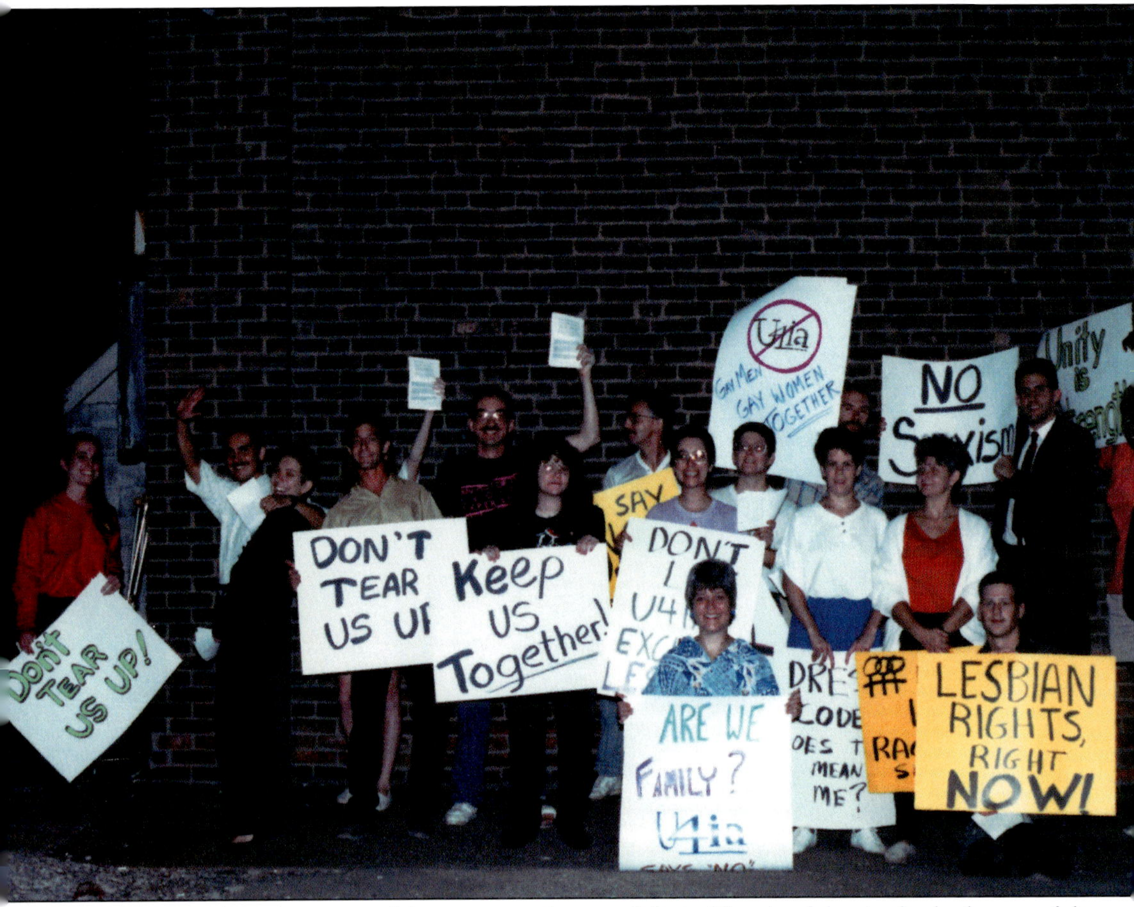

U4IA may have been one of the most popular gay clubs in Cleveland, but it also had some of the most questionable practices when it came to their different treatment of gay men and lesbians. In October 1989, Brynna Fish was supposed to sell tickets to a play to benefit AIDS organizations in Cleveland. She was informed that she had to wear a skirt to be able to enter the club. The U4IA manager confirmed this fact to *Gay People's Chronicle* and declared that U4IA was bringing back a gender-specific dress code to the club (which the community had successfully argued against previously). The coverage in the newspaper brought together men and women to raise their voices against the club's attempt to divide the community. This protest caused U4IA to (again) rescind its dress code and to add programming for women in the club. (Brian DeWitt.)

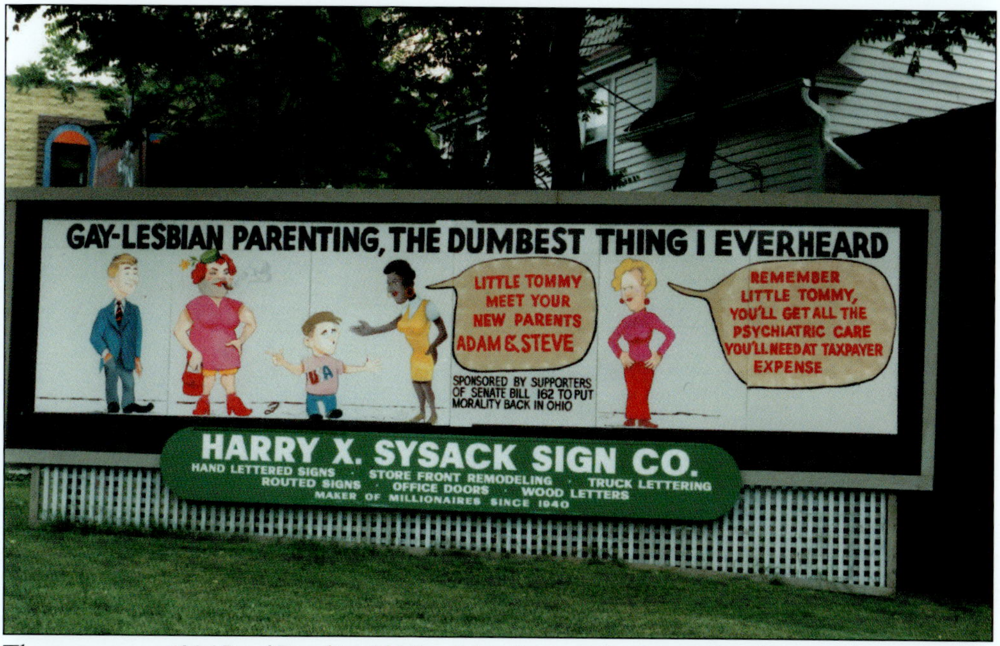

The property at 4306 Pearl Road in Old Brooklyn (just south of State Road) was a constant source of disgust for the LGBTQ community in the early 1990s. Russell Sysack, sign maker and unabashed bigot, regularly used his street level billboard to broadcast his hateful antigay views: from his homophobic views on same-sex adoption to his childish denouncement of Buck Harris's radio show *The Gay 90s*. In June 1991, Sysack displayed another offensive billboard, this time denouncing the NAMES Project AIDS Memorial Quilt, which included the phrase "Gay Today, Gone Tomorrow." When he received word that a picket was planned outside the billboard, he quickly repainted the offensive sign with the "Serenity Prayer." The new display did not stop the community from showing up in force to denounce his detestable public displays. (Both, Brian DeWitt.)

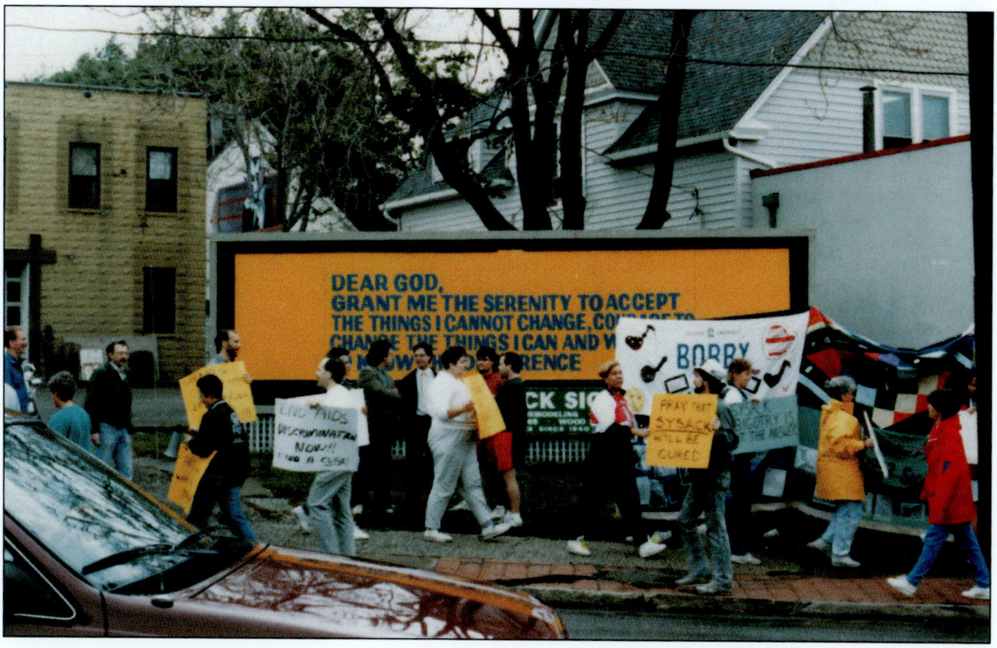

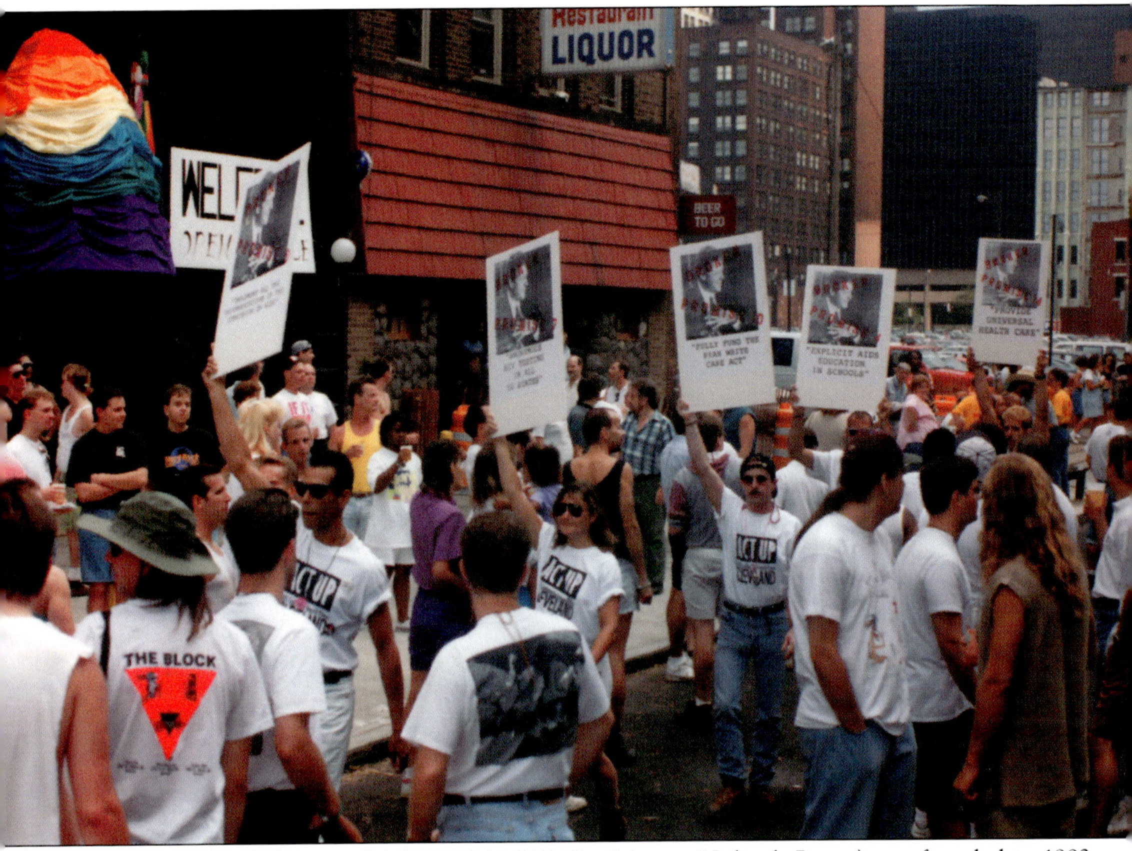

The Cleveland chapter of ACT UP (AIDS Coalition to Unleash Power) was founded in 1993 and worked to create change in a manner consistent with the mission of the original group in New York City: as a diverse, nonpartisan group of individuals united in anger and committed to direct action to end the AIDS crisis. In Cleveland, ACT UP staged various actions over the years from disrupting an event in 2004 held to honor health and human services secretary Donna Shalala, to demanding an end to a federal funding ban on needle exchange programs, to one of their famous die-ins: shutting down a major Cleveland thoroughfare as protesters laid down in the street, chalk outlines around them, to draw attention to the lack of resources being devoted to the devastation brought by HIV/AIDS. Additional protests included a disruption of a visit by Newt Gingrich, several actions on the steps of city hall, and a visible presence at both Cleveland Pride and Dancing in the Streets. (Brian DeWitt.)

In 1986, the LGBTQ community was collectively outraged by the Supreme Court's decision in *Bowers v. Hardwick* to uphold anti-sodomy laws persecuting consenting adults in the privacy of their homes. This anger helped motivate hundreds of thousands of citizens, including many Clevelanders, to attend the second annual March on Washington for Lesbian and Gay rights on October 11, 1987, and the subsequent acts of civil disobedience at the US Supreme Court two days later on October 13. (Western Reserve Historical Society.)

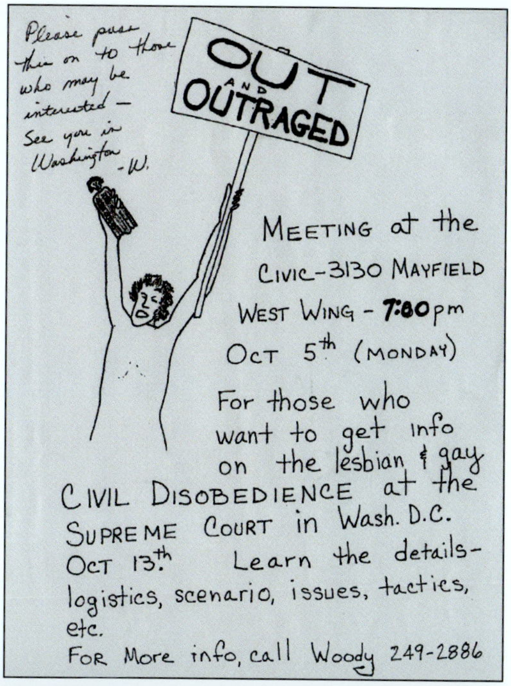

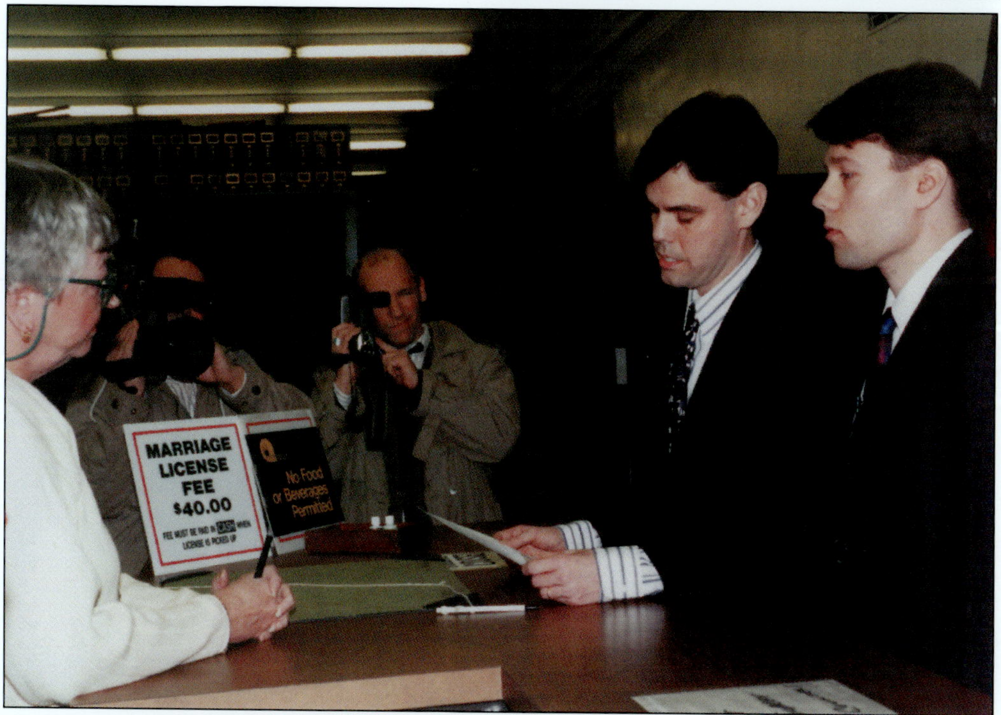

Nothing says Valentine's Day like flowers, roses, chocolate, and an attempt to draw attention to the lack of legal equality. On February 14, 1994, a total of 10 gay couples donned their Sunday best and gathered at the Cuyahoga County Courthouse in an attempt to file marriage licenses. Though, as expected, their applications were denied, their actions created much-needed media exposure on a day when love—all love—reigns supreme. (Brian DeWitt.)

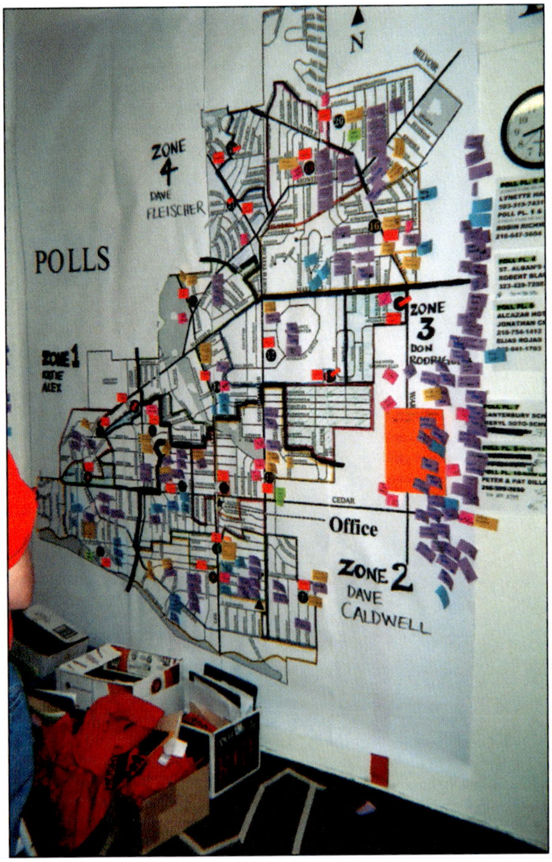

Cleveland Heights made history in 2003 when it became the first city in the United States to pass a domestic partner registry by voter initiative. Heights Families for Equality (HFE) was formed in 2002 in response to an attempt by a councilmember to pass a referendum invalidating an ordinance granting health benefits to domestic partners of gay and lesbian city employees. Though this referendum failed to get the requisite number of signatures and was later defeated in court, HFE moved forward to create proactive legislation to create a registry for the entire community. Hundreds of volunteers spearheaded an inspiring grassroots initiative to collect nearly 5,000 signatures to put the proposal on the ballot. On November 4, 2003, voters in Cleveland Heights overwhelmingly approved Issue 35, creating a municipal domestic partner registry, a direct result of the 10,000 one-on-one conversations HFE had with registered voters. (Both, Brian DeWitt.)

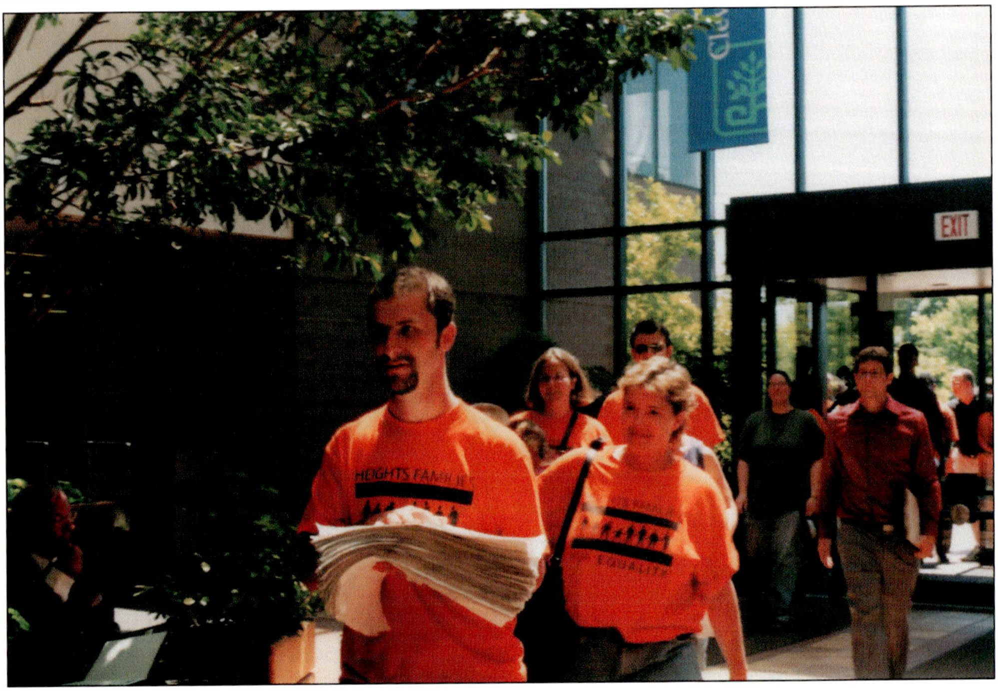

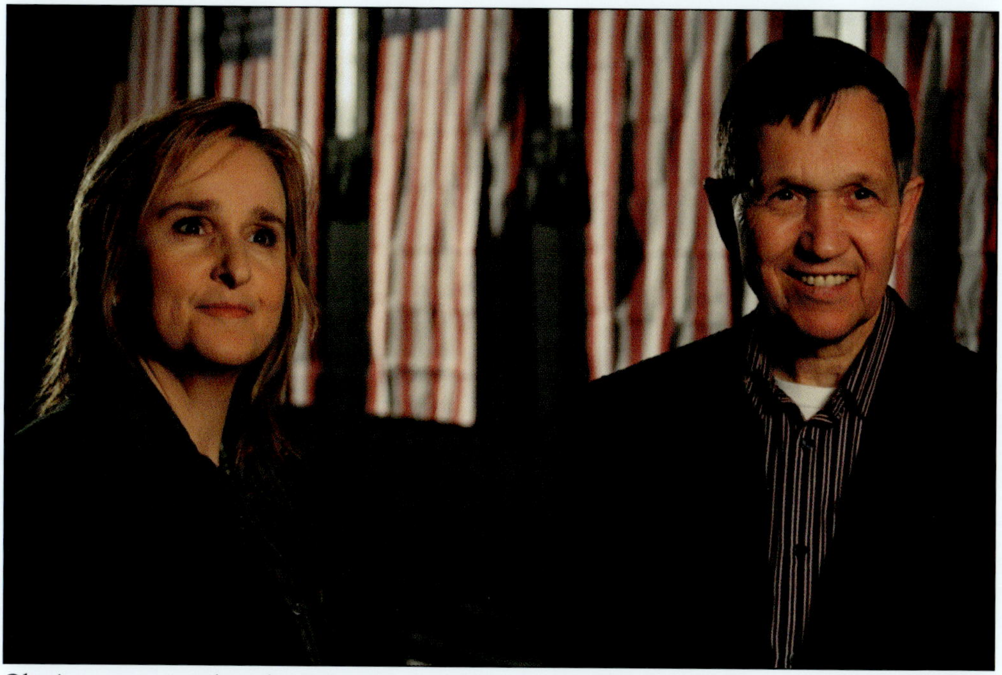

Ohio's status as a political swing state results in an extended election season and a cavalcade of celebrities passing through the Midwest to increase the star wattage of their candidate of choice. One week in October 2008 alone saw a flurry of famous—and distinctly LGBTQ—activity within Cleveland's borders. First, superstar rocker Melissa Etheridge performed a special intimate concert to benefit the Dennis Kucinich congressional campaign. A few days later, *The L Word* creator Ilene Chaiken and star Jennifer Beals appeared at The Nickel in Old Brooklyn to stump for presidential candidate Barack Obama. Both candidates were successful in their election bids. (Both, Janet Macoska.)

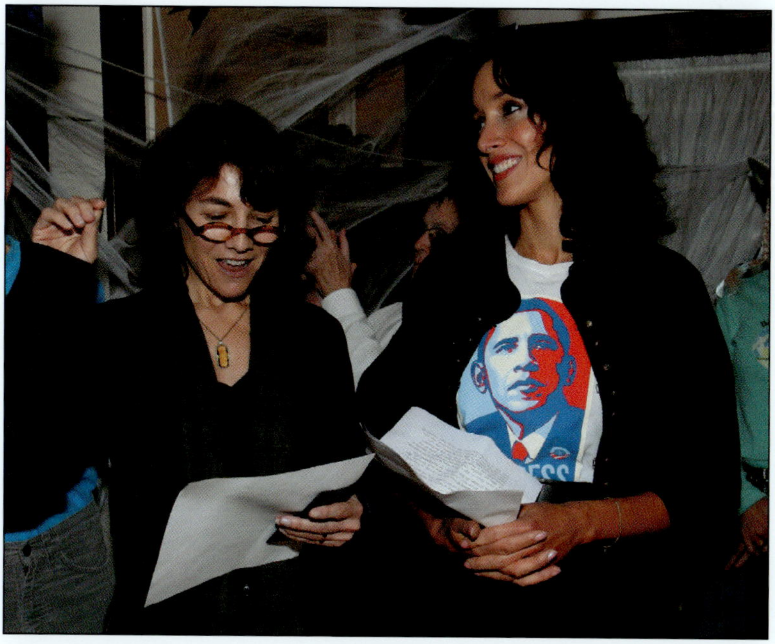

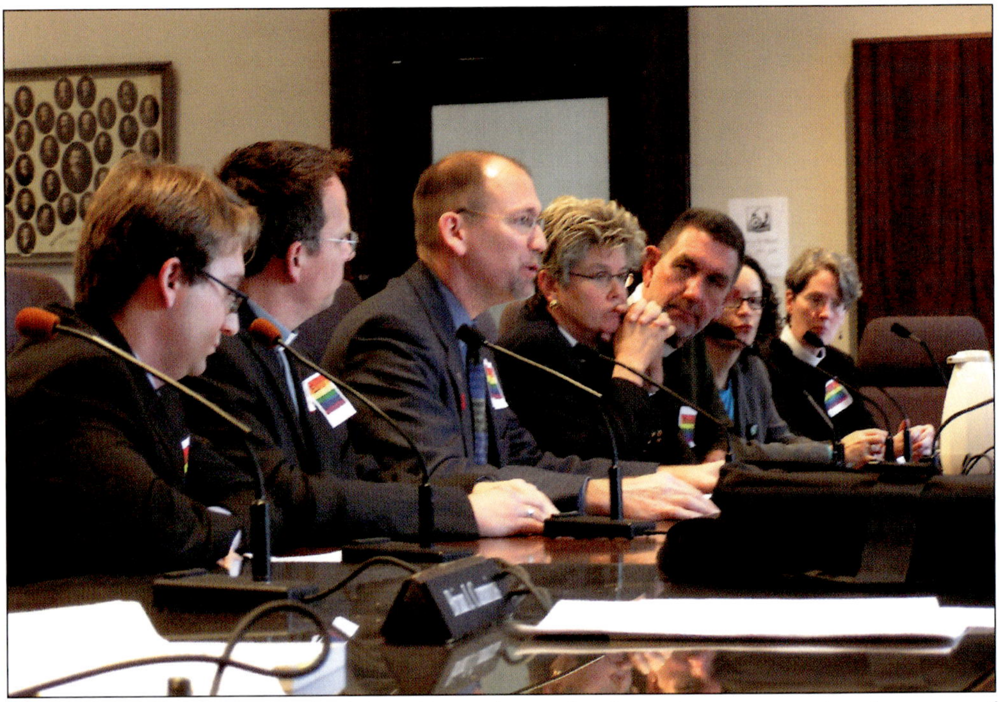

On December 8, 2008, Cleveland City Council passed a domestic partner registry by a vote of 13-7. Mayor Frank Jackson signed it into law within 48 hours, and it went into effect on April 9, 2009. Despite objection from religious leaders, Cleveland joined Cleveland Heights and Toledo as the third city in Ohio with such a registry (Columbus was first in 1998, but the Columbus City Council quickly repealed these benefits two months later after residents voiced their opposition). The public participation at the Cleveland City Council hearings proved key to the success of this legislation, as LGBTQ leaders from across Cleveland spoke passionately and compellingly in support of this major step toward equality. (Both, Brian DeWitt.)

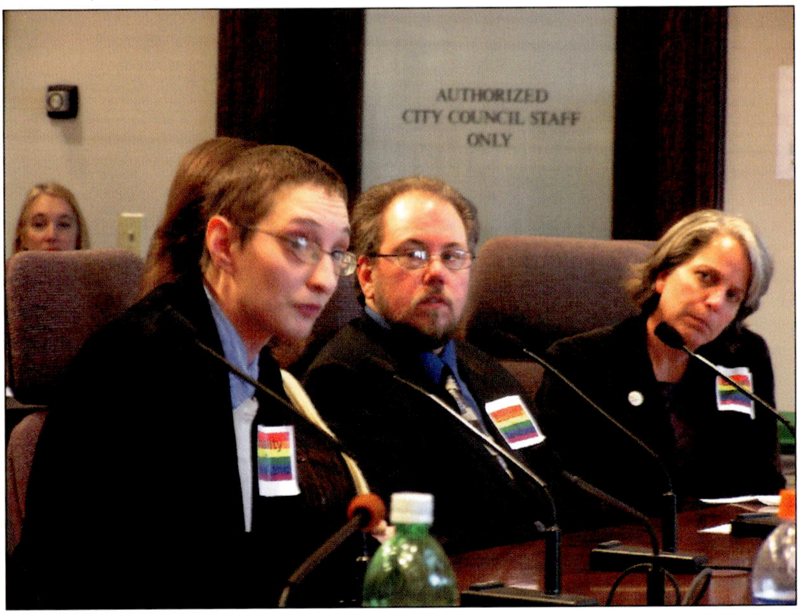

The relationship between the LGBTQ community and the Cleveland police has often been tense (in the most mild terms) and never more so than when there was documented evidence of the practice of entrapment: police officers posing as private citizens, baiting men into a sexual encounter, and then arresting them for it. From 1992 to 1998, one particular ranger made a series of arrests, prompting local activists to fight back against his duplicitous targeting. (Doug Braun.)

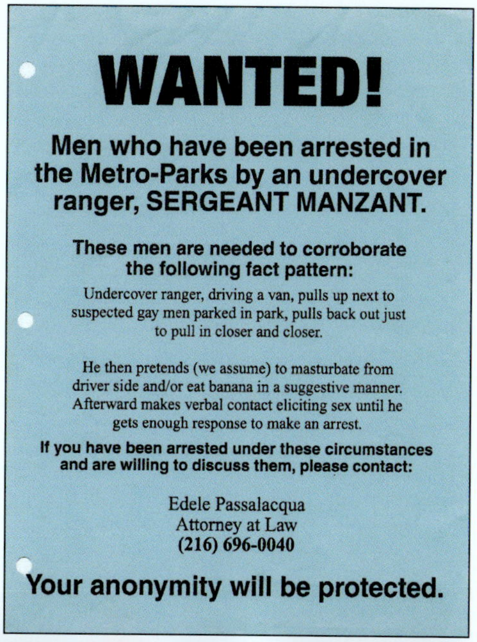

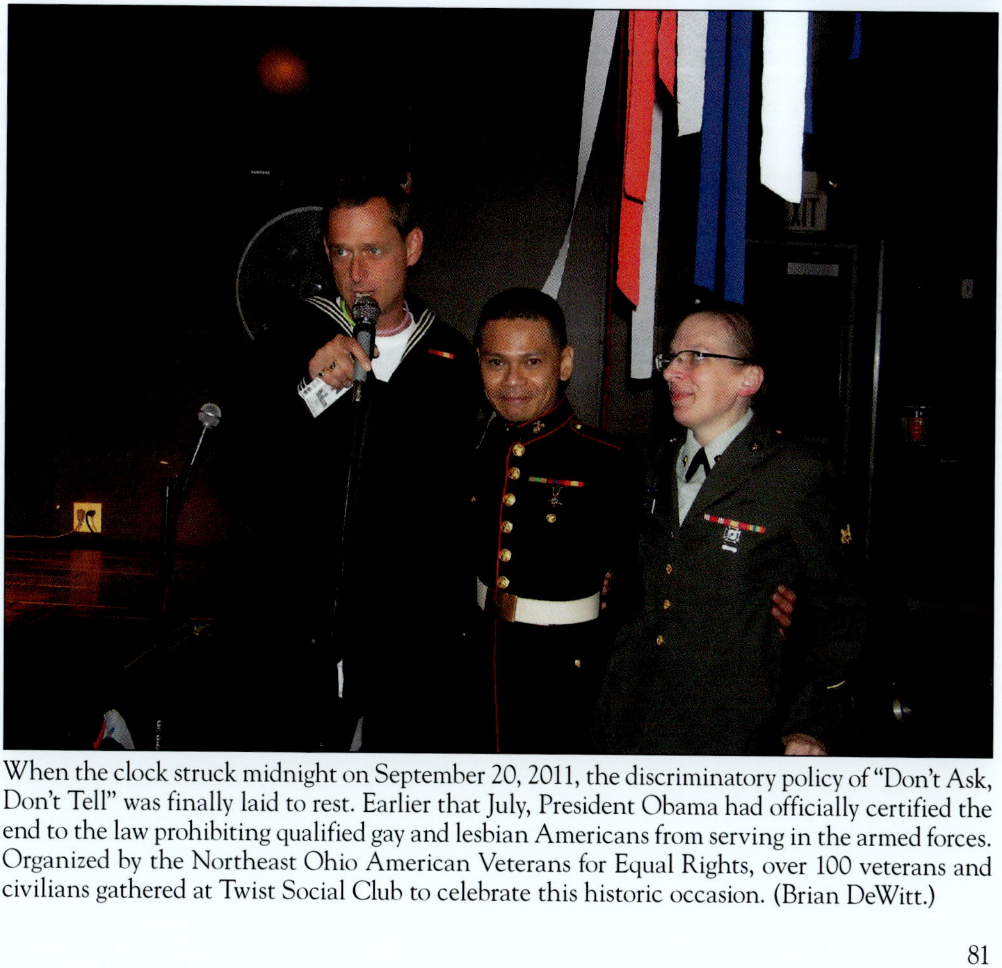

When the clock struck midnight on September 20, 2011, the discriminatory policy of "Don't Ask, Don't Tell" was finally laid to rest. Earlier that July, President Obama had officially certified the end to the law prohibiting qualified gay and lesbian Americans from serving in the armed forces. Organized by the Northeast Ohio American Veterans for Equal Rights, over 100 veterans and civilians gathered at Twist Social Club to celebrate this historic occasion. (Brian DeWitt.)

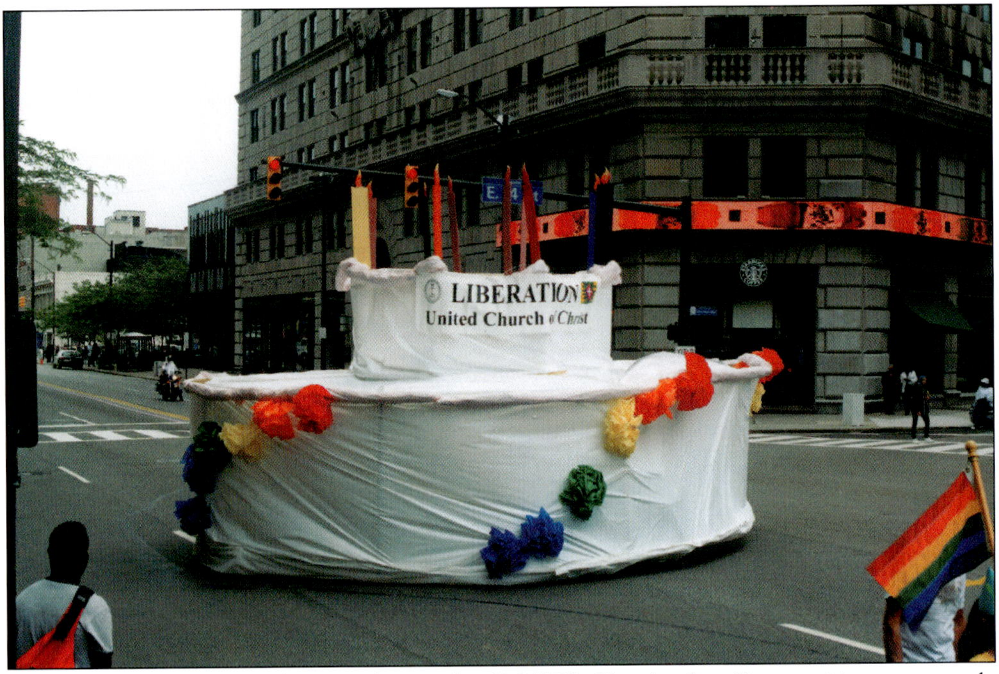

Marriage equality has long been on the minds of LGBTQ Clevelanders. From petitions constantly circulating at events, to floats in the many Cleveland Pride parades (above), to the countless actions of heroes working legislatively to have unions of love officially recognized, it has been a long march toward enshrining "love is love" within the law. On March 24, 2012, following a marriage equality rally, almost 250 couples were wed in the Galleria in a symbolic mass wedding, witnessed by 3,645 enthusiastic congregants (a greater attendance than had previously been counted at any Cleveland Pride parade to that date). The event was the brainchild of Adam Hoover, a 17-year-old who had organized similar events in Cincinnati and Columbus. (Both, Brian DeWitt.)

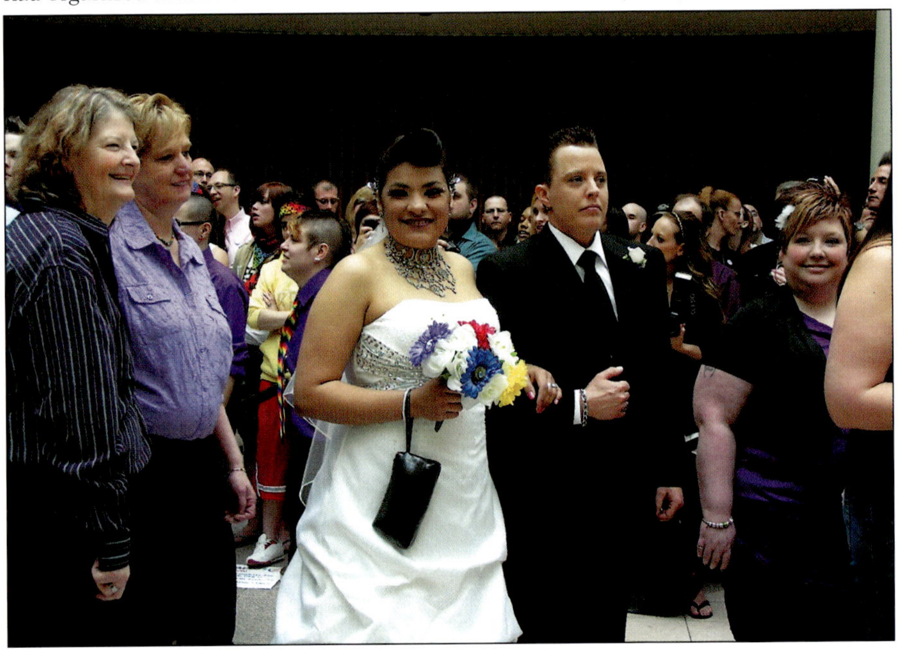

After serving five years on the Lakewood City Council, Nikki J. Antonio was elected in 2010 to serve as the state representative for Ohio District 13, making her the first openly gay person to serve in the Ohio General Assembly. She was reelected three times and is widely regarded as a champion of civil rights, a strong proponent of civic engagement, and a reliable voice for Cleveland in the state capital. (Brian DeWitt.)

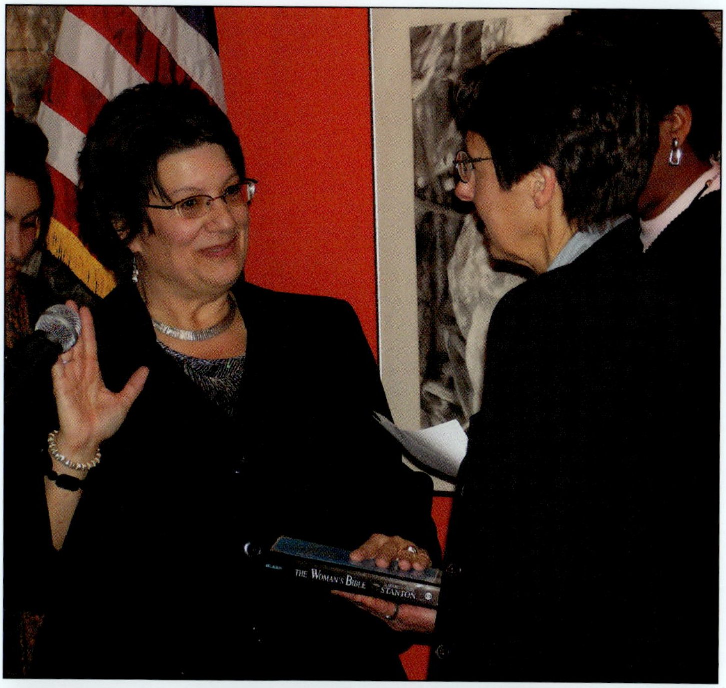

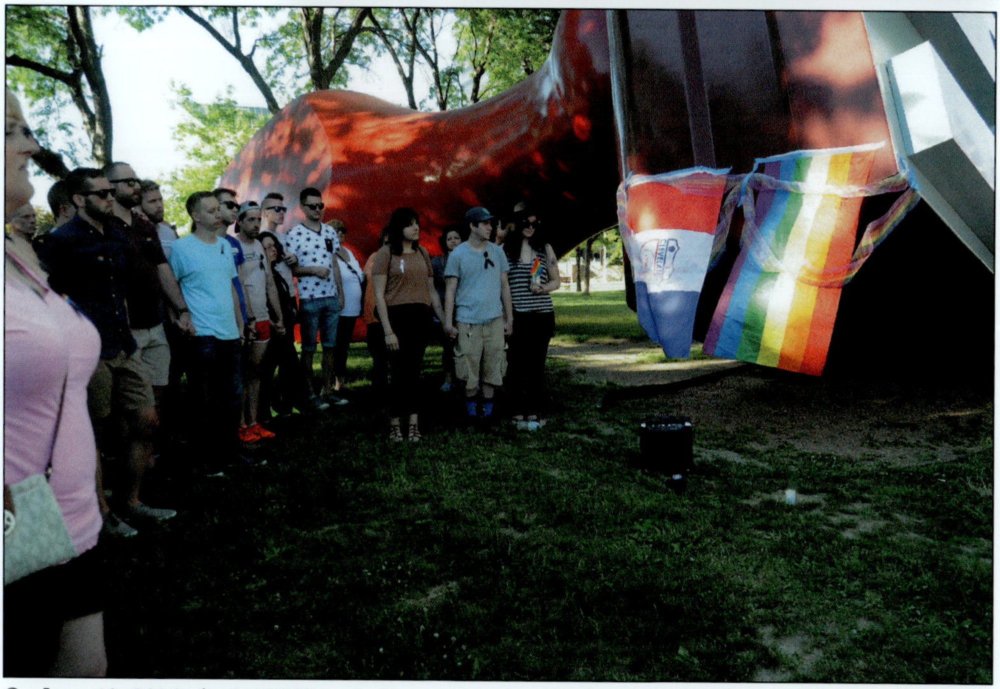

On June 12, 2016, the LGBTQ and ally community was devastated to learn of the mass shooting at Pulse, a nightclub in Orlando, Florida, where 49 people were murdered and 58 injured during the club's Latin Night. In response and in community, hundreds of Clevelanders gathered together at the Free Stamp in downtown Cleveland that evening for a vigil (pictured), and hundreds more assembled the next day to walk together from the LGBT Center of Greater Cleveland to the West Clinton Labyrinth Garden. (Anastasia Pantsios.)

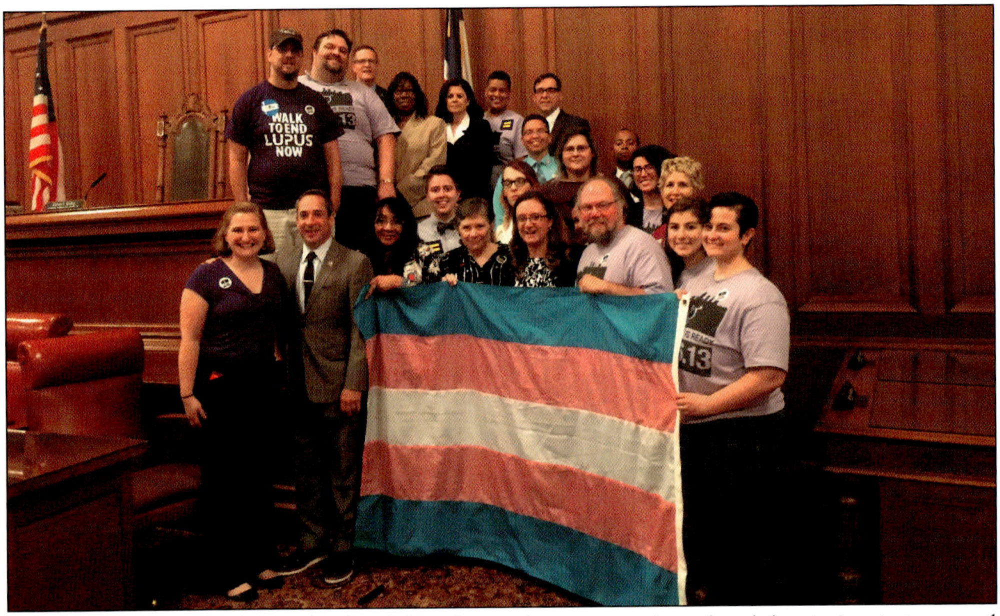

On November 30, 2009, the Cleveland City Council unanimously updated the city's existing equal rights code to include gender identity or expression. However, earlier that day, amendments were suddenly introduced, one of which included language exempting bathrooms, locker rooms, and showers from certain parts of the measure. In 2013, Councilpersons Joe Cimperman and Matt Zone introduced language to repeal this language. After three years of unyielding advocacy by Cleveland Is Ready, a robust coalition coordinated by Equality Ohio, funded by Human Rights Campaign, the National LGBTQ Task Force and including the LGBT Center of Greater Cleveland, Margie's Hope and many more, the Cleveland City Council unanimously passed Ordinance 1446 on July 13, 2016—three days before the Republican National Convention descended upon the city. When Mayor Frank Jackson signed it into law on July 22, the discriminatory language was finally removed from the city's code. (Above, Alana Jochum; below, William Rieter.)

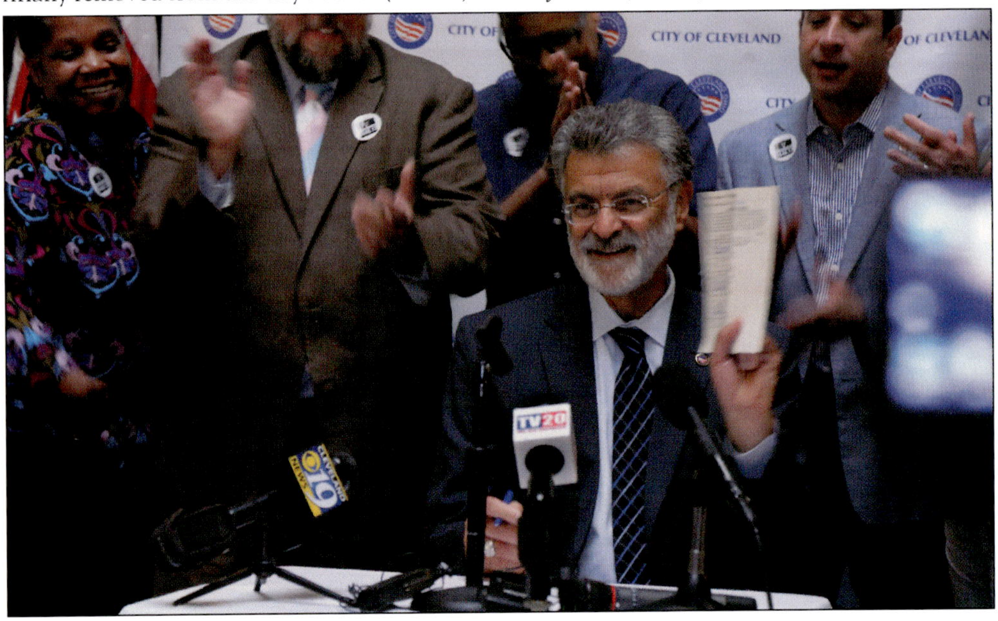

Six

We Nest
LGBTQ Centers

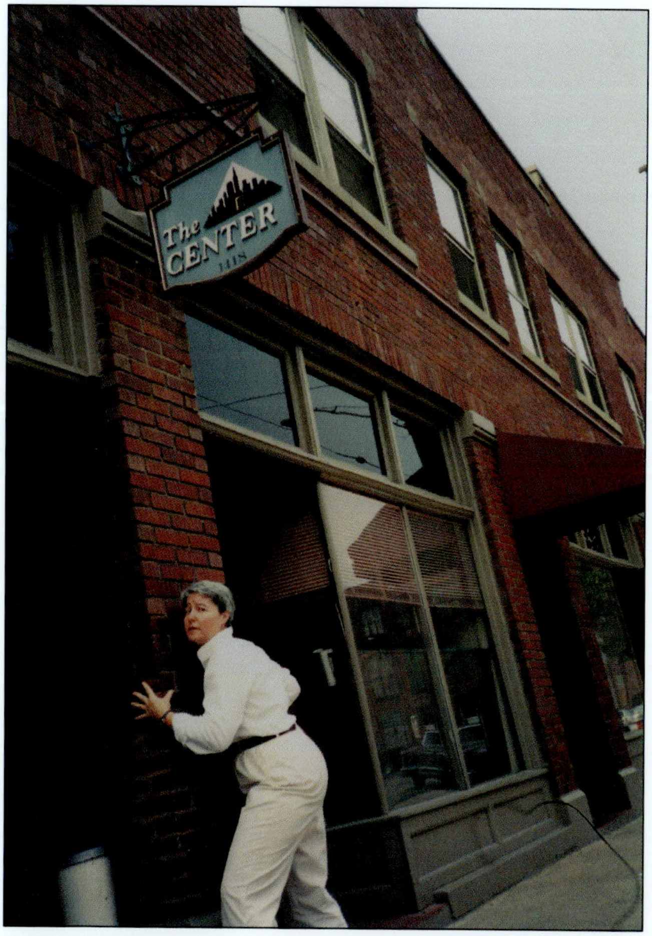

Organizations come and go. Events can be sporadic. Pride parades eventually reach their destination. At the end of the day, the Cleveland LBGTQ community has always needed a home, a physical structure that would be there for them no matter what. Since 1977, the LGBT Center of Greater Cleveland has sported a variety of names and has been found at six different locations, but that commitment to providing this vital space to the community has never wavered. Pictured here is Judy Rainbrook, the executive director of the center, at its location on 1418 West Twenty-Ninth Street. (Western Reserve Historical Society.)

G.E.A.R.

Gay Educational and Awareness Resources Foundation
P.O. Box 6177 Cleveland, Ohio 44101

First Annual Meeting: May 14, 1977, 4:00

A G E N D A

1. Call to order, welcome, and approval of agenda (Mr. Levy)
2. Reports of officers
   a. Secretary, including membership (Mr. Brown)
   b. Treasurer, including tax exemption (Mr. McGuire)
3. Reports of committees
   a. Community center lease (Mr. Levy)
   b. Community center operations (Mr. Skaggs)
   c. High Gear (Mr. Nosek, Mr. Stevens)
4. New Business
   a. Plans for Gay Pride Week, June 20-27 (Mr. Nosek)
   b. Proposal to amend bylaws to require elections by ballot (Mr. Brown)
   c. Election of trustees: six two-year terms
   d. Election of trustees: six one-year terms
   e. Other new business and general discussion
5. Adjournment

What began as a gay activists group at Cleveland State University in the early 1970s soon became the launching pad for much of the LGBTQ activity in Cleveland for decades to come. The GEAR (Gay Educational and Awareness Resources) Foundation filed its articles of incorporation in 1975 with the following purposes: to do scientific research on, and collect and disseminate educational material concerning human sexuality and sexual orientation; to provide facilities and rehabilitative services of a positive nature for the homophile community in the areas of mental health, physical health, and social alternatives; and to provide endowment funding for qualifying homophile organizations, persons, and events. As this agenda for the first annual meeting in 1977 illustrates, the board was largely populated by gay men, as the LGBTQ community had not yet come together to work as one. (Western Reserve Historical Society.)

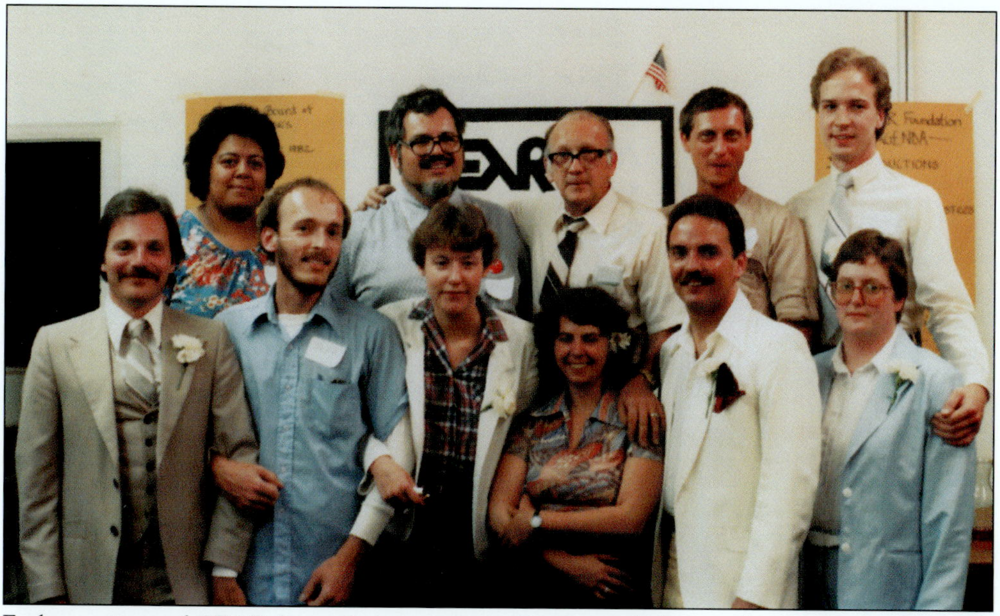

Early meetings of GEAR focused on a variety of topics including updates on the publication of *High Gear* magazine, responses to high profile LGBTQ incidents of the time, plans for Pride celebrations, and the almost constant search for a permanent space to house an LGBT community center. It was this last item that would prove to be the source of so much stress, joy, anxiety, and hope for decades to come. From a devastating fire that destroyed the first center to abandoned leases on proposed property due to antigay graffiti and threats of firebombing, from east side locales to near-west side sites, and from living rooms to basements, GEAR never wavered in its forward movement to provide the energy and spirit of the Cleveland LGBTQ community with bricks and mortar that they could call home. (Both, Brian DeWitt.)

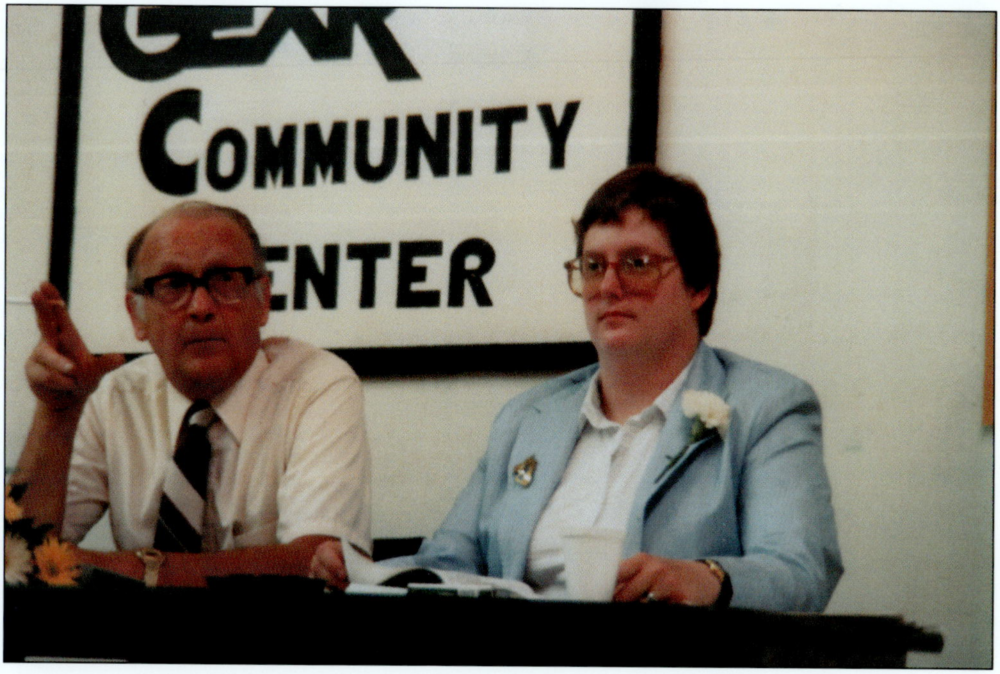

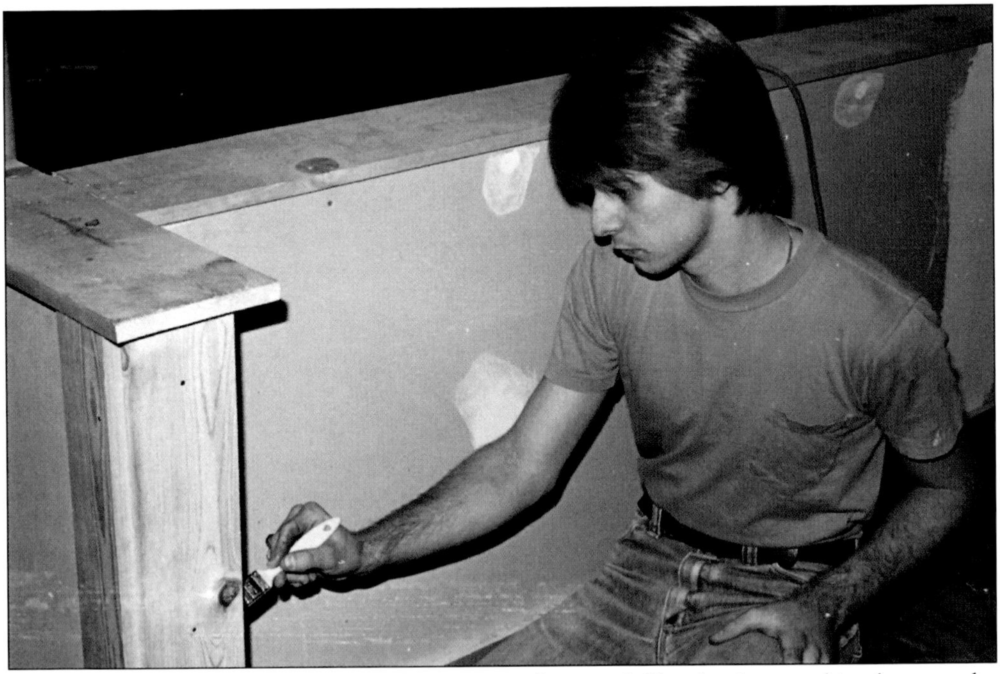

On March 27, 1977, the GEAR Gay Community Center of Cleveland opened its doors to the public for an open house in a three-room suite on the third floor of the Coventryard building, at 2785 Euclid Heights Boulevard in Cleveland Heights. This was a true community endeavor: with no named permanent director of the center, volunteers showed up at all hours to plan, build, paint, and assemble. The following passage from *High Gear* covering the open house best captures the spirit: "Though the rooms were unfurnished at the opening, a feeling of cohesiveness and optimism permeated the center. If any word of mouth has been skeptical up to now, that skepticism has been proved unfounded: The Gay Community Center of Cleveland is alive and the people of our community will soon have a comfortable drop-in and services center at their disposal." (Both, Western Reserve Historical Society.)

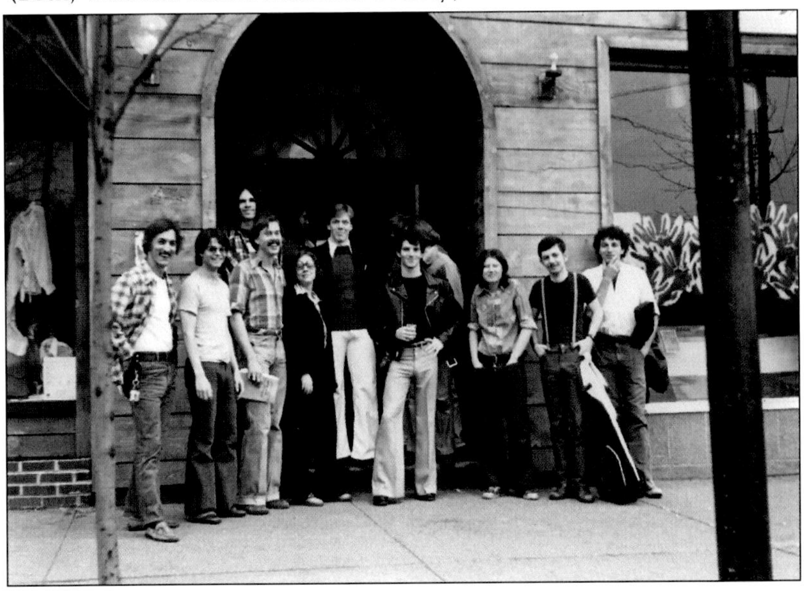

Less than a year after the Gay Community Center of Cleveland opened its doors on the east side of Cleveland in March 1977, a fire destroyed the space and all of its contents in February 1978. Some say it was an electrical fire, while others claim it was arson. Regardless, the community was never able to determine the cause and the damage had been done. The decision was made to relocate the center to downtown so as to "be more accessible to the gay community." A benefit event was held at After Midnight in March asking for donations of $2 "just this once." The center reopened downtown one door east of Dimensions on Sumner Court in April 1978. (Both, Western Reserve Historical Society.)

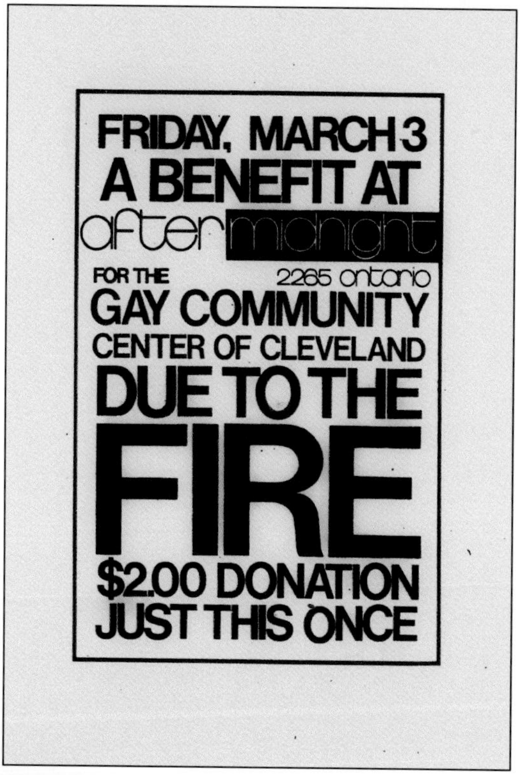

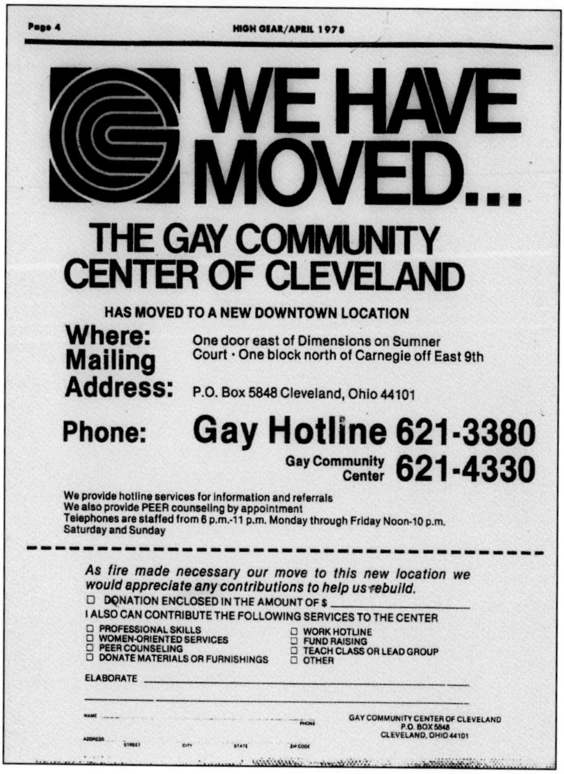

Page 4 HIGH GEAR/APRIL 1978

WE HAVE MOVED...

THE GAY COMMUNITY
CENTER OF CLEVELAND

HAS MOVED TO A NEW DOWNTOWN LOCATION

Where: One door east of Dimensions on Sumner Court · One block north of Carnegie off East 9th

Mailing Address: P.O. Box 5848 Cleveland, Ohio 44101

Phone: Gay Hotline 621-3380
Gay Community Center 621-4330

We provide hotline services for information and referrals
We also provide PEER counseling by appointment
Telephones are staffed from 6 p.m.-11 p.m. Monday through Friday Noon-10 p.m. Saturday and Sunday

As fire made necessary our move to this new location we would appreciate any contributions to help us rebuild.

☐ DONATION ENCLOSED IN THE AMOUNT OF $ ______
I ALSO CAN CONTRIBUTE THE FOLLOWING SERVICES TO THE CENTER

☐ PROFESSIONAL SKILLS
☐ WOMEN-ORIENTED SERVICES
☐ PEER COUNSELING
☐ DONATE MATERIALS OR FURNISHINGS
☐ WORK HOTLINE
☐ FUND RAISING
☐ TEACH CLASS OR LEAD GROUP
☐ OTHER

ELABORATE ______

GAY COMMUNITY CENTER OF CLEVELAND
P.O. BOX 5848
CLEVELAND, OHIO 44101

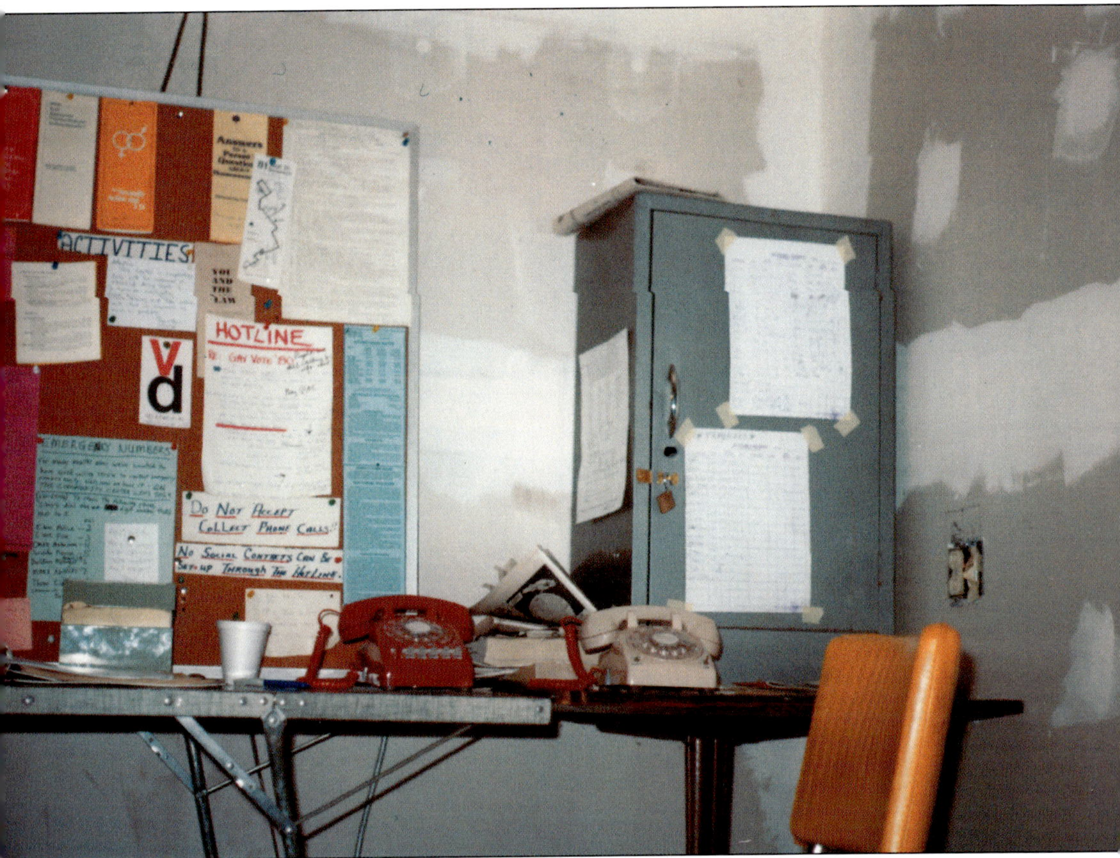

One vital feature that has remained consistent throughout the years has been the presence of a telephone hotline to provide the LGBTQ community with counseling options, referrals, and general information. GEAR established the Gay Hotline in 1976, and it was briefly operated out of a dingy second-floor office at West Twenty-Fifth Street and Clark Avenue before being call-forwarded to volunteers' homes. After the fire that destroyed the center in 1977, GEAR was quick to inform the community that the hotline would quickly be back up and running, far before they knew their plans to reopen the actual center. "Working the phones" is the narrative thread that connects so many volunteers in the Cleveland LGBTQ community, from fielding calls reporting discrimination in the 1970s, to linking callers with HIV/AIDS-related services in the 1980s and early 1990s, to the daily calls connecting new Clevelanders to the social scene and services no matter the decade. Pictured here is the Gay Hotline room in 1980 in the center, located at that time on West Fourteenth Street and Auburn Avenue. (Brian DeWitt.)

HUGS (Hope, Understanding, Giving, and Support) East was established in 1984 when a group of individuals sought to provide the gay and lesbian community of Lake, Geauga, and Ashtabula Counties with a support network and to act as an extended family, similar to what they saw being offered just east in Cleveland. These efforts led to a lavender ribbon cutting in January 1989 for a physical space to serve the local LGBTQ population. (Brian DeWitt.)

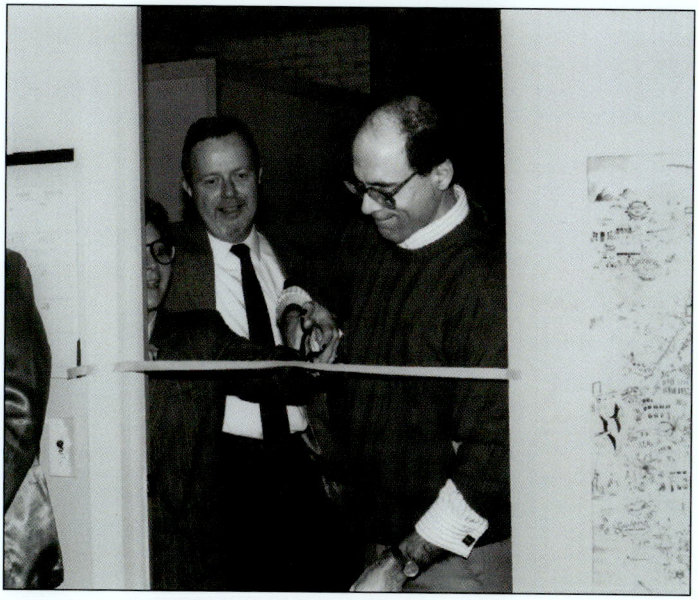

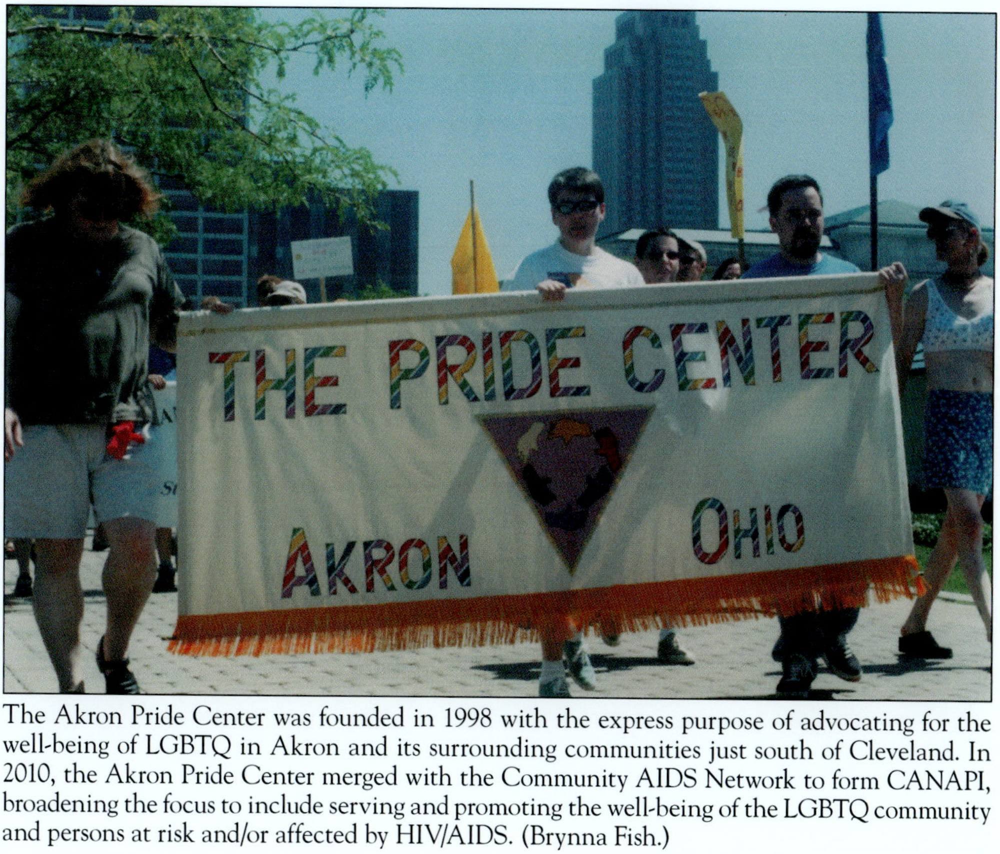

The Akron Pride Center was founded in 1998 with the express purpose of advocating for the well-being of LGBTQ in Akron and its surrounding communities just south of Cleveland. In 2010, the Akron Pride Center merged with the Community AIDS Network to form CANAPI, broadening the focus to include serving and promoting the well-being of the LGBTQ community and persons at risk and/or affected by HIV/AIDS. (Brynna Fish.)

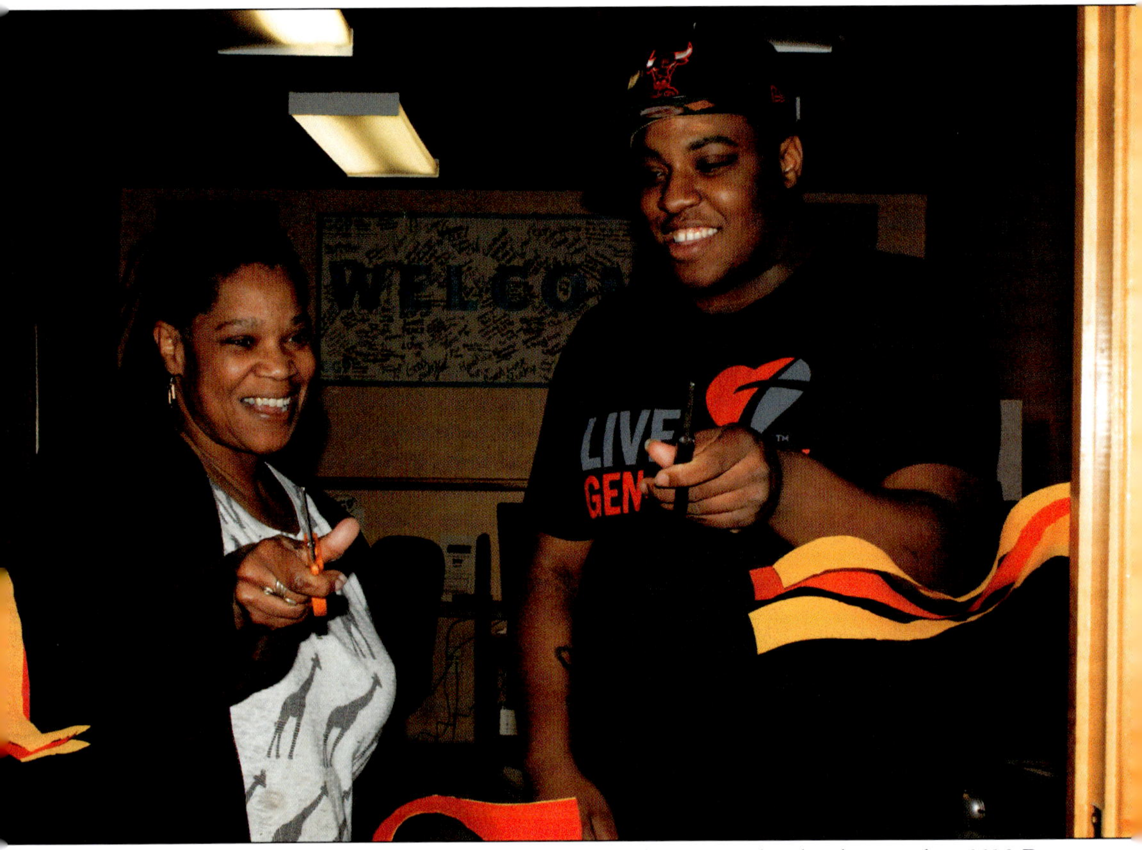

On May 21, 2000, the LGBT Community Center of Greater Cleveland opened at 6600 Detroit Avenue in the basement of the historic Gordon Square Arcade in the Detroit Shoreway Neighborhood, the farthest west the LBGT Center has been situated. At 7,000 square feet, it almost doubled the size of the previous location on West Twenty-Ninth Street. Over the years, the space has housed the Living Room program providing support to those living with and affected by HIV/AIDS and the David Bohnett Cyber Center for use by the entire community. Programs and services have been designed for members of all ages, from drop-in groups for teens to the robust slate of SAGE offerings for LGBTQ seniors. The center has also remained committed to providing free and rapid HIV testing multiple times a week. (Ryan Clopton-Zymler.)

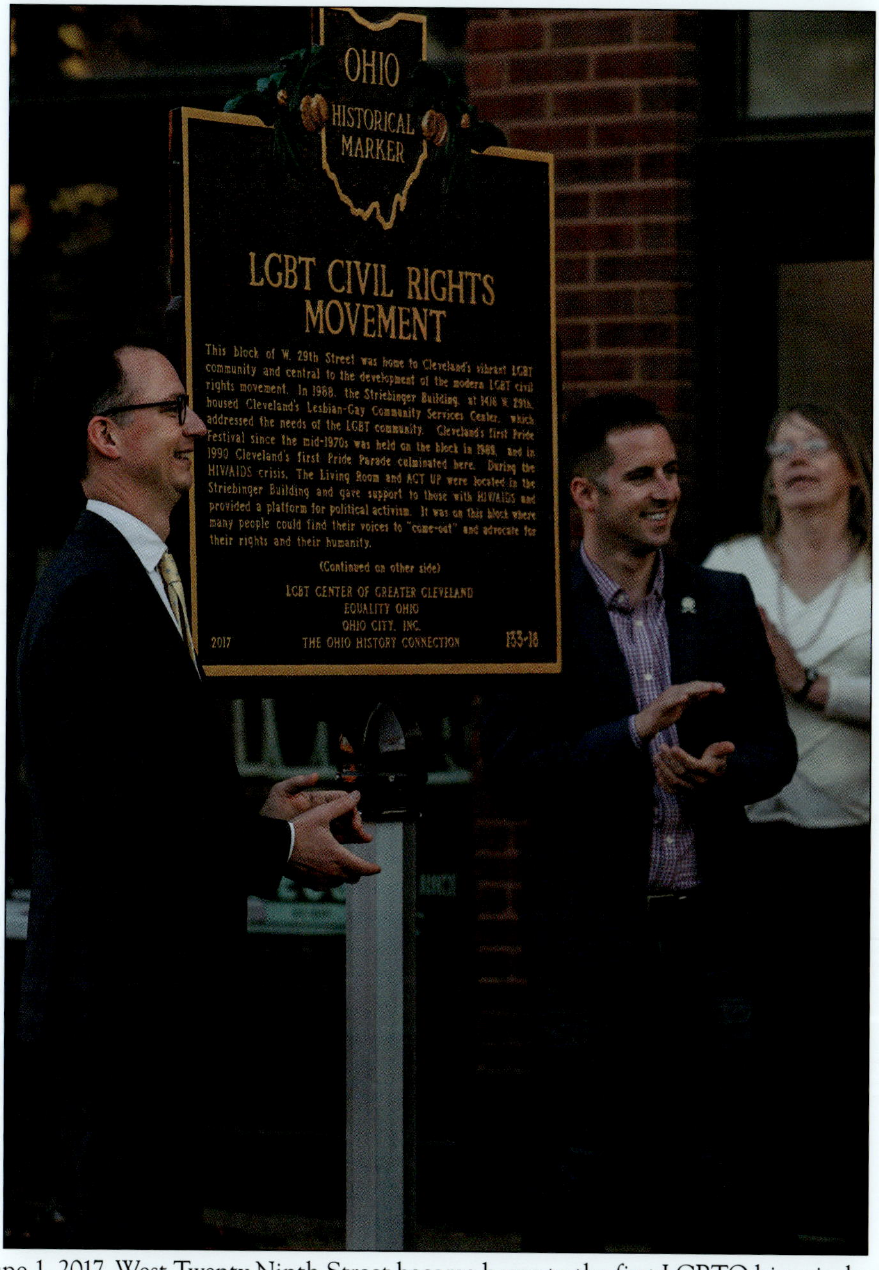

On June 1, 2017, West Twenty-Ninth Street became home to the first LGBTQ historical marker in the entire state of Ohio. Over the decades, the Ohio city street has been the geographic focus of much energy, activism, and pride. It served as the home of the Lesbian-Gay Community Services Center from 1988 to 2000, which at that point was the longest stretch in one location for the center. The Living Room, the offices of ACT UP, and well over a dozen LGBTQ-themed bars and businesses could all be found in the immediate area. Twenty-Ninth Street was also the site of the 1989 Cleveland Pride festivities as well as the celebration grounds at the end of the 1990 Pride parade. Pictured here at the unveiling ceremony attended by hundreds of community members are Alex Frondorf (left) and Councilman Kerry McCormack, who were instrumental in installing this visual reminder of Cleveland's rich LGBTQ history. (Jacqueline Zema.)

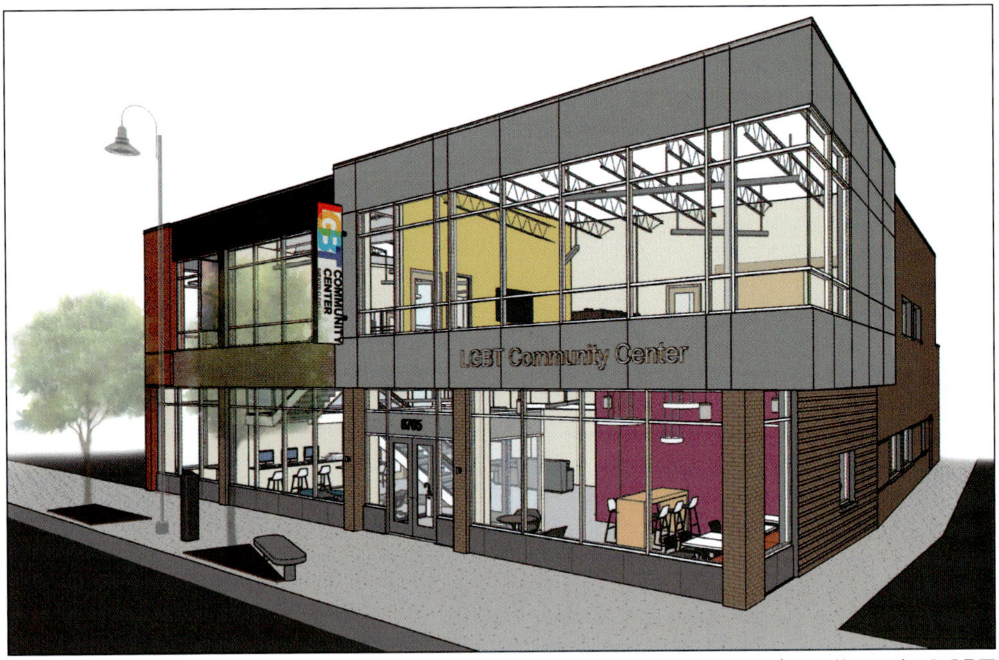

Due to the generosity of an anonymous angel donor who contributed nearly $5 million, the LGBT Center of Greater Cleveland broke ground on a new site on December 13, 2017, at 6705 Detroit Avenue, across the street and a few doors down from the current location. The expansion is a realization of the community center's goal to solidify Northeast Ohio as a place where LGBTQ people are embraced and celebrated as integral members of the community. The new facility will offer expanded programming and meeting areas totaling almost three times that of the current space. It will be accessible, visible, and welcoming to the LGBTQ community and the surrounding neighborhood. A few of the many amenities of the new site will include a visible façade on one of Cleveland's busiest thoroughfares, a dedicated youth space, community areas, and public Wi-Fi access. With this move, the center will own its property for the first time in its history. (Above, Weber Murphy Fox; below, Alana Jochum.)

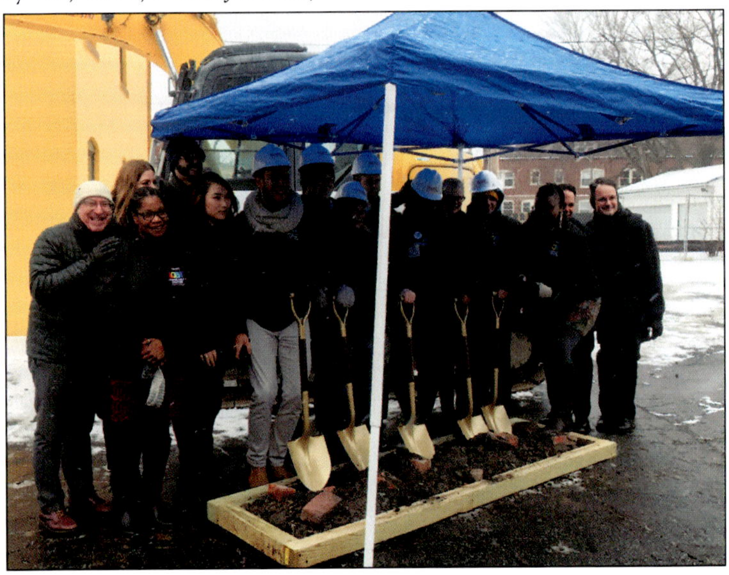

About the Organizations

LGBT COMMUNITY CENTER
GREATER CLEVELAND

The Lesbian Gay Bisexual Transgender Community Center of Greater Cleveland works to advance the rights, respect, and diversity of the LGBT community while seeking to create a community that celebrates the inherent worth and dignity of every person regardless of sexual orientation, gender identity, or gender expression, and inclusive of class, race, and ability. The center works collaboratively with other LGBT and ally groups to address community needs and issues. Founded in 1975, the center was the third LGBT center in the United States and among the first Cleveland organizations to provide services to individuals living with HIV, LGBT youth, homeless LGBT individuals, and LGBT elders.

CLEVELAND HISTORY CENTER
of the WESTERN RESERVE HISTORICAL SOCIETY

Western Reserve Historical Society's mission is to inspire people to discover the American experience by exploring the tangible history of Northeast Ohio. The core values of the Western Reserve Historical Society rest upon four common words with particular meaning for an institution dedicated to preserving and sharing the history of the people and communities of Northeast Ohio. These words, and the manner in which they relate to its mission, constitute a promise to the community: a promise of integrity, stewardship, connectivity, and innovation.

DISCOVER THOUSANDS OF LOCAL HISTORY BOOKS FEATURING MILLIONS OF VINTAGE IMAGES

Arcadia Publishing, the leading local history publisher in the United States, is committed to making history accessible and meaningful through publishing books that celebrate and preserve the heritage of America's people and places.

Find more books like this at
www.arcadiapublishing.com

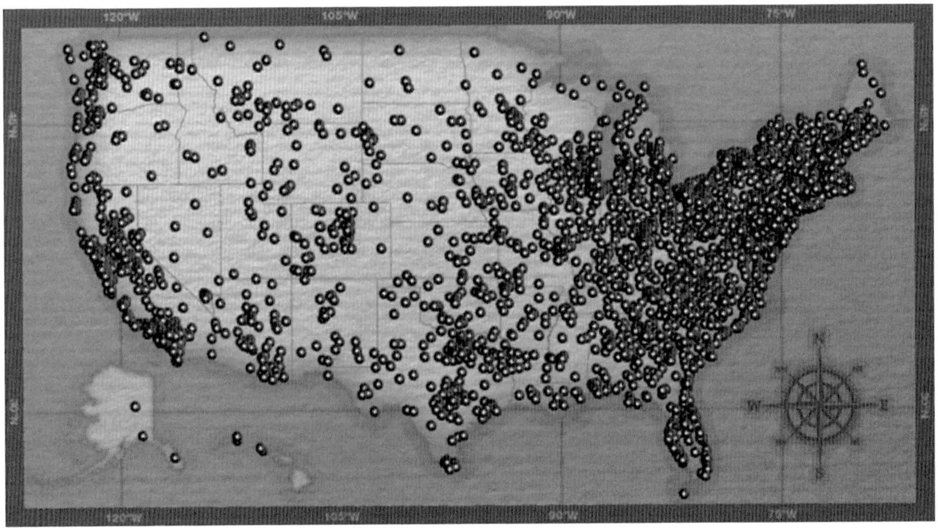

Search for your hometown history, your old stomping grounds, and even your favorite sports team.

Consistent with our mission to preserve history on a local level, this book was printed in South Carolina on American-made paper and manufactured entirely in the United States. Products carrying the accredited Forest Stewardship Council (FSC) label are printed on 100 percent FSC-certified paper.

MADE IN THE USA